22830

ANGLICAN ORDERS:
THE DOCUMENTS IN THE DEBATE

Anglican Orders: the documents in the debate

Edited by

CHRISTOPHER HILL

and

EDWARD YARNOLD, SJ

CANTERBURY
PRESS
Norwich

British Library Cataloguing in Publication Data

A catalogue record for this book is available
from the British Library

ISBN 1–85311–163–5

*Typeset by David Gregson Associates, Beccles, Suffolk and
Printed and bound in Great Britain by Biddles Ltd
Guildford and King's Lynn*

TO:
FR GIUSEPPE RAMBALDI, SJ

Foreword

The years 1996–97 offer significant anniversaries for all who are concerned with the relations between Rome and Canterbury. This year is the celebration of the 1400th anniversary of the landing of St Augustine in Kent at the bidding of Pope Gregory the Great. Last year, there was a moving 75th celebration of the anniversary of the Malines Conversations, which heralded the beginnings of new initiatives for friendship and reconciliation between the Roman Catholic Church and the Anglican Communion. It was also the Centenary of an Apostolic Letter of Pope Leo XIII entitled, 'Apostolicae Curae', which asserted that Anglican Orders were null and void and to which an official response was made by the Archbishops of Canterbury and York. Two distinguished former members of the Anglican/Roman Catholic International Commission (ARCIC), Christopher Hill, Bishop of Stafford, and Fr Edward Yarnold, S.J., have therefore decided to publish the documents which were at the heart of the debate in 1896–97. They have gathered together significant material, not with a view to changing past positions, but to help us to look at the controversies of one hundred years ago in the light of recent history.

The Second Vatican Council resulted in new initiatives for ecumenical dialogue, prominent among which was the creation of ARCIC, of which we are now Co-Chairmen. Despite the difficulties and obstacles which still remain between us on the road to full Christian unity, there is now a new atmosphere of friendship and understanding, thanks in no small part to ARCIC's work. It is in this new ecumenical context that we welcome the publication of these documents. We congratulate and thank the co-editors, with all their collaborators, for their perseverance and the hard work they have put in to making this material available to all who are interested in the growth of ecumenical understanding and truth between our two Communions.

✠ CORMAC MURPHY-O'CONNOR
      Roman Catholic Bishop of Arundel and Brighton

✠ MARK SANTER   *Anglican Bishop of Birmingham*

Co-Chairmen of the Anglican–Roman Catholic International Commission

Contents

Preface

In 1995 a conference was held at General Theological Seminary, New York, in preparation for the centenary of *Apostolicae Curae*, Leo XIII's Apostolic Letter of 1896, which declared that Anglican ordinations were invalid; its papers have been published in the USA in *Anglican Theological Review* ((LXXVIII/1) Winter 1996), and in England under the title *Anglican Orders: Essays on the Centenary of Apostolicae Curae 1896–1996*, ed. R. W. Franklin, with a Foreword by H. Montefiore (London 1996). The proposal was made at the conference that the centenary would provide a good occasion for publishing a collection of the 1896 documentation in English translation. The present volume is the realisation of this project.

The authoritative version of most of these documents is held in the archive of the Congregation for the Doctrine of the Faith. The editors of this collection have not enjoyed access to this archive; our work is based on the original versions which Fr G. Rambaldi of the Gregorian University, Rome tracked down in a number of other archives and libraries, and published piecemeal in several journals. The present collection owes everything to his dedication and encouragement. In the course of our work we learnt that the Congregation for the Doctrine of the Faith was planning to publish their own dossier in the original languages. Nevertheless the fact that we were publishing translations rather than original texts persuaded us that it was worth while to continue with our project.

For ease of reference we refer to paragraph numbers,

specifying the document by the following abbreviations:

A   *Votum* of E. De Augustinis
AC   *Apostolicae Curae*
G   *Votum* of P. Gasparri
D   *Votum* of L. Duchesne
FP   Letter of F. Portal
H   Letter of Lord Halifax
I   Introduction of the present volume
L   *Diary* of T. A. Lacey
P   Report and *votum* of R. Pierotti
S   Letter of T. B. Scannell
SO   *Saepius Officio*
W   Exposition of the Westminster theologians, J. Moyes, F. A. Gasquet and D. Fleming

If the authors have numbered paragraphs, we have followed their numbering; if not, we have inserted our own numbers in square brackets. The Lacey *Diary* is unparagraphed but is referred to by date. Editorial footnotes or other material are indicated by square brackets [ ].

In preparing the translations contained in this collection for publication, the Editors have attempted to introduce some degree of consistency in the use of initial capitals and in the spelling of names; however the use of capitals for emphasis and other typographical devices has been reproduced where possible.

We have not edited this collection in order to establish a case for the withdrawal of *Apostolicae Curae*. We had two other aims in mind. The first was to provide the material which would help our churches to decide if circumstances had changed so much in the last hundred years that the verdict of 1896, which was perhaps almost inevitable granted the categories of thought in which the investigation had been pursued, now needed revision. Our second hope was that, if readers could see the thoroughness and fairness with which certain of the issues were explored by the theological commission in 1896, some of the resentment and frustration which is still provoked by the decision would evaporate, particularly since it can be seen that the discussions of the theological Commission represented a wide spectrum of opinion, and indeed the members were unable to reach the unanimity which would be required if a change in practice were to be justified.

We wish to express our warmest thanks to Fr Francis Sullivan, SJ, who first conceived the idea of this volume; to our industrious and cooperative team of translators, who have considerately allowed us to tinker with their versions, so that criticisms should be levelled against the editors rather than against them; to the Archivist of the Westminster Archdiocese, Fr Ian Dickie, who tracked down for us the papers compiled by the Westminster theologians, and to The Canterbury Press Norwich for generously agreeing to publish a volume which is not likely to find a place on the list of best sellers. Our thanks also go to the Catholic Truth Society and to the Society for Promoting Christian Knowledge for their respective co-operation as previous publishers of *Apostolicae Curae* and *Saepius Officio*.

It goes without saying that we owe a great debt to two contemporary writers both of whom we think of as friends: Fr John J. Hughes (whom one could regard as a living piece of teaching material) and Dr Francis Clark. Though perhaps neither will agree with everything we have written, the clear focus of their debate has helped us to sharpen our perception of some of the key issues.

Above all we wish to acknowledge our debt to Fr Giuseppe Rambaldi, SJ, of the Gregorian University, Rome, whose persistent searches in various archives over many years have unearthed several of the documents contained in this collection, and who had the imagination to grasp their importance. To him we have great pleasure in dedicating this volume, with out warmest admiration.

We can find no better note on which to introduce this study than that sounded by Pietro Gasparri in his gracious and ecumenical concluding remark (G 81):

Christian charity compels us to promote and hasten the

return of the great English nation to Catholic unity, in the first place by the courtesy of our discussions, inspired by the respect we owe to virtue, learning and good faith, and above all by our prayers. May there be 'one flock and one shepherd'. Amen.

CHRISTOPHER HILL
EDWARD YARNOLD, SJ

Introduction

THE DEVELOPMENT OF EVENTS

1. In 1889 Lord Halifax spent the winter in Madeira with his sickly eldest son. There he met a French priest, the Abbé Fernand Portal of the Society of S. Vincent de Paul. This chance encounter was to have considerable ecumenical consequences. Portal interested himself in the problem of the 'reunion' of separated Christians and his continuing and profound friendship with Halifax gave him a special impetus to study the 'English schism'. It seemed to him that the most helpful approach would be to interest Catholic opinion in France. So the idea of an 'Anglo-Roman' campaign was born. Halifax was encouraged (unsuccessfully) to write a number of articles. By 1890 Portal judged that it was time to take advantage of the broadmindedness of Leo XIII and focus on an attainable first goal: the resolution of Anglican orders, which Portal considered to be an 'easier' question 'in that the answer depends upon questions of fact, not of faith'.[1] Halifax at first doubted whether good would come of such a request. Indeed by 1893 there was already an antagonistic public debate between Cardinal Vaughan of Westminster and Archbishop Benson of Canterbury on the subject.

In 1894 Portal, using the pen-name Fernand Dalbus, published a widely read and reviewed pamphlet on Anglican orders. He concluded against their validity on the grounds

---

1. Letter of Portal to Halifax, November 1890; *Fernand Portal*, Hemer and Macmillan, London 1961, p. 22.

of intention and the suppression of the handing over of the chalice, paten and host. It was probably intended to provoke positive responses. The well-known Church historian the Abbé Louis Duchesne indeed responded to 'Dalbus' in favour of Anglican ordinations. This was widely noticed. Portal next visited England and met Anglican dignitaries including the Archbishops of Canterbury and York, but missed an appointment with Cardinal Vaughan.

Later in the year Portal went to Rome at the request of the Cardinal Secretary of State, Rampolla, who took Portal to see Leo XIII. Portal proposed a series of conferences between the two churches on the subject of orders. In the event Rampolla was to write to Portal who showed the correspondence to Halifax for the Archbishops of Canterbury and York. Rampolla's letter approved of the impartiality of the debate and the opening up of the question.[2] Portal and Halifax again visited the – somewhat reluctant – Archbishop of Canterbury who took Cardinal Vaughan's negatives to be the authentic voice of the Roman Catholic Church rather than a private letter from the Secretary of State to a French priest.

2. Early in 1895 T. A. Lacey and E. Denny published *De Hierachia Anglicana*, a Latin examination and defence of the Anglican episcopal succession. Duchesne responded very amiably to this study. Duchesne had also been approached through Rampolla for a study on Anglican orders for the Pope. Duchesne concluded in favour of the presbyterate and episcopate in a Mémoire distinct from his later votum. Mgr Pietro Gasparri, the distinguished Italian canonist, future Secretary of State, also printed a booklet and circulated it to the Holy Office. It favoured conditional ordination. Meanwhile Cardinal Vaughan, who was regularly kept informed of all developments by Halifax, travelled himself to Rome and gave the Pope a negative account of Portal's proceedings and affirmed that nothing short of individual submission should be offered to the Anglican church and

2. *Fernand Portal* op. cit. p. 45.

that this would be quite unacceptable to the Protestant bishops. At the same time, at Vaughan's request, Dom Francis Gasquet was working in the archives of the Holy Office[3] with the assistance of the learned lay-liturgist Edmund Bishop. In March Halifax was received in audience by Pope Leo. Halifax explained the misgivings of the Archbishop of Canterbury and that it would be essential for the Pope to propose theological conversations directly to the Archbishops, in view of the known opposition of Cardinal Vaughan. But the Pope had already decided to write to England in what became the letter *Ad Anglos*. This was drafted by Vaughan, Gasquet, Bishop and Mgr Merry del Val, a protégé of the Pope with regard to English affairs. It was well received and encouraged prayer for unity but made no mention at all of the Church of England.

During the summer Halifax and Vaughan spoke on various public platforms. Vaughan was clear that a new investigation of Anglican orders would only confirm existing practice. Merry del Val and Rampolla presented different perspectives to the Pope, Merry del Val keeping in close touch with Vaughan, Rampolla with Halifax. In August Vaughan wrote to the Pope in the strongest terms against any change in practice without the fullest investigation and co-operation of English Catholics and that he was forming a commission of his own to investigate the matter. In September Vaughan announced that Rome would investigate Anglican orders, while continuing to press his view in Rome that a condemnation of Anglican orders would facilitate individual conversions.

3. The members of the Commission were announced in March 1896. The English members of the commission were nominated by Cardinal Vaughan and were the leading members of the Cardinal's own committee of investigation: Dom Adrian Gasquet, Canon James Moyes and the Franciscan Fr. David Fleming. The other original members were Mgr Duchesne, Mgr Gasparri and the Italian dogmatician Jesuit

---

3. Now the Congregation for the Doctrine of the Faith.

Fr A. M. De Augustinis. Its President was to be Cardinal Mazzella with Mgr Merry del Val as Secretary, who kept closely in touch with Cardinal Vaughan. Two additional members were appointed after the first meeting, the Spanish Franciscan (and later Cardinal) de Llaveneras, a Consultor at the Holy Office, and the English secular priest the Revd T. B. Scannell (at the suggestion of Baron von Hügel through Rampolla) who had written several letters to *The Tablet* in favour of Anglican orders. Among the ordinary members of the Papal Commission opinion was fairly evenly balanced. T. A. Lacey and F. W. Puller SSJE (who had contributed to Portal's *Revue Anglo-Romaine*) were present in Rome as unofficial Anglican experts and were consulted by those favourable to a change in the Roman position.

4. The Commission met twelve times between 12th March and 7th May 1896 and came to a somewhat abrupt conclusion. It could not reach a common view. The Pope put all the position papers into the hands of the Papal theologian Raffaele Pierotti, Master of the Sacred Palace, with the mandate to summarise the Commission's work for the members of the Holy Office, who would in turn come back to Leo with a final recommendation. This volume includes the known *vota* or written opinions of the members of the theological Commission (in the case of Scannell a short letter published in *The Tablet*), an edited version of T. W. Lacey's diaries, together with Pierotti's painstakingly fair summary for the Holy Office (though making no bones about his own negative views and conclusions). The Holy Office met with the Pope on July 16th, in the absence of only the Cardinal Secretary of State Rampolla, who may have been in favour. The vote was unanimously against.

5. To complete the picture it would have been good to have included the minutes of that decisive meeting of the Holy Office. But their decision will have been based on Pierotti's summary and conclusions. The first draft of *Apostolicae Curae* is by the hand of Cardinal Mazzella, in Italian. The second draft, in Latin, follows Holy Office discussion with Mazzella. It is also certain that Merry del Val was involved

in the draft as he turned to Gasquet more than once in July and August for historical information. He sent the Latin draft to Gasquet in August for final comment.[4] The final draft includes many small corrections by Leo himself. The Pope will also, rightly, have been influenced by the feelings of his Catholic subjects in England: and perhaps by their conviction that a negative decision would speed the re-conversion of England. To top and tail the collection we include Portal's letter suggesting the project of Anglican orders, the official English translation of the Bull, and the important Response to it by the Archbishops of Canterbury and York, *Saepius Officio*, together with a moving letter from Lord Halifax to Portal after the publication of *Apostolicae Curae*.

6. The documents we have collected enable the reader to identify the arguments put forward on both sides of the question. But as the debate was complex, readers may be grateful for a thread to help them to pick their way through the maze of controversy. In what follows we shall try to provide such a thread, tracing the discussions point by point in three stages: first the *vota* formulated by the individual commissioners, then the discussion of the issues in the Commission as reported by Pierotti, and the Letter *Apostolicae Curae* itself. Finally we shall look briefly at the Answer of the Anglican Archbishops entitled *Saepius Officio*, and appraise the prospects of reaching agreement.

THE HISTORICAL FACTORS

7. In the discussion a distinction was commonly made between historical and theological factors. The most important historical factor concerned the precedent already set as early as the reign of Mary I and the papacy of Julius III and Paul IV, when Catholicism was restored with the help of the Papal Legate Cardinal Reginald Pole, and the question arose

---

4. We owe the discovery of the authorship of the draft (as of many other things) to Fr Rambaldi. Granted this Merry del Val's role was in connection with Gasquet as documented by J. J. Hughes, *Absolutely Null and Utterly Void*, Sheed and Ward, London, 1968, pp. 192–198.

whether clergy ordained according to the 1552 'Edwardine' Ordinal would need to be re-ordained. The ordinations performed during the schism under Henry VIII presented no difficulty, as no change had been made in the ordination ritual or in its interpretation; the validity of these ordinations was never called into question. The Catholic assessment of ordinations performed according to the Edwardine Ordinal, however, was quite different. As early as the time of Pole they were regarded as invalid. On several subsequent occasions the question was reopened, but the same answer was always given.

8.   The first decision to this effect is contained in the Bull of Julius III appointing Pole in 1553, which implied that only those 'rightly (*rite*) and legitimately promoted and ordained' were allowed to continue to exercise their orders; others had to receive ordination. Next year a papal Brief, in which Julius III confirmed Pole's faculties, helped to clarify the meaning of this right and legitimate ordination: a distinction is implied between those who were ordained by schismatical bishops according to 'the customary form of the Church' (as happened under Henry VIII) and those who had received orders 'less rightly and without the customary form of the Church being maintained' (as occurred once the new Ordinal was introduced under Edward VI).[5] A letter written by Pole to the Bishop of Norwich in 1555 shows that the Cardinal understood that the 'customary form of the Church' included the right intention as well as the spoken formula. Julius' successor Paul IV confirmed Pole's arrangements in a Bull dated 1555, and ordered the reordination of those who had been ordained by bishops who had themselves not been 'rightly and correctly (*rite et recte*) ordained'; in a Brief of the same year the Pope explained that ordination could be judged right and correct only if it was conferred 'in the form of the Church'. As a consequence there are several documented cases from the sixteenth century of Anglican clergy being

---

5. The phrase 'less rightly' (*minus rite*) is perhaps an elegant way of saying 'wrongly', and should not be taken as implying that the defects in the ordinations were only trivial.

reordained when they became Roman Catholics.[6] Nevertheless the historical evidence does not allow us to conclude that this happened in every case.[7]

9. The theologians of the Commission varied in their knowledge of these historical facts. Duchesne, for example, when he composed his *votum*, knew nothing of the two documents of Paul IV, which did not come to light until 1895; Duchesne, Gasparri and De Augustinis fail to distinguish Julius' Bull from his Brief; Duchesne and De Augustinis deny knowledge of any reordinations of former Anglican presbyters at this time. Pierotti records that detailed evidence for reordinations performed under Mary came to light only at the end of the Commission's work.

The theologians also varied in their interpretation of the facts. Gasparri notes that the ordinations were held to be invalid because the ordaining bishops had not themselves been consecrated according to the form of the Church; the silence concerning the adequacy of the form used in the ordination of presbyters, he argues, shows that the objection is raised only against the rite for the consecration of *bishops*. He contends that the requirement that ordination rites should follow the form of the Church does not mean that they must conform in every detail; it is enough if they are substantially in agreement with the Catholic rites (G 62). In any event, Paul IV was giving 'a practical guideline for a specific situation, ... not a definitive and irrevocable settlement of the question' (G 17). De Augustinis observes that the introduction of an insufficient rite was not included among the charges levelled against Cranmer when he was excommunicated in 1555; moreover the Holy Office's decision to 'defer' judgment in 1685 shows that the case was not yet regarded as closed (A 2). Scannell concludes that, as Rome had no wish to condemn all rites apart from that of the Pontifical, the Pope

---

6. Pierotti's report gives details of the documents dating from the time of Julius III and Paul IV.

7. Practice during the Marian restoration does not appear to have been consistent: cf. W. H. Frere, *The Marian Reaction*, London 1896.

must simply have meant that 'the external rite must be one which the Church would recognize as sufficient'. For the Westminster theologians on the other hand Paul's Bull and Brief laid 'the foundation for the original and invariable practice' of requiring ordination 'absolutely and *de novo*' (W 2); the 'form of the Church' was lacking in the sense that its 'essence' had been 'destroyed' (W 50, 62). They take Cardinal Pole to be stating that the lack of the 'form of the Church', which was the basis of the condemnation, meant that the form contained in the Roman Pontifical was not observed.

10. After this material had been discussed at length in the Commission, the President, Cardinal Mazzella, sought to clarify the mind of the members by asking each to state whether the directives given by Paul IV and Julius III settled the question of orders conferred according to the Edwardine rite. Four members, evidently Moyes, Gasquet, Fleming and Llevaneras, answered Yes, the other four No.

Pierotti set out five arguments which the defenders of validity used during the Commission's discussions, but judged that they had 'no force at all to negate or to put in doubt the strength of the papal documents and the historical facts' (P 19). The arguments and Pierotti's counterarguments were as follows: (1) The documents nowhere state explicitly that the ordinations were invalid simply because they were performed according to the Edwardine rite. To this Pierotti replied that, since no other rite is known in this connection, the condemnation of ordinations 'not in the customary form of the Church' must refer to the Ordinal of Edward VI. (2) The description of ordinations as 'invalid' may be a loose expression denoting rites that are illicit. Pierotti in answer maintained that there is no evidence for the use of the term *nulliter* as the equivalent of *illicite*. (3) The requirement that a rite to be valid must be performed according to 'the customary form of the Church' does not mean that it must necessarily conform to the Roman Pontifical but rather that it must contain the essential elements of ordination rites. Pierotti however held that Julius III's words concerning the lack of 'the *customary* form of the Church' show that the defect was the use of any new form. (4) Further to argument (3), it was maintained that since Paul IV, unlike Julius, did not use the word 'customary', he accepted that other forms besides that of the Pontifical could be valid. Pierotti's reply is that, if that is so, Paul's directive would have given no help to the legate in deciding which rites were valid. (5) Julius' instruction that those who had not been 'promoted' should be ordained need not imply that 'ordination' received according to the Edwardine Ordinal was invalid; the reference could be to those who had never received any form of ordination to the priesthood. Pierotti regards this as 'a mere hypothesis without any foundation'.

Apostolicae Curae also analysed these declarations by Popes Julius III and Paul IV, and concluded that they clearly show the origin of the rule, which has now been constantly observed for more than three centuries, of treating ordinations according to the Edwardine rite as null and void (AC 15).

11. The question of the validity of ordinations performed according to the Edwardine rite continued to be raised after the accession of Elizabeth in 1558, since she reintroduced that rite for the consecration of Matthew Parker as Archbishop of Canterbury in 1559. One case involved an unnamed French Calvinist who, after receiving the orders of deacon and priest in the Church of England, had become a Catholic and sought to have his orders declared invalid so that he could marry. He saw that his petition depended on two questions: whether there was a valid hierarchy in England, and whether the Anglican form for ordination was sufficient. The Holy Office accordingly set up an investigation of the case. After receiving the opinion of Cardinal Casanata, who observed that the words of the Edwardine Ordinal 'in no way signify the most essential power of the priest and bishop, i.e. the power to offer the sacrifice and to consecrate the Body of Christ', in 1685 the consultors of the Holy Office voted unanimously in favour of invalidity. However when this recommendation was passed on to the cardinals of the Holy Office, in whose competence it lay to pass a formal judgment, these

cardinals, apparently for pastoral reasons, decided to defer their verdict indefinitely (P 26–27).

The Westminster theologians, observing that the consultors' judgment of the insufficiency of the Anglican rite was based on the augmented form of 1662, concluded 'a fortiori that this verdict clearly tells against the sufficiency of the Anglican Ritual of 1552' (W 3). De Augustinis, on the other hand, pointed out that the decision to defer judgment showed that 'the question concerning the validity or nullity of Anglican ordinations had not been decided in Rome before 1684, nor was a decision taken in 1685' (A 2). *Apostolicae Curae* noted the opinion of the consultors, and attributed the postponement of the verdict to 'considerations of expediency' (AC 18). Pierotti however fairly records that according to Genetti the question of the validity of Anglican ordinations was still being 'hotly discussed among Catholics' in 1686 (P 29).

12. Another case came up in 1704, that of the convert Anglican bishop John Gordon, who sought presbyteral but not episcopal ordination in the Roman Catholic Church. Pope Clement XI, after hearing the recommendations of the cardinals of the Holy Office, determined that he should be reordained unconditionally (P 31).

Gasparri and Duchesne argued that this decision can be questioned, because the main reason alleged in the report of the proceedings of the Holy Office was the Nag's Head fable (G 19; D 47).[8] The Westminster theologians, on the other hand, placed more weight on the reasons stated in Genetti's *votum*, and concluded that the Gordon verdict was based on the defect of form in the Anglican Ordinal (W 4). Similarly Pierotti took Clement's decision to be 'an explicit and formal declaration of the invalidity of Anglican ordinations, by reason of the defect of form' (P 32). So too, according to *Apostolicae Curae*, although the decree

---

8. In fact, the papal decree itself gives no reasons for the verdict, even though the document relates Gordon's own contention that his episcopal consecration was invalid 'both by reason of the lack of legitimate succession in the bishops of England and Scotland who consecrated him, and for other reasons' (see P 31).

refers to a particular case, yet the ground upon which it was based was not particular. This ground was the 'defect of form', a defect from which all Anglican ordinations suffer equally (AC 21).

However the Archbishops' Answer gives four reasons for regarding the judgment to have a 'weak and unstable foundation', one of which is the use made of the Nag's Head story (SO 7). They refer also to an alleged judgment by the Holy Office given in 1704, which apparently accepted the validity of Abyssinian ordination conferred by the imposition of hands with the simple formula: 'Receive the Holy Ghost'. Gasparri's treatment of 'this difficult question' is given in G 69, note 39.[9]

Pierotti, Gasparri and the Westminster theologians referred also to later decisions by the Holy See. Pierotti cited the Holy Office's rebuttal in 1724 of Canon Courayer's defence of the validity of Anglican orders (P 34); the others, the Holy Office's negative reply to Cardinal Manning's inquiry in 1875 whether the Roman attitude to Abyssinian orders described above implied the validity of the rites of Anglicans (G 19; W 6).

13. Summing up the historical evidence, Gasparri and De Augustinis concluded that it is not decisive against validity. Thus according to Gasparri:

> the practice and the decisions of the Holy See opposed to the validity of Anglican ordinations, while carrying great weight among theologians, do not seem to settle the question. Catholics can discuss the question freely without fear of being accused of temerity (G 20).

De Augustinis went further and maintained that the historical evidence shows that:

> there has never been a Pontifical doctrinal decision which demonstrated the nullity of Anglican ordinations; nor

---

9. The Westminster theologians devoted to the Ethiopian question a scholion which, like much of their thorough documentation, we did not have space to include in our compilation.

was there any act of the Holy See which even implicitly affirmed this nullity in the first years of the new rite; on the contrary, there are documents which lead one to believe that the ordinations were held to be valid *at that time*. Later, that is from perhaps the first half of the 18th century, these ordinations were considered *from a practical point of view* to be invalid (A 8).

Duchesne recalled several occasions in history when ordinations by validly ordained popes were subsequently declared invalid, and concluded that such practical decisions, however solemnly proclaimed, do not constitute a definitive precedent (D 44–46).

For Pierotti, on the other hand, the examination of the question had been 'brought to a practical and decisive conclusion' with the decision in the Gordon case in 1704 (P 3); consequently 'the question regarding the Anglican Ordinations *is not an open one*, it cannot be said to be left to the free discussion of Catholic theologians, because the absolute invalidity of the same orders has been solemnly declared by the Supreme Authority of the Church, even from the year 1555.' (P 16).

Similarly Leo XIII's Bull, making use of the fuller evidence which came to light during and after the sessions of the commission, drew the following conclusion:

> It thus becomes quite obvious that the controversy which has recently been revived had already long ago been settled by the judgement of the Apostolic See (AC 22).

14. The weight to be attached to the decisions of the Holy See was not however the only historical factor. The validity or otherwise of Matthew Parker's episcopal consecration in 1559 was regarded as a matter of crucial importance because he was the principal channel of the apostolic succession of Anglican orders. 'The origin of all Anglican orders can be traced back to Matthew Parker'; validly consecrated bishops, like de Dominis, who participated in Anglican consecrations

later did not repair the break in the chain, because they acted only as assistants, and did not pronounce the sacramental form (W 44). If Parker's episcopal orders were invalid, the hierarchy became 'extinct', so that subsequent changes to the rite were irrelevant (AC 26). Gasparri however was more cautious, regarding Parker as the 'main' but not the 'sole' source (G 7).

None of the parties in the 1896 discussions allowed any credibility to the 'Nag's Head fable', according to which Parker had been consecrated in a tavern with minimal rites; the records showed that the ceremony was carried out in the chapel of Lambeth Palace according to the Edwardine Ordinal. The Westminster theologians however argued that there were grave doubts whether the four bishops who consecrated Parker had themselves been validly consecrated; they devoted their greatest efforts to impugning the consecration of Barlow, the principal consecrator. Gasparri, Duchesne and De Augustinis on the contrary all maintained that Parker's consecration was not open to doubt from this point of view, as the episcopal orders of Barlow at least were beyond reasonable doubt. This seems to have been the area in which Lacey and Puller were able to be of most help to the Commission.

THEOLOGICAL FACTORS: (I) FORM

15. As we have seen, one of the reasons which was given in the 1550s for requiring the reordination of priests ordained according to the Edwardine Ordinal was the failure to use 'the customary form of the Church'. So far we have been considering the discussion concerning the historical and canonical implications of such decisions; but in addition all of the *vota* went into the theological question concerning the form of words required for an ordination to be valid.

16. The Westminster theologians insisted that the imposition of hands must be accompanied by words which unambiguously determine the nature of the ordination (W 52). In the Edwardine rite the words 'Receive the Holy Ghost ...'

which go with the imposition failed in their sixteenth-century form to distinguish between the orders of priest and bishop, and so did not fulfil this criterion (W 55–56). Moreover the formula for the consecration of a bishop – 'remember that thou stir up the grace of God . . .' – was inadequate because it refers not to a person being ordained, but to one who has already been ordained (W 57). Although the Preface to the Ordinal declared the intention that the orders of bishops, priests and deacons, which have existed from the time of the Apostles, should be 'continued', it must be presumed that the Preface understands these three orders according to the heretical and inadequate conception of Cranmer and his associates (W 55, 59). In any event, the reformers' heretical understanding of Eucharist and priesthood prevents the words accompanying the laying on of hands from giving a sufficient determination to the action; 'the forms contained in the Edwardine Ritual cannot be given any Catholic sense' (W 62).

17. De Augustinis, in assessing the Anglican rite for episcopal consecration, takes into account not only the prayer for grace and the declaration ('Receive the Holy Ghost . . . stir up the grace of God which is given thee by this imposition of our hands; for God hath not given us the spirit of fear, but of power, and love, and holiness'), but also the words with which the candidate is presented to the Archbishop 'to be ordained and consecrated Bishop'. In any event he judges that the allusion to 2 Timothy 1.6–7 in the declaratory formula constitutes a sufficiently clear reference to episcopacy (A 19–21). On the same principles he concludes that the rite for priestly ordination is also sufficient, not only because of the mention of priesthood in the formula of presentation and the prayer for grace, but also because the declaratory formula ('Receive the Holy Ghost . . . Whose sins thou dost forgive, they are forgiven . . . And be thou a faithful Dispenser of the Word of God and of his Sacraments') implies priestly powers (A 22). The validity of these sacramental signs is not destroyed by the reformers' errors concerning the Eucharist, because the minister does

not act by his own power but as an instrument for the power of Christ (A 23–24).

18. Gasparri subscribed to the view that Jesus Christ instituted the imposition of hands as the matter of the sacrament, and a prayer for grace as the form; the imperative formula ('Receive the Holy Ghost ...') was a later addition by the Church, and is not by itself sufficient (G 57). The prayer for grace needs to specify the particular order in some way, but there is no *a priori* way of determining how that specification is to be made: the only criterion is the practice of the Church (G 59). The Anglican rite for the ordination of a deacon is probably insufficient because it contains no prayer for grace, though Gasparri acknowledges that some Catholic theologians believe the handing over of the Gospels with the accompanying words is sufficient (G 64–5). The rite for the presbyterate is better because it includes the prayer preceding the laying on of hands; but as this prayer does not contain a petition specifically for the grace of priesthood, but only a general petition for all the Church, it is not 'certainly sufficient' (G 74). The corresponding prayer in the consecration of a bishop, while not mentioning episcopate explicitly, is made for the candidate, and is sufficiently 'focused on the episcopate' by its context (G 79).

19. Duchesne argues that it is not consistent to demand a more explicit mention of the pristhood or episcopate in the Anglican rite than is found in various rites regarded as sufficient by the Roman Catholic Church (D 16, 30). If one takes into account the prayer for grace which precedes the imposition of hands and the declaration 'Receive the Holy Ghost ...' which follows it, the Edwardine rite is sufficiently explicit (D 25–29). In any event, the clearer the ritual action and the teaching of the church, the less need there is for precise specification by the accompanying words (D 32). It is only in the Anglican rite for the ordination of deacons that Duchesne finds these criteria unfulfilled (D 24–5).

20. Pierotti relates that the president sought to clarify the question of form by putting two questions to the commission. The first question asked whether it was essential for

the form to express the particular order being conferred; the four opponents of Anglican validity all answered Yes; two of the defenders of Anglican orders also answered Yes (one of them 'more probably Yes'), the other two replied No, one of them explaining that there can be sufficient determination from the whole rite. Pierotti's own answer, based on both theological reasoning and historic precedent, is 'absolutely in the affirmative' (P 40–41). The president then asked whether this designation of the order to be conferred was to be found in the Anglican rite. For his own part, Pierotti answers No on the grounds that the words 'Receive the Holy Ghost' (the following words not being part of the form) are not sufficiently definite to be able to serve as the form of the sacrament. Those who maintained invalidity all answered No. The other four gave affirmative responses for various reasons: because the form was sufficiently definite, or because it was determined by other words or by its setting in the rite. Pierotti for his own part argued against their appeal to the prayer for grace contained in the litanies, or to the words 'Receive the Holy Ghost' themselves (P 42–46).

21. The president then proposed two further questions concerning the form for episcopal ordination: were the words so ambiguous as to need further determination? If so, where was that determination to be found? In reply the eight theologians did little more than refer back to their previous answers. Pierotti himself agreed with the invalidity party that the Anglican rite fails to express episcopacy unambiguously, and that the missing determination of meaning is not to be found in other parts of the rite. He concluded therefore that 'the *form* of the Ordinal, looked at objectively in itself, *is invalid*' (P 47).

22. *Apostolicae Curae* itself accepted with some modifications the argument against the sufficiency of the Anglican form. The form must give precise determination to the indeterminate act of the laying on of hands (AC 24); however this determination cannot be present in a rite from which all reference to sacrificing priesthood has been systematically removed (AC 27). Even though similar words may have

been adequate in rites accepted by the Catholic Church, they cannot be sufficient in the Anglican case because of the *objective* 'native character and spirit of the Ordinal' (AC 31).

23. The president then proposed a fifth and a sixth question. The fifth asked whether formulas which could bear a Catholic sense but had been twisted into the opposite meaning could be said to retain their Catholic sense in the new rite. The four opponents of validity, with the approval of Pierotti, gave a negative answer, on the grounds that the meaning given to the words by the one who pronounces them is decisive. Gasparri, Duchesne and Scannell also replied No, if there was the intention to convey a substantial error. De Augustinis adopted a solitary position, answering that the decisive factor was the meaning of the words as instituted by Christ (P 49).

The sixth question asked the members of the commission whether the Ordinal had been so framed as to exclude the Catholic doctrine of Orders. Pierotti summarised and endorsed the evidence collected by the Westminster theologians in support of their emphatic affirmative answer. He also set out some of the arguments which the defenders of validity put forward in justification of their negative reply. Gasparri argued that the Ordinal, though omitting elements of Catholic doctrine, did not positively propose heretical views. De Augustinis maintained that the compilers' aim was to return to the practice of the early Church. The retention of the threefold ministry of deacons, priests and bishops was also seen to be significant. Pierotti himself rebutted each of these arguments (P 50–55).

24. In the written *vota* and the deliberations of the commission attention was concentrated on the original Edwardine version of the declaration 'Receive the Holy Ghost', without the determining clauses 'for the office of a bishop/priest' which were added in 1662. Presumably the understanding was that Anglican orders had to be attacked and defended at their root. For the Westminster theologians in fact the addition amounted to an admission that the form had not been sufficiently determined originally (W 56, 67). The

Anglican Archbishops, however, pointed out that historically the words were not added in 1662 to meet Roman objections, but 'to enlighten the minds of the Presbyterians' (SO 15).

THEOLOGICAL FACTORS: (II) INTENTION

25. In traditional sacramental theology, if a sacrament is to be valid the minister must have the intention of doing what the Church does.[10] One of the charges brought against Anglican ordinations has been that this intention was not present. However this alleged defect was not always distinguished from the question of form.

Gasparri, Duchesne and De Augustinis did discuss this issue at considerable length. All three give credit to the declaration made in the Preface to the Ordinal, that the purpose of the new rite is to continue the orders of bishops, priests and deacons, which have existed in the Church since the time of the Apostles (G 28; A 33; D 38). Errors about the effect of a sacrament do not necessarily imply that the requisite intention is lacking: it is sufficient to intend what the Church *does*, even if one does not intend what the Church *intends* (A 28–32; G 42; cf above, n. 12). However, Gasparri and Duchesne indicate a further difficulty: if the ordainer not only does not intend, but *positively intends to exclude*, the effect of the sacrament, the two acts of the will – both to do and not to do what the Church does – would be mutually exclusive and the sacrament consequently invalid (G 42; D 39–40). But did the ordaining bishops positively will the exclusion at the time of ordaining? Duchesne thought not (D 40); for Gasparri however the changes which the reformers introduced into the Mass make the supposition plausible, so that 'a shadow falls across all Anglican ordinations' (G 49). However the adoption of a rite which is not approved by the Catholic Church is not in itself evidence of

---

10. Cf Council of Trent, Session VII, Canons on the Sacraments in General, canon 11 (DS 1611).

the lack of due intention; firstly, the argument would prove too much, namely the invalidity of all rites apart from the Catholic ones (D 37; G 32); secondly, although the intention of using the rite of the Catholic Church was clearly lacking, all that was needed was the intention of doing with the non-Catholic rite what the Catholic Church does with the Catholic rite. Duchesne and De Augustinis believe that this was the case in the 1560s. Gasparri is more critical: the intention can be presumed only if the essential elements of ordination are retained – which was sadly not the case with regard to Anglican ordinations, so that at Barlow's consecration 'a defective intention in the external forum was probable without being certain' (G 80).

26. The Westminster theologians also concentrated less on the personal intention of the ordainer than on the 'Intention of the Rite'. This they understand as 'what the Ordinal was designed to express'; 'common sense and unquestionable theological principles' show that the intention was the suppression of the Catholic doctrines of priesthood and sacrifice W 48. Consequently Parker's consecrators did not have the necessary intention of doing what the Church did (W 62); indeed it was positively excluded (W 63).

Pierotti discusses the question briefly in terms of the intention of the ordaining bishop. Quoting historic precedent and St Thomas Aquinas, he argues that if an ordaining bishop employs a rite which has been changed with a heretical intention, he cannot be intending to do what the Church does (P 48).

27. In some of this discussion there was a failure to distinguish between the various senses of intention: the intention of the compilers of the Ordinal, the intention of the Ordinal itself, the intention of Parker's consecrators, and finally the intention of bishops who followed the Ordinal on subsequent occasions, though Duchesne draws some valuable distinctions (D 39).[11] *Apostolicae Curae* however introduced a degree of

---

11. This question is discussed with precision by Francis Clark, *Anglican Orders and Defect of Intention*, London, 1956.

precision, disclaiming any purpose of judging the internal intention of ordaining bishops; the key factor was the choice of rite. The use of the Catholic rite would have created a *presumption* of the intention to do what the Church does; on the other hand, the use of a rite which rejects Catholic doctrine is evidence not merely of the absence of the intention to do what the Church does, but of the presence of an intention which is incompatible with it (AC 33).[12]

THEOLOGICAL FACTORS:
(III) *TRADITIO INSTRUMENTORUM*

28. The Anglican Ordinal of 1552 discarded the rite of the *traditio* or *porrectio instrumentorum*, by which the bishop handed to the ordinands the sacred objects of their order, namely a paten with the host and a chalice with the wine. Gasparri (G 67) seems to be the only commissioner to regard this omission as a reason possibly telling against Anglican ordinations, and even he is speaking as a canonist in terms of practical jurisprudence. Pierotti shows that the absence of the *traditio* was not regarded as a relevant consideration in the case of the French Calvinist (P 26); similarly the Bull noted that the verdict in the Gordon case 'was in no way influenced' by the omission (AC 21).[13]

THE FINAL RECOMMENDATION

29. In the light of the responses to the six questions the president now sought the commissioners' verdicts in a seventh: 'What judgment, therefore, should be made about the form and intention in this new rite?' The Westminster theologians and Llaveneras, consistently with their earlier replies, now

---

12. Clark showed that this argument was based on what he called 'the principle of positive exclusion' (*Anglican Orders and Defect of Intention*, p. 201). Gasparri expounds the principle, but does not believe that positive exclusion can be proved to have existed in the case of Anglican ordinations (G 42ff).

13. This does not touch on the question of whether the omission of the *traditio* was thought to be relevant at the time of the Marian restoration; a point noted in the Archbishops' reply.

answered that both a valid rite and the requisite intention were missing; Pierotti himself supported this verdict.

Among the defenders of Anglican orders, on the other hand, a degree of weakening was now evident. Duchesne and Gasparri seem to have adhered to their belief that there was some possibility but no certainty that the orders were valid; De Augustinis and Scannell however seem now to have abandoned their unqualified acceptance of validity, and now went no further than maintaining the 'probable' validity of Anglican orders. It follows that four of the commissioners would require the absolute reordination of former Anglican presbyters, while four would require them to be reordained conditionally (P 56).

It scarcely needs repeating that the Bull came down in favour of absolute invalidity:

> Therefore adhering entirely to the decrees of the Pontiffs Our Predecessors on this subject, and fully ratifying and renewing them by Our own authority, on Our own initiative and with certain knowledge, We pronounce and declare that ordinations performed according to the Anglican rite have been and are completely null and void (AC 36).

30. However *Apostolicae Curae* did not endorse the arguments of the Westminster theologians and Pierotti at every point, as Rambaldi points out.[14] Thus Leo XIII did not insist that the matter and the form must be virtually simultaneous, and consequently did not place as much emphasis on the words 'Receive the Holy Ghost' as the invalidity party had done. The Bull gives as its reason for discussing these words the fact that Anglicans themselves 'until recent times' had taken them to constitute the 'proper form' of the sacrament (AC 25). For the Pope the decisive factor was the 'native character and spirit' of the whole rite (AC 31). *Apostolicae Curae* concluded that the Anglican Ordinal failed this test;

---

14. G. Rambaldi, 'La bolla "Apostolicae Curae" di Leone XIII sulle Ordinazioni Anglicane – II', *Gregorianum*, 66 (1985), pp. 53–88.

but the logic leaves open the possibility that new circumstances might remove the defects of the native character and spirit. Cardinal J. Willebrands envisaged this possibility when he suggested that ARCIC II would do well to re-examine current Anglican ordination formularies to see if they accorded with the theology of the Final Report of ARCIC I.[15] Indeed in 1994 the Vatican implied that the native character and spirit of the Ordinal might change, when it gave this as the reason why conditional rather than absolute ordination was judged appropriate when Dr Graham Leonard, the former Anglican Bishop of London, was ordained priest in the Roman Catholic church in 1994.[16]

THE ARCHBISHOPS' ANSWER

31. The Bull itself was published on 13th September 1896. By the 19th July the following year the Archbishops of Canterbury and York had issued a reply (the official version of which was in Latin) entitled *Saepius Officio*. It was addressed 'to the whole body of Bishops of the Catholic Church'. As the letter itself observes, Edward Benson, Archbishop of Canterbury, who died soon after the publication of the Bull, had already begun to outline a response. The new Archbishop of Canterbury, Frederick Temple made major contributions to the important chapters on eucharistic sacrifice (11) and the 'form' of the sacrament (19). But the text was really the work of the Bishop of Salisbury, John Wordsworth, who had already been working on questions to do with Anglican orders in connection with the early Anglican dialogue with the Dutch Old Catholics. Wordsworth had also written the Preface to T. E. Lacey's work on the Anglican episcopal succession. The Archbishop's

---

15. J. Willebrands, Letter to the Co-chairmen of ARCIC II, 13 July 1985, included in *Anglican Orders – a New Context*, CTS, London, 1986.

16. Some of the documentation can be read in *The Tablet*, 30 April 1994. Cf E. J. Yarnold, 'A New Context: ARCIC and Afterwards', *Anglican Orders*, ed. R. W. Franklin, Mowbray, London 1996, pp. 70–73.

Letter focuses first on the historical question of what in fact happened during the Marian reaction; and then on the more important and theologically related questions of the form of the Anglican rite and its intention.

On the historical questions the reply admitted some ignorance but showed evidence of inconsistency and unevenness in the Marian re-ordinations. Many Edwardine clergy were deprived, especially for marriage, but rarely for a defect in order.[17] Some were re-ordained. Others were not, yet they continued in their benefices, even being promoted. Others received anointing as a supplement to their previous ordination. Moreover very few of them were actually re-ordained after Pole's arrival. It also notes that Pole appended to his Legatine Constitutions the Decree of Pope Eugenius IV for the Armenians which understood the matter of the sacrament of Order to be the giving of the chalice with wine and the paten with bread. The Archbishops argued here that the Edwardine ordinal restored the essential matter of the sacrament of Order (the laying on of hands) to its proper centrality. They note that Pope Leo himself rejects the *porrectio instrumentorum* (the handing over of chalice and paten with bread and wine) in the Bull (SO 6). They identify the Holy Office's decision in the Gordon case of 1704 as the point at which a tradition was established from which Leo XIII could hardly depart, but they question the grounds on which that decision was based (SO 7).

32. The Archbishops agree with the Pope that the question of sacramental intention is central. This can be ascertained from the Church of England's formularies and 'definite pronouncements'. They cite the Preface to the Ordinal which speaks explicitly of the Orders of Bishop, Priest and

---

17. The most recent survey of the complex historical evidence is found in G. H. Tavard *A Review of Anglican Orders*, Liturgical Press, Collegeville, Minnesota, 1990. He summarises the evidence for the early Marian deprivation of Edwardine clergy on grounds of marriage rather than defective orders. He further argues that the Papal documents cited by *Apostolicae Curae* only concern bishops ordained by the Ordinal not necessarily those ordained by such bishops. This is argued because Pope Paul IV was concerned with papal jurisdiction, not the modern question of matter and form.

Deacon as existing from the 'Apostles' time' and 'the intent that these orders should be continued. ... in this Church of England', noting that the Bull is entirely silent about the Preface. (SO 8, 17).

The Archbishops also respond to the argument that the rejection of the doctrine of the eucharistic sacrifice nullifies any catholic intention. They argue that the Anglican Church teaches such a doctrine and that it is compatible with one of the interpretations of the eucharistic sacrifice promulgated by the Council of Trent (SO 11). The Archbishops also argue that the Anglican Ordinal is compatible with the ancient Roman ordination prayers. Moreover the requirement that the form for the presbyterate must specify the power of 'offering the sacrifice of the Body and Blood of Christ' is not met by the earliest extant ordination rites. Thus it would follow that the Roman Catholic hierarchy had become extinct in the same way as the Anglican hierarchy was said by the Bull to be extinct. 'Thus in overthrowing our orders, he [Pope Leo] overthrows all his own, and pronounces sentence on his own Church' (SO 20). They also note that the additional specification of bishops, priests and deacons in 1662 was directed not against Roman Catholic criticism but the Presbyterian doctrine of a single order of ministry (SO 15).

FUTURE PROSPECTS

33. Leo XIII, Cardinal Vaughan and the Westminster theologians intended *Apostolicae Curae* to put an end to the prospect of a reunion between Rome and Canterbury based on the recognition of Anglican orders. They hoped that the removal of false hopes would move Anglican clergy to acknowledge the nullity of their orders and so to seek ordination within the Roman Catholic Church; but the number of Anglicans who have taken this road has been relatively small. The centenary of *Apostolicae Curae* should be an opportunity for asking whether after all there may be other paths leading to a less ultramontaine unity.

One approach accepts the force of Leo XIII's decision

when applied to the situation of 1896, but asks whether the changed circumstances of 1996 would justify a different verdict. Thus, as we have seen, Cardinal Willebrands envisaged that the Roman Catholic and Anglican processes of reception of the ARCIC I Final Report might constitute a change, from the traditional Roman Catholic viewpoint, in the native character of the Anglican Ordinal and in the other rites that have been introduced since then. It must however be confessed that not every change that has taken place in the last hundred years has made the native character of the Ordinal more acceptable to the Roman Catholic Church; the ordination of women to the priesthood and the episcopate has certainly added a new problem to the many that already existed.[18]

34. However, as Cardinal Willebrands noted, recognition of a change in the native character of the Anglican rite would still leave the question of the apostolic succession to be solved. This could be done by absolute or conditional reordinations; a more radical solution might be sought in a reexamination of the doctrine of apostolic succession in the hope of establishing that a succession of churches in faith and Christian life could supply for a breach in a chain of episcopal ordinations. Anglicans themselves have pursued this line of reasoning in coming to recognise the orders of the Danish Lutheran Church in which the episcopal succession was broken;[19] the Roman Catholic Church, however, has not itself adopted such a procedure in its relations with other churches.

35. Though the canonical force of *Apostolicae Curae* is not in doubt, the Bull leaves a number of questions not yet fully resolved.[20] (1) Does Pius XII's decision of 1947, that the essential act in the sacrament of Order is the imposition of

---

18. Pope John Paul II wrote to the Archbishop of Canterbury in 1988 stating that the Anglican decision to ordain women appeared to 'block the path to the mutual recognition of ministries'.

19. *Together in Mission and Ministry: The Porvoo Common Statement*, Church House Publishing, London, 1993.

20. Some of these points are discussed in G. Rambaldi, 'La bolla "Apostolicae Curae" ... II', pp. 77–87.

the bishop's hands together with the prayer for the power and grace of the order conferred, affect the principles on which the judgment of 1896 was based? What are the limits of the power of the Church to modify sacramental signs? (2) Do the decisions to reordain absolutely taken under Julius III and Paul IV necessarily constitute precedents which will remain in force in perpetuity? Were the decisions dogmatic, concerning faith, or were they merely pastoral and disciplinary? (3) Could the Anglican Churches claim to have the same power as the Eastern Orthodox to make unilateral liturgical changes? (4) Does the argument of *Apostolicae Curae* lose some of its cogency now that Vatican II has broadened the Roman Catholic conception of ordained ministry so that priesthood is no longer understood so exclusively as the power to offer sacrifice? (5) Does Vatican II's acknowledgment that elements of sanctification and truth exist outside the Roman Catholic Church mean that the recognition of the validity of orders has become less important since even invalid orders may be means of grace?

The Documents

LETTER OF F. PORTAL TO THE EDITOR OF THE *MONITEUR DE ROME*

Sir,

[1] Various circumstances have prevented me from thanking you earlier for publishing in the *Moniteur* the concluding section of my pamphlet on Anglican ordinations. I wanted to wait until I had discovered the impression made in England by the brief remarks with which you introduced it; then I was led to expect a very important letter, and I did not want to write to you before I had received it.

The impression made was excellent, I can positively assure you, and you can judge the value of the letter for yourself from the enclosed copy.

[2] The author of the letter, who has honoured me with his friendship, is Lord Halifax. Lord Halifax holds a high position in England, and is the friend – indeed, the intimate friend – of the Prince of Wales. His [grand]father was Prime Minister, and if he has not himself gained a name in active politics, this is because he has dedicated his life to the Church, and in particular to the unity of the Church. He is a member of the Anglican Church, but he is a man of unimpeachably good faith, great piety, and solid virtue; I like to call him my very dear holy heretic. In addition, he is very well informed, and a very good theologian. In the Anglican Church he is a leading member of the Church Union, a society which includes seventeen bishops; he does battle fiercely against the dissenters, the protestants, and even wages a campaign against the government over the schools question and disestablishment.

[3] I got to know Lord Halifax at Madeira, where over a period of four months I spent a considerable amount of time with him. My superiors kindly allowed me to continue my

contacts with him, and I have been able to spend a week with my friend every year. Our talks and interminable tête-à-têtes have all borne on a single subject to which everything else leads us: the Church, the unity of the Church. In the end we made up our minds to try something out. It seemed to us that the question of Orders offered an excellent battlefield. Hence my pamphlet. I can assure you that, despite my negative conclusion, its effect has been excellent. The Archbishop of Canterbury, the Archbishop of York, the Bishop of Salisbury and many others have taken an interest in our initiative; they have been struck by my loyalty, and when they heard of the excitement which my work aroused among our theologians they declared candidly that this was something to be taken seriously.

[4] This evening or tomorrow I shall send you two articles, one by P.Duchesne, the other from the review published by the Jesuits, which met with their strong approval. In a private letter P. Duchesne had asked me to make his opinion known; this letter has made a favourable impression with the highly placed Anglican clergy to whom I communicated it by the good offices of Lord Halifax.

[5] As a Catholic of no official standing, I have told the Anglicans that it was up to them to refer the matter to Rome. This was the only position open to me. However, in view of the genuinely good dispositions of several figures in the Anglican Church, of several members of the Anglican episcopate whose support I seem to have enlisted for our campaign, would it not be possible to venture on a step which would add impetus to the movement and put pressure on hesitant wills? You can see what Lord Halifax thinks; and he is too prudent, too experienced in handling people, and has discussed the matter too much with his coreligionists to be mistaken. You can rely on him and proceed confidently. I believe then that if one could at the present moment draw the attention of Cardinal Rampolla and His Holiness to the way people are thinking, this would be a skilful manoeuvre which would yield great results.

[6] What is needed is that in one way or another the Holy

Father should let the Anglican bishops know that the Roman Church is prepared to examine the question of Anglican ordinations, etc. etc., to quote Lord Halifax. If a direct letter is thought to be inopportune, a letter could be addressed to me as the author of the pamphlet on Anglican ordinations. But it is not for me to suggest the most appropriate means; that would certainly be too bold on my part. I will simply add that I leave for London in a few days' time. I beg you, Sir, to be so good as to send me a reply at the address below and to forgive me for writing so long a letter. If I have taken the liberty of writing to you, the reason is that one of my confrères, who are friends of M. Monteuuis, has assured me that I could find no better intermediary with Cardinal Rampolla than the Editor of the *Moniteur de Rome*. It is my fervent hope that our Lord is making use of us, Sir, to do some good in his Church.

[7] I do not need to add, Sir, that none of all this is for the journal, and I beg you to observe the strictest discretion in the use you make of it. Here, in the *l'Univers* and in *le Monde*, gentlemen seem inclined to meddle in my affairs and to wage a campaign against my friends.

I have the honour to be, Sir, your humble and very devoted servant,

Portal
c/o Viscount Halifax
79 Eaton Square, London

ON THE VALIDITY OF ANGLICAN ORDERS

P. Gasparri

I
A HISTORICAL SUMMARY TO ESTABLISH THE STATE OF THE QUESTION

1. The question of the validity or invalidity of Anglican ordinations is put before us today, and all those who follow the movement of ideas must examine the question and provide an answer. I had a particular reason for devoting serious study to this fascinating question. In my treatise *De Sacra Ordinatione* I had been unusually blind in following the Roman schools; I accepted the fable of the ordination at the Nag's Head (n.18), and as a result I concluded that Anglican ordinations were evidently invalid. When M. Dalbus's pamphlet *Les ordinations anglicanes* in 1894 revived the controversy, I soon recognised that the story of the Nag's Head was a fabrication, and that the question was more difficult and important than I had thought. I now intend to examine it, and I shall begin by examining the state of the question.

2. Schism in England dates from the spring of 1534. But Henry VIII, the author of this sad separation, in the course of his reign did not want to go beyond a mere schism. As a result, up to the time of his death on 28 January 1547 liturgical books in England did not undergo any change; ordinations to the diaconate, presbyterate and episcopate were carried out by schismatic bishops according to the ancient Catholic rites.

3. HenryVIII's successor in 1547 was his son Edward VI, a boy of nine, placed under regents whom Henry had appointed before his death. Shortly before Edward's reign began, parliament set up a commission to compose a book in the vernacular containing morning and evening prayer, the liturgy, and the rites for the administration of the sacraments. The part of the book which related to the rites of ordination was called an Ordinal, and appeared in 1550. From this time onwards ordinations to the diaconate, presbyterate and episcopate (the Ordinal suppressed the other ministries) were carried out by schismatic English bishops according to the rites of the Ordinal of Edward VI of 1550. Earlier ordinations had been carried out according to Catholic rites.

4. In 1552 this first Ordinal of Edward VI's reign was expurgated again. The only important change referred to the presbyterate: the handing over of the chalice and the bread was suppressed. The new Ordinal was in use by All Saints 1552. Only one bishop was ordained under Edward VI according to the rites of the Ordinal: John Harley, Bishop of Hereford, ordained on 26 May 1553 by Cranmer, assisted by Ridley and Aldrich, the Bishop of Carlisle. It is more than likely that ordinations of deacons and presbyters were carried out according to this Ordinal in Edward VI's time, before Queen Mary came to the throne.

5. Edward's successor was Mary, his legitimate sister, who reigned from 1553 to 1558.[1] As a Catholic she wanted to bring England back into communion with the Church of Rome. She suppressed Edward VI's Ordinal and restored the original Catholic rite with all the degrees of the hierarchy of orders. To undo the damage of the past and to prepare for the future, Pope Julius III appointed Cardinal Pole his legate in England with very extensive powers. It goes without saying that all the ordinations in Mary's reign were carried out according to Catholic rites.

6. Mary's successor was Elizabeth, the daughter of Henry

---

1. Mary entered London on 19 July 1553; on 14 September she imprisoned the Archbishop of Canterbury, Cranmer, in the Tower of London; her coronation was celebrated on 2 October.

VIII and Anne Boleyn; she reigned from 1558 to the end of 1603. When she came to the throne Elizabeth again pulled England from the centre of unity and into a state of schism. Mary died on 15 November 1558, and in February 1559 Parliament restored the Prayer Book of Edward VI including the Ordinal of 1552. This book thus became for the second time the official liturgical text of the Anglican Church.

7. The see of Canterbury became vacant, because Cardinal Pole only lived a few hours longer than Queen Mary. Elizabeth decided to choose her own candidate, and favoured Matthew Parker, who had been her tutor and her mother's chaplain. He was consecrated on 17 December 1559; according to which rites? Here we find the famous story of the Nag's Head. This legend tells us that the candidates for the episcopate in the new church came together in an inn whose sign was a horse's head. There they were consecrated in a way that was as cursory as it was original. As they knelt, Bishop Scory placed the open Bible on each one's head, saying: *Receive the power to preach the word of God in all sincerity*. Then, taking each one by the hand, he is said to have added: *Arise, Bishop of London*, etc. Now Parker, the Archbishop of Canterbury, is alleged to have been among these candidates. Nowadays nobody believes this story, which is totally improbable and has been rightly rejected. The truth is that Parker was consecrated by four bishops: Barlow, Bishop of Chichester; Miles Coverdale, former Bishop of Exeter; John Scory, former Bishop of Chichester; and John Hodgkins, coadjutor of Bedford, who had been consecrated in 1537 according to the old Catholic rite. The principal consecrator was Barlow, and the consecration was carried out according to the rites of the Ordinal. However, there was one peculiar feature which was pointed out by the authors of the *Dissertatio apologetica de Hierarchia Anglicana*,[2] n. 17: whereas usually only the

---

2. E. Denny and T. A. Lacey, *De Hierarchia Anglicana Dissertatio apologetica*, London 1895. In this dissertation, which favours Anglican orders, the discussion is conducted vigorously, but at the same time with a courtesy which many Catholics would do well to imitate. This defence of Anglican orders must be read by anyone interested in the question.

consecrating archbishop imposed hands on the candidate saying: *Receive the Holy Ghost*, etc, on this occasion, as there was no archbishop present, the four bishops all imposed hands and pronounced the formula: *Receive the Holy Ghost*, etc. Once he had been consecrated, Parker ordained several other bishops nominated by the Queen, so that he must be considered the main source of the Anglican clergy, even if he cannot be called the sole source.

8. Finally in 1662, that is to say almost a century later in the reign of James II (*sic!*),[3] the Ordinal received certain alterations, some of which were important. In Edward VI's Ordinal, the bishop when ordaining a presbyter imposed his hands on the candidate and said: *Receive the Holy Ghost. Whose sins thou dost forgive, they are forgiven; and whose sins thou dost retain they are retained: and be thou a faithful dispenser of the word of God, and of his holy sacraments. In the name of the Father, and of the Son, and of the Holy Ghost.* In 1662 this formula was extended as follows: *Receive the Holy Ghost for the office and work of a priest in the Church of God, now committed unto thee by the impositon of our hands. Whose,* etc. In the consecration of a bishop, according to the Ordinal, the bishop imposed his hands on the candidate, saying: *Receive the Holy Ghost. And remember that thou stir up the grace of God which is given thee by this imposition of our hands: for God hath not given us the spirit of fear, but of power, and love, and soberness.* In 1662 this formula was changed to: *Receive the Holy Ghost for the office and work of a bishop in the Church of God, now committed unto thee by the imposition of our hands: in the name of the Father and of the Son and of the Holy Ghost. Amen. And remember that thou stir up the grace of God which is given thee by this imposition of our hands: for God,* etc.

9. Such are the main facts about the history of Anglican ordinations. Now the ordinations according to Catholic rites under Henry VIII and in Edward VI's reign before the Ordinal have always been considered certainly valid.

---

3. [The author has confused his kings; he should of course have said Charles II.]

Ordinations conducted according to the rites of the 1550 Ordinal have been challenged, but they are not under consideration in this study. We shall not need to refer to the changes made in the 1662 Ordinal. The only question for this study will be to know whether Anglican ordinations carried out by bishops using the 1552 Ordinal are to be considered as certainly invalid, or as certainly valid, or as doubtful.[4]

10. I shall make one last observation before embarking on the topic. If Anglican baptisms were invalid, or if they had been invalid at a certain stage of their history, their ordinations would also be invalid, and it would be useless in practice to argue about Barlow's episcopal consecration, about the intention of the Anglican minister, about the adequacy or inadequacy of the Ordinal. In this study I prescind from this indirect cause of invalidity; I assume that Anglican baptisms are valid and have always been valid. Beginning from this hypothesis I ask whether their orders are equally valid.

II
IS THE THEORETICAL QUESTION STILL AN OPEN ONE FOR CATHOLICS?

11. After the Ordinals of 1550 and 1552 (see nn. 3, 4) replaced the old Catholic pontificals, Catholic church authorities naturally had to ask themselves whether deacons, priests and bishops, ordained since the schism in the new rite, were real deacons, real priests and real bishops. One can take it for granted that these ordinations were considered invalid. Nevertheless one should not exaggerate: the few documents we still possess on this subject are not particularly clear, nor do they indicate decisively that Catholics are not allowed to discuss the matter. Surely the present attitude of the Holy See to this controversy strongly confirms this impression.

12. For a full understanding of these documents we are

---

4. [Gasparri refers the reader to an Appendix setting out the text of the Ordinal in its three recensions.]

about to discuss it is highly necessary to point out that at the accession of Queen Mary there were four types of ordained Anglicans: (1) those who as Catholics had been ordained by Catholic bishops according to the Catholic rites and then went into schism in the reigns of Henry VIII and Edward VI; (2) those who as schismatics had been ordained by schismatic bishops according to Catholic rites before the Ordinal of 1550 (see nn. 2, 3); (3) those who as schismatics had been ordained by schismatic bishops according to the 1550 Ordinal (see n. 3); (4) finally those who as schismatics had been ordained by schismatic bishops according to the 1552 Ordinal (see n. 4). The ordinations of those in the first two categories were not challenged (see n. 9). It was different for the other two groups.

13. In her letter to the bishops of the kingdom on 4 March 1554, Queen Mary gave the following instructions: 'Touching such persons as were heretofore promoted to any orders, *after the new sort and fashion of order*, *considering they were not ordained in very deed*, the bishop of the diocese finding otherwise sufficiency and ability in those men, may supply that thing which wanted in them before, and then, according to his discretion, admit them to minister.' The invalidity of Anglican orders according to the 1550 and 1552 Ordinals is clearly indicated. Nevertheless a command from Queen Mary cannot settle a serious theological controversy.

14. Julius III in a series of letters gave his legate the powers he needed to reconcile the Church of England; powers which are partly found in the Bull of 8 March 1554 addressed to Cardinal Pole.[5] According to this Bull the Cardinal, in spite of all kinds of irregularities, censures and other penalties that had been incurred, could authorise those who had been ordained to exercise the sacred ministry, 'provided that prior to falling into this heresy, they were rightly and legitimately promoted and ordained'. It would seem that the

---

5. [Actually this is a papal Brief; the original Bull was dated 1553. Pierotti (n. 6) explains that the distinction between the Bull and the Brief was not recognised until after the commission had completed its work.]

Cardinal Legate could only authorise those who belonged to the first category of those who 'prior to falling into this heresy ... were rightly and legitimately promoted and ordained'. Nevertheless this restriction does not prove that the Pope regarded as invalid all the Anglican ordinations performed by schismatic bishops even according to Catholic rites; the refusal to dispense may have been based on other reasons.

On the other hand Julius III, putting an end to doubts that had been raised, said in this Bull[6] that the Cardinal Legate could exercise all these powers in Flanders as well as in England; that in Flanders he can exercise them '... also in favour of other persons to whom we have referred in any way in each of the aforenamed letters [the letters previously addressed to the Cardinal], if they should come or send to you as occasion offers, *also with regard to Orders which they never received or have received badly, and the consecration which was conferred on them by other Bishops or Archbishops, even heretics and schismatics, or otherwise less rightly and without the customary form of the Church being maintained.*' Anglican[7] and Catholic advocates of the validity of Anglican orders are pleased to quote these words in support of their thesis. While recognising that these words are not entirely clear, I believe that the interpretation these writers give is not strict enough. It is permissible to let them refer to certain other dispensations without going so far as the recognition and acceptance of ordinations performed after the schism according to the rites of the Ordinal.

It is true that the Pope adds further on that the Cardinal Legate will have the right to keep in their sees, or to transfer elsewhere, heretical or schismatical archbishops and bishops who have renounced heresy and who can then 'make use of the consecration previously conferred, or if it has not yet been conferred on them [archbishops or bishops who have been merely elected and not yet consecrated], to receive it freely and lawfully from such Catholic bishops or archbishops as

---

6. [Actually the words come from Julius' subsequent Brief (see P 6).]

7. Cf *De Hierarchia Anglicana*, p. 223ff.

you shall name'. The Legate will also have the right to allow them 'even to minister at the altar if they have been less rightly ordained'. But there is nothing to prevent us from referring these words to ordinations performed before or after the schism according to the old Catholic Pontificals in spite of some accidental defects.

Thus neither the validity nor the invalidity of Anglican orders is affirmed by Julius III in his Bull of 8 March 1554.[8]

15. To ease the return of those who had strayed from Catholic unity, the Cardinal made generous use of the powers he had been given; he even sub-delegated powers to other bishops. In his letter of 29 January 1555 to the Bishop of Norwich, he authorised him to dispense from all sorts of irregularities and to allow the exercise of orders which had been received *even from heretical and schismatic bishops, even less rightly, provided that in their ordination the form and intention of the Church was maintained*'. Clearly he went beyond the restrictions of Julius III; we must therefore assume that he had received more extensive powers. Anglicans and supporters of the validity of Anglican orders think that the words *even from heretical and schismatic bishops, even less rightly*' include all Anglican ordinations, even those conducted according to the rites of the Ordinals; and that the expression *provided that in their ordination the form and intention of the Church was maintained*' is a general clause covering those cases where the valid form or the necessary intention had not been observed. It seems to me more probable that the words *even from heretical and schismatic bishops, even less rightly*' only envisage ordinations carried out by schismatic bishops according to the old rites in the reigns of Henry VIII and Edward VI before 1550; and that *provided that in their ordination the form and intention of the Church was maintained*' refers to and excludes ordinations carried out according to the new rites of the 1550 and 1552 ordinals. Nevertheless I admit that this reservation does not

---

8. [The author gives the Latin text of the passage of the Brief in a footnote.]

prove that Cardinal Pole regarded the latter ordinations as invalid; such reasons as the difficulty of a question which had perhaps not yet been settled or adequately clarified could be more than enough to justify this reservation. It is necessary to understand in the same way and with the same restrictions the Cardinal's words in a letter which he wrote a few days earlier on 24 December 1554 to King Philip and Queen Mary: 'All those ecclesiastical persons, whether seculars or regulars of whatever orders, who have, by the alleged authority of the supremacy of the Anglican Church, received invalidly and merely *de facto* various grants, dispensations, concessions and indults, and Orders as well as ecclesiastical benefices, or other spiritual goods, once they have sincerely returned to the unity of the Church, shall be mercifully received in their Orders and benefices either by ourselves or by those deputed for this by us, as indeed many have already been received, and we shall take these steps in due time in the Lord'.

16. At the beginning of his pontificate Julius III's successor Paul IV was quick to confirm by a Bull of 19 June 1555 the powers of the Legate and to ratify all his actions. In reference to orders, he approved of what had been done and added a new clause: *'in such a way that if some were promoted to ecclesiastical orders, whether sacred or not sacred, by someone other than a bishop rightly and correctly (rite et recte) ordained, they are bound to receive the same orders again from their Ordinary, nor can they exercise those orders in the interim.'*[9]

Naturally the Holy See was asked who were the bishops 'rightly and correctly ordained', and the Pope, wishing 'to put an end to such hesitation and ... to serve the peace of conscience of those who had been admitted to orders in the course of this schism', replied by a Brief of 30 October of the same year that the bishops 'rightly and correctly ordained' were the bishops *'ordained in the form of the Church'.*[10] I have

---

9. [In a footnote the author gives a long quotation from the Bull, published in *Civiltà Cattolica*, 1 June 1895.]

10. [The author gives the full text of the Brief in a footnote.]

no doubt that the form of the Church must have meant the Catholic rites as opposed to the Ordinals of 1550 and 1552.

There is no point in observing that according to this reply of Paul IV all Anglican ordinations – of bishops, priests and deacons – would today be considered invalid.

17. This reply was bound to create serious problems. Orders conferred according to Catholic rites were not challenged (nn.9, 14, 15 above); the question only arose in connection with those ordained according to the rites of the Ordinal. Should they be re-ordained, at least conditionally, or could they be accepted with a simple dispensation? To this question the Pope replied: Those who have been ordained (according to the rites of the Ordinal) by a bishop consecrated 'not rightly and correctly', that is to say 'not in the form of the Church', that is to say according to the rites of the Ordinal, must be re-ordained absolutely. On the other hand those who had been ordained (according to the Ordinal) by a bishop consecrated 'rightly and correctly', that is to say 'in the form of the Church', which means according to Catholic rites (either an apostate bishop or a schismatic consecrated before the Ordinal) could be received back by a simple dispensation. The words 'rightly and correctly' in the Bull as well as the explanatory words 'in the form of the Church' in the Brief only refer to the bishop and archbishop, the ordaining minister. Once this interpretation has been accepted – and I do not see how it can be avoided – it follows that deacons and priests ordained according to the Ordinal of 1550 and even that of 1552 by an heretical or schismatical bishop consecrated according to Catholic rites would be validly ordained. It follows that Paul IV recognised in the minister the intention which is necessary for a valid ordination, and recognised the adequacy of the Ordinal rites of 1550 and 1552 in so far as the diaconate and priesthood were concerned; he only denied the adequacy of the Ordinal rites in so far as the episcopate was concerned. Certainly neither the opponents nor the supporters of the validity of Anglican orders would want to accept all these conclusions, which nevertheless follow in strict logic

from the texts of the Bull and the Brief.[11] Without disrespect for Paul IV's reply, I think one can consider it as a practical guideline for a specific situation, although we know nothing about the reasons behind it. It was not a definitive and irrevocable settlement of the question.

18. After the Bull and the explanatory Brief of Paul IV it is not surprising that Anglican orders were regarded in England as certainly invalid. Gordon, whom we shall meet later on, said in his request to the Holy Office: 'Finally it has been the constant practice in England that if any heretical minister returns to the bosom of the Church, he is to be regarded as the equivalent of a layman. Consequently if he is bound in marriage, he is to remain in that state; but if he is free and wishes to pass to the ecclesiastical state, he is to be ordained like other Catholics or, if he so chooses, to marry.' Fr Sidney Smith has sufficiently shown that not one Anglican minister was simply received [as a priest], and that not a single reordination of an Anglican cleric was conditional.

19. Later the Holy Office also declared that Anglican ordinations were certainly invalid. The first decision recorded by the authors is that of Thursday, 17 April 1704, approved by Clement XI. Gordon, the Anglican Bishop of Glascow (*sic*)[12] in Scotland, had followed the unhappy James II, King of England, when he took refuge in France. After several discussions with the Bishop of Meaux, the immortal Bossuet, he was converted to Catholicism. Gordon went to Rome, where he asked the Holy Office to declare his ordination and consecration invalid, and to authorise him to receive orders according to Catholic rites. The Holy Office replied:

---

11. If these conclusions represent the Pope's thinking accurately, Paul IV's Bull and Brief were on the whole much more favourable than not towards Anglican ordinations. This statement may appear paradoxical, but it is true. To be sure, the absolute invalidity of Anglican ordinations is the final conclusion of Paul IV's Bull and Brief; but if you allow that the Anglican bishop who was the minister of ordination had the necessary intention, and if you allow that the rite of the Ordinal, despite the modifications it introduced, was sufficient with regard to the diaconate and presbyterate, it will not be possible to find serious theological arguments against the sufficiency of the rite for the episcopate.

12. [Actually Galloway.]

'The aforesaid petitioner John Clement Gordon should be ordained again to all orders, including holy orders and the presbyterate, and since he has not been confirmed, he should first receive the Sacrament of Confirmation.'[13]

Cardinal Patrizi in his letter of 3 April 1875 wrote in the name of the Holy Office with reference to the diaconal and presbyteral ordinations of the Copts in Ethiopia; in this letter, as I reported in my *Tractatus canonicus de sacra ordinatione*, n. 1058, he also clearly rejects all Anglican orders in general.

Nevertheless these replies and the legal practice of the Holy See, which go against the validity of Anglican orders, can be questioned. Among the reasons claimed in favour of the nullity in the decree of 17 April 1704, the main one ('*which is the source of all doubt in the matter*') is the notorious story of the Nag's Head (n. 7 above), told with variations and other obvious errors: 'Clearly null...invalid and null'.[14] This legend, now abandoned, removes all authority from the decision, or at least makes it doubtful. The subsequent juridical practice of the Holy Office was perhaps determined by this decision.

20. Thus the practice and the decisions of the Holy See opposed to the validity of Anglican ordinations, while carrying great weight in the scales of theologians, do not seem to settle the question. Catholics can discuss the question freely without fear of being accused of temerity. They can even take the risk of declaring themselves in favour of validity. It is nonetheless clear that everyone must respect the present jurisdiction of the Church and accept in advance any decision that the Holy See might choose to make on the subject.[15]

---

13. [The author in a footnote quotes the full text of the Holy Office's reply. The version of the Holy Office's decree given by Pierotti (P 31) contains the word 'unconditionally' (*absolute*) after 'again'.]

14. [The quotation is from the official account written by the secretary of the Holy Office.]

15. The question arises whether the movement for unity which is, thank God, constantly growing in England would be fostered or impeded by a hypothetical papal declaration concerning the validity of Anglican ordinations. Some say the process would be fostered, others that it would be impeded. Perhaps both are right; for it often happens in this world that the same thing can attract some people and repel others. But if this consideration of pious opportunism and utilitarianism might determine the Holy See to make a pronouncement or to remain silent, it can have no bearing on the theological solution of the question.

III
WAS BARLOW REALLY A BISHOP?

21. This specific question may have a general bearing on our topic. It is connected with the consecration of Parker, the main source of the Anglican episcopate.[16] In my humble opinion Barlow's episcopal consecration must be considered as a historically certain fact.

22. (1) William Barlow, a priest and an Augustinian monk, was elected as Bishop of St Asaph on 16 January 1536 in Henry VIII's reign, and transferred on 10 April in the same year to the see of St David's. He took possession of his see, where it is impossible to find the least trace of the slightest opposition from the chapter. Shortly afterwards he was at loggerheads with his chapter over the custom there of making the bishop the dean. There is no evidence that in the heat of the argument the chapter ever accused him of not being consecrated. We have to conclude that the chapter was convinced of his consecration, either because at the outset he gave them satisfactory proof, or because the fact was well known.

(2) As a bishop Barlow took his place in the House of Lords, where he sat above many bishops who were clearly consecrated. It is true that the Upper House admitted bishops who had been elected and confirmed and not yet consecrated, but these bishops certainly sat below those who had been consecrated. Therefore when Barlow came to Parliament he must have provided proof of his consecration.

(3) Barlow took part in the consecration of several bishops apart from Parker: for example Skip, Bishop of Hereford in 1539, Bulkeley, Bishop of Bangor in 1542, etc. Certainly these bishops and Parker himself, jealous of their claim to be

---

16. If Barlow was not a bishop, it would be necessary, if the validity of Parker's consecration is to be upheld, to prove that all the consecrating bishops laid on their hands and said together: 'Receive the Holy Ghost', etc., and that this rite is sufficient. In that case, even if Barlow was not a bishop, Parker's ordination would have been valid on the part of the other consecrators, particularly John Hodgkins. However, the sufficiency of the words: 'Receive the Holy Ghost', etc. as the form is much more debatable than the sufficiency of the preceding prayer, which was pronounced by Barlow alone (nn. 77–79); consequently the case of the defenders of Anglican orders, which is already shaky, would be made even weaker.

validly consecrated, would not have invited or welcomed him, nor would the assistant bishops have agreed to take part, if they had known that he was not consecrated, or even if they had doubts about his consecration; all the more so when the laws of the state, as shown for example in the famous *Praemunire* law, forbade with serious penalties the participation of a non-consecrated bishop.

(4) In Mary's reign Barlow was stripped of his office in 1554 because he was married, and he went to Germany. He was recalled by Queen Elizabeth and appointed Bishop of Chichester. Barlow was thus a leading Anglican who naturally had ferocious opponents, especially in the reign of Mary. No one claimed that he had not been consecrated or cast doubts on his consecration. Even better, his nephew, the author of the pamphlet *Speculum Protestantismi*, a fervent Catholic and a strong opponent of his uncle, affirms that he was consecrated as Bishop of St David's.

(5) Barlow took part in various provincial synods, where he appeared among bishops who were certainly consecrated and shared in their deliberations without any questions being asked about his status. It is remarkable that among these bishops there were some who zealously defended Catholic doctrines in opposition to Barlow and nevertheless said nothing about his non-consecration.

(6) Neither Henry VIII nor Elizabeth nor public opinion would have accepted and tolerated Barlow as a bishop if they had known that he lacked episcopal consecration or if they had the slightest doubt on the subject. Above all, how can one believe that Elizabeth, who wanted her own personal episcopate, would have chosen Barlow to consecrate Parker? Queen Mary in various documents also calls Barlow 'bishop' without any reference to non-consecration.

23. These observations and similar ones which could easily be gathered clearly prove that Barlow was at the time considered a bishop by everyone: by his chapter, by Parliament, by Catholics and Protestants, by the faithful and the clergy, by kings and queens. The first person to raise a doubt was Champnay in 1616, that is to say 40 years after Barlow's

death. If indeed Barlow was never consecrated one would have to assert that he had passed himself off as consecrated, had forged the records of his consecration, and had managed to deceive everyone until 40 years after his death. To admit this massive trick and this general delusion one would need to possess clear, unequivocal proof. The proof that is offered is far from carrying such weight in so far as it has any weight at all.

24. Firstly it is pointed out that we do not know the date of Barlow's consecration. That is true, but what does it prove? Absolutely nothing. Those who have studied Barlow's papers, even Catholics, admit that there is a period of about 15 days during which he could have been consecrated; that is to say the second half of June 1536.[17] In addition it is argued that Barlow believed that the royal nomination was enough to make a bishop, and consequently would not have asked to be consecrated. Similarly Henry VIII shared the same conviction and is unlikely to have forced Barlow to be consecrated. It is easy to answer these arguments. Barlow knew that consecration was necessary for him if he wished to win promotion in the hierarchy, and that no one, even those who shared his religious beliefs, would have accepted him without consecration. It is not likely that in lieu of consecration he would have preferred deceit and lying, thus running the risks of the severe penalties attached to the law of *Praemunire*. Cranmer shared the same views, and yet he was certainly consecrated. If this alleged opinion of Barlow's did not prevent him from consecrating other bishops throughout his life, why should he have felt obliged to neglect or to refuse consecration himself, when it was so necessary for him? Moreover it is far from proven that Henry VIII shared the same ideas about the superfluousness of episcopal consecration; it is quite clear that in practice he demanded consecration. Finally it is said that the register of Cranmer's consecrations makes no mention of Barlow's consecration and that no record of it or

---

17. Estcourt, *The Question of Anglican Orders Discussed*, quoted by Dom Bede Camm, in *Revue Bénédictine*, December 1894.

reference to it is inscribed there. This omission has been the sole motive and reason for doubting the reality of Barlow's consecration. Without destroying the contrary proofs this negative argument would carry a certain weight if Barlow had been the only bishop whose consecration was missing from the records of Cranmer's register. But it so happens that other bishops, unquestionably consecrated and recognised by everyone, are in the same situation. At the time of Warham and Cranmer the registers were badly kept, and one can notice that in Warham's episcopate from 1503 to 1533 six entries and in Cranmer's episcopate from 1533 to 1553 nine entries are missing out of a total of 42 consecrations.[18] Lingard in his *History of England* has good reason to affirm: 'The objection we can have to Barlow is that the record of his consecration is not to be found in the register, but the same defect is true of many other bishops, for instance Gardiner. No one questions whether these bishops were consecrated. Why should we question Barlow's consecration and accept Gardiner's? The only reason, I fear, is that Gardiner did not consecrate Parker, whereas Barlow did.'[19]

25. This question of Barlow's consecration is discussed at length in the *Dissertatio apologetica de Hierarchia Anglicana*, chapter 2. I have carefully read the arguments for and against, and I confess that no doubt remained in my mind. As Barlow's consecration took place in Henry VIII's reign we cannot question its validity (n. 9 above). The consecration of the other bishops according to Catholic rites or those of the Ordinal is an uncontested matter of fact. Consequently Anglican orders can only be invalid because of defective intention in the minister or because of inadequacy in the rite. I shall address these two objections in the following sections.

---

18. Dalbus [F. Portal], *Les ordinations anglicanes*, p. 17.

19. [This seems to be not so much a quotation as an expansion of Lingard's *History*, Vol. 6, pp. 671–2.]

IV
WHETHER ANGLICAN ORDERS ARE INVALID OR DOUBTFUL ON ACCOUNT OF DEFECTIVE INTENTION IN THE MINISTER

26. It is hardly necessary to repeat that for the validity of sacraments in general and of the sacrament of orders in particular one of the necessary conditions is the intention of the minister: the *'intention at least of doing what the Church does'*. This is Catholic doctrine as defined by the Council of Trent in canon 2 of Session VII: 'If anyone says that the intention at least of doing what the Church does is not required in ministers while they perform sacraments, let him be anathema.' Furthermore, it is a theologically certain doctrine that the interior intention of the minister is necessary for the validity of a sacrament; a purely exterior intention would not be enough. If it had been proved that, when they were ordaining, the Anglican bishops did not have this intention or that they did not have it at a certain moment in the history of the English schism, then it would follow that their ordinations only had the appearance of ordinations. Catholics who challenge the validity of Anglican orders mainly stress the defective intention. Dom Bede Camm, in *Revue Bénédictine* of December 1894, goes as far as to say that the question of the invalidity or validity of Anglican orders should be reduced today to this single question of the minister's intention. H.E. Cardinal Vaughan in his letter of 2 October 1894 to M.I.D Howell, which makes interesting reading in Appendix II[20], confined himself almost exclusively to this point.

27. I must now investigate the question whether this defective intention has been really proven in the external forum. I shall begin with the arguments in favour of the intention and I shall go on to the arguments against.

28. The supporters of the validity of Anglican orders say that Anglican bishops, as they conferred orders, wanted to create real deacons, priests and bishops. If it was necessary to

---

20. [Omitted here for lack of space.]

establish this general intention, it would follow from an examination of the Ordinal. Indeed we can read in the Preface which introduces the Ordinal: 'It is evident unto all men diligently reading the holy Scripture and ancient Authors, that from the Apostles' time there have been these Orders of Ministers in Christ's Church; Bishops, Priests, and Deacons ... And therefore, to the intent that these Orders may be continued, and reverently used and esteemed, in the Church of England; no man shall be accounted or taken to be a lawful Bishop, Priest, or Deacon in the Church of England, or suffered to execute any of the said Functions, except he be called, tried, examined, and admitted thereunto, according to the Form hereafter following, or hath had formerly Episcopal Consecration, or Ordination.' The prayers and the ceremonies in the Ordinal for each ordination contain the same ideas. Thus, for example, for episcopal consecration the archbishop begins by reciting a prayer in which he says: *Give grace, we beseech thee, to all Bishops, the Pastors of thy Church*', etc., after which passages of Scripture referring to bishops are read; finally the two assistant bishops present the candidate to their archbishop with the words: '*Most Reverend Father in God, we present unto you this godly and well-learned man to be Ordained and Consecrated Bishop*', etc. The Ordinal is therefore conceived to create deacons, priests and bishops according to the wishes of the Redeemer, the Apostles and the early Church, as these orders had existed up to that time in the Church of England. As Anglican bishops made precise use of the Ordinal in their ordinations, we must conclude – unless there is proof to the contrary – that they shared the intention of the Ordinal. This intention was certainly sufficient for the validity of the ordinations since it was the equivalent of the '*intention at least of doing what the Church does*'.

29. To this argument, which one could call intrinsic, one can add another drawn from certain documents which I have quoted in Section II of this study. Thus, for example, Queen Mary said that all ordinations ought to be regarded as invalid if they had been carried out 'after the new sort and fashion of

order', that is according to the Ordinal of 1550 and 1552 (n. 13 above). Consequently all the ordinations performed by schismatical or heretical bishops according to Catholic rites are valid; after the Ordinal they are invalid, because of the inadequacy of the rite rather than on account of defective intentions. No doubt Cardinal Pole seems to prescind from the question of intention (n. 15), but Paul IV only attributes the invalidity of the episcopate to the inadequacy of the rite '*not in the form of the Church*'. He seems to accept the validity of orders conferred by a bishop consecrated '*in the form of the Church*' – schismatics and heretics along with others. He therefore recognises the necessary intention in the bishop as the minister of consecrations and ordinations (n. 17).

30. Such are the arguments in favour of the intention of the ministers who performed Anglican ordinations. They apply to Barlow, the principal consecrator of Parker, as well as to the other Anglican bishops who conferred orders according to the rites of their Ordinal. It would not be honest to question the seriousness of these arguments. We must now examine the contrary arguments, and we shall see that, if some inspired by polemic are worthless, they are not all to be despised.

31. The advocates of the invalidity of Anglican ordinations say that, when an Anglican bishop confers orders, he uses an ordinal created by heretics with heretical intentions, altogether different from catholic Pontificals. That clearly shows that the bishop does not intend to do what the Catholic Church does in ordination. This is the argument of Pope Zachary in the canon *Retulerunt*, dist. 4, *De consecratione*, in Gratian's Decretum. The pope had been told that a priest who did not know Latin mangled the form of baptism as follows: 'In nomine Patria et Filia et Spirita Sancta', and that St Boniface, the apostle of Germany, ordered that all those who had been baptized in this way must be baptized again. The pope wrote on this subject to St Boniface and said: 'But, holy brother, if the priest in question did not use this formula in baptism out of the desire of introducing an error or heresy, and if, as we have said, he simply mangled the

language out of ignorance of grammar, we cannot approve of rebaptism.' Thus the pope recognised that the baptism was invalid if the form was changed 'out of the desire of introducing an error or heresy', because the change is then a clear sign of the minister's intention not to do what the Church does. This is St Thomas's argument in III, q. 60, art. 8, when he asks whether it is permissible to add or subtract from the form of the sacraments. He replies: 'If one intends by such an addition or subtraction to introduce another rite which is not accepted by the Church, it seems that the sacrament is not performed, because he does not seem to intend to do what the Church does.' Several distinguished authors argue along the same lines; for instance, de Lugo (*De sacramentis in genere*, disp. 11, n. 116 end); and d'Annibale (*Summula Theologiae Moralis*, 3rd edn, vol. III, §241, not. 21): 'Some authors propose that a sacrament is not valid if the minister makes an inessential change so as to introduce a new rite or an error; this is to be understood to be true because he is believed not to have the intention of doing what the Church does... . The question therefore reduces to a presumption, and becomes a matter of fact, not of law.' In our situation the Ordinal was surely composed precisely 'to introduce a new rite and error or heresy'.

32. The argument is certainly plausible, but it does not appear to me to be conclusive. In the first place one must comment that it is not only Anglican ordinations which are affected by the argument; it applies to all sacraments administered according to a rite that differs from the Catholic rite. Secondly, it is important to observe that the person who administers a sacrament using a rite that is not the Catholic rite clearly does not have the intention of doing what the Church does in the material sense of the words, that is to say observing exactly all the rites of the Catholic Church. But that is not necessary for the validity of a sacrament. So far as intention is concerned, it is sufficient that the minister should have the intention of doing with his rite what the Catholic Church does with its rite, even though the rites are different. The question is therefore: if the sacrament is admi-

nistered according to a rite that is not Catholic, is that a reason to conclude in the external forum that the minister did not have the intention of doing what the Catholic Church does?

33. In all questions of revealed theology, but above all in those connected with sacraments, where the subject-matter is positive, leaving aside all *a priori* theories, we must draw inspiration solely from the doctrine and practice of the Church, the faithful guardian of Christ's will in the institution of the sacraments. In this situation what is the doctrine and practice of the church?

34. Many non-Catholic sects (heretical or schismatic) have kept baptism, which they administered with the necessary matter and form; but they certainly varied their non-essential rites, suppressing some, adding others, influenced by heretical ideas.[21] When the question of the validity or invalidity of baptism has been discussed, the Church was only concerned with one thing: whether the matter and form were exactly observed; if so, the Church always pronounced in favour of validity without paying attention to other differences; if not, the verdict was in favour of invalidity because of the inadequacy of the rite rather than because of defective intention. This can be proved by numerous examples. As it is so certain I shall simply recall the reply of the Holy Office quoted in n. 40 below, and the declarations of the same Congregation approved by Pius VIII on 17 November 1830: '1. With regard to heretical sects whose rituals prescribe the conferring of baptism without the necessary use of the essential matter and form, each case must be examined on its own merits; 2. With regard to others who baptize validly according to their rituals, their baptism is to be regarded as valid.' The same verdict can be passed on ordinations: the Holy See declared valid the ordinations of several heretical or schismatical sects which had clearly suppressed or modified Catholic rites and had introduced new rites coloured by heretical ideas, while still maintaining the essential matter and form.

---

21. [In a note Gasparri quotes the Council of Trent, Sess. VII, canon 13.]

35. This constant practice of the Church does not contradict the authorities I quoted earlier. In fact the suppression or the alteration of a Catholic rite in the administration of a sacrament creates the presumption in the external forum that the minister did not have *the intention of doing what the Church does*. St Thomas did not mean anything else, and it was the understanding of his commentators, some of whom seem to have taken the presumption too far. But this presumption must give way to other, stronger presumptions which prove that the minister did intend to do with his rite what the Catholic Church does with hers. An example of this would be the preservation of the necessary matter and form. Cardinal Petra in his commentary on the second constitution of Gregory XI, n. 10, speaks of heretics as follows: 'If they retain the matter and form, it is to be presumed that they have the intention of baptizing; otherwise they would not baptize. This is enough to make baptism conferred by Calvinists valid, even though they do not themselves allow that baptism has any efficacy.' That is why the Church always pronounces in such a case in favour of the validity of the sacrament in the external forum in spite of other changes in the rite. If even the necessary matter and form are not kept, there could be grounds for accepting the intention of the minister, but the question would be superfluous because the sacrament would be invalid *by reason of the rite*. That was true in the case of the words *in nomine Patria et Filia et Spirita Sancta* in the reply of Pope Zachary. If it is not a question of a mere fault in pronunciation and the change was introduced deliberately 'in order to introduce an error or heresy', in its grammatical sense this form means that baptism is conferred in the name of three women; consequently the form is inadequate, even if the minister who used this form wanted to do what the Church does when she uses hers.

36. The application of these principles to Anglican ordinations leads us to the following conclusions. From the new rites introduced into the Ordinal and from the changes made in Catholic rites by heretical ideas we deduce the presumption that the minister does not intend *doing what the*

Church does. But if the essential elements of an ordination are kept, the stronger presumption in favour of the minister's intention must prevail in the external forum. If on the other hand the essential elements of an ordination are not kept, the presumption remains that the minister's intention is inadequate; in which case it is pointless to look for the invalidity in the minister's intention, because it already exists in the rite.

37. The advocates of the invalidity of Anglican ordinations bring forward another argument to prove the absence of sufficient intention. They say that Anglican bishops are the ministers or representatives of the Anglican Church. Now the Anglican Church does not accept the real presence or at least the sacrifice of the Mass, the sacrament of Order, or the sacramental character. Therefore we must infer that Anglican bishops do not accept these truths either. And as our intention is determined by our beliefs, we must conclude that when Anglican bishops confer orders, they do not have the intention of conferring the power to ordain, the power to consecrate, the power to offer the sacrifice and to serve the altar as a deacon. They do not have the intention of making a sacrament or of imprinting the sacramental character; that is to say they do not have *the intention at least of doing what the Church does*. This argument has a particular strength so far as Barlow is concerned, because he certainly did not accept these truths.

38. It is not easy to say precisely what is or was the doctrine of the Anglican church concerning the real presence of Jesus Christ under the sacramental species, the sacrifice of the Mass, the sacrament of Order, the sacramental character and grace, although these are major areas of religious doctrine. To speak only of the holy sacrifice of the Mass, many Anglicans today accept it as a dogma of their church and answer more or less satisfactorily those who object that their Church once taught the opposite position. Others deny the sacrifice, as Cardinal Vaughan observes in the letter quoted in Appendix II,[22] claiming that they are thus following the teaching

---

22. [Letter to *The Times*, 2 Oct. 1894, reprinted in H. Vaughan, *The Reunion of Christendom*, Westminster, 1894?.]

of the Anglican Church. If we go back to the origins of the schism, it seems unquestionable that at the end of Edward VI's reign and under Elizabeth this was the doctrine of the Anglican church or of the majority of the bishops. In fact n. XXXI of the Anglican Articles says explicitly: 'The offering of Christ once made is that perfect redemption, propitiation, and satisfaction, for all the sins of the whole world, both original and actual; and there is none other satisfaction for sin, but that alone. Wherefore the sacrifices of Masses, in the which it was commonly said, that the priest did offer Christ for the quick and the dead, to have remission of pain or guilt, were blasphemous fables, and dangerous deceits.' The article was adopted in 1552 and included among the authorised 42 Articles; it was suppressed by Queen Mary and restored by Elizabeth to take its place among the authorised 39 Articles. As a commentary on the article, the Mass was suppressed and replaced by a communion service, altars were destroyed and replaced by tables; every trace of sacrifice was removed from the services and in particular from the ordination rite. The authors of the *Dissertatio Apologetica de Hierarchia Anglicana* (n. 189ff) claim that Article XXXI was motivated by errors opposed to the sacrifice of the Mass. That may be so, but in reacting in this way Anglicans may have gone too far. The obvious meaning of the article and the surrounding facts seem to show that this is the case. Let us see now how far these heresies vitiate the minister's intention.

39. In the first place, everyone admits as a general principle that the minister's heresy or schism does not necessarily bring about the invalidity of ordinations or of other sacraments; as a result they do not presuppose a defective intention. Thus the Catholic Church has recognised many heretical or schismatical ordinations as valid, such as those of the Nestorians or Monophysites. This teaching is certain; it was defined at least so far as baptism was concerned by the Councils of Trent and Florence, and there is no point in repeating it. Would the same principle hold for a heresy that was opposed to the essence of ordinations? Surely a heresy which denies the essential truth of the sacrament of Order, for example, fatally

undermines the general intention of *doing what the Church does*, that is the intention of making real deacons, real priests and real bishops? Far from being applicable only to the sacrament of Order, it is easy to see how the question is relevant for all the sacraments. In this question we can seek illumination from the teaching and practice of the Church.

40. A Vicar Apostolic put the following query to the Holy Office: 'In certain places some (heretics) make use of the proper matter and form in baptism, but *expressly warn the candidates not to believe that baptism has any effect in the soul*: for they say it is the purely external sign of entry into their sect. Accordingly they often deride Catholics for their "superstitious" belief in the effects of baptism. I ask: (1) Whether baptism administered by these heretics is doubtful on account of the lack of the intention of doing what Christ willed, if before the minister baptizes he expressly declares that baptism has no effect in the soul; (2) Whether baptism administered in the same circumstances is doubtful if the minister has not made this declaration immediately before baptism, but he has often made it within the sect, and it forms part of the sect's public teaching.' We can agree that the question could not be nearer to our problem; it concerns Protestants who deny that baptism has any interior effect, whether of grace or sacramental character. They are not satisfied with publicly preaching this doctrine, but sometimes they repeat it immediately before the administration of baptism. The Holy Office replied on 18 December 1872; 'To the first question: No, because despite the error about the effects of baptism, the intention of doing what the Church does is not excluded. To the second question: the answer follows from the first.'

41. Similarly, does a Jew marry validly when he does so in the conviction that the marriage bond is broken by the 'bill of divorce'? In *De consanguinitate et affinitate* (chap. 4) and *De divortiis* (chap. 7), Innocent III replies in the affirmative. Again, marriage is valid for those who believe that the marriage bond is broken by adultery, or that marriage is not a sacrament, or that polygamy is permissible, etc. Many of such

cases have been submitted to the Holy See for judgment, which has always pronounced in favour of the validity of the marriage.[23] Benedict XIV, *De synodo* (book XIII, chap. 22, n. 2) teaches the same doctrine concerning the marriages of Calvinists, who do not accept the indissolubility of the marriage bond: 'It follows that if both partners at the time of the marriage belong to the Calvinist sect, it is to be held valid and certain, even though like the rest of the members of their religion they believed wrongly that adultery caused the dissolution of a marriage, and even of the marriage bond, etc.'

42. Thus, according to the doctrine and the practice of the Church, even when heresy contradicts the essence of the sacrament it does not necessarily exclude the *intention of doing what the Church does*. The explanation is quite simple. Intention is an act of the will. The act of the will of *doing what the Church does*, can exist alone in the soul at the time of the administration of the sacrament; for instance, if the minister at that moment does not give a thought to his heresies. In such a case why should this act of the will be vitiated by heretical opinions? It can moreover exist alongside the heresy without being infected; for example, if the minister in conferring baptism wants to do *what the Church does* while thinking that baptism has only exterior effects. In this case as well the act of the will is not undermined by heresy. After the words we have just quoted. Benedict XIV adds: 'For we must believe that they had the general will to contract according to Christ's law a marriage which was valid and consequently not to be dissolved even on account of adultery. For a private error does not carry more weight than the general will of which we have spoken, nor can it remove the presumption in favour of this will, on which the validity and perpetuity of the marriage depends.' In other words, in this situation the act of the will of *doing what the Church does* alone directs the administration of the sacrament; the heresy, which is merely concomitant, does not affect the act of the will; it is an *error* rather

---

23. See my *Tractatus canonicus de matrimonio*, n. 192.

than the *intention* of the minister. Finally if the act of the will of *doing what the Church does* in the soul of the minister were to be *positively* affected by the heretical doctrine contrary to the substance of the sacrament – for instance, if the minister while conferring were to say interiorly: 'I want to do what the Church does, but I do not want to confer grace or to impress a character'; or while effecting marriage: 'I want to do what the Church does, but I do not want to perform a sacrament or to contract an indissoluble bond', etc. – in these cases the *intention of doing what the Church does* would in reality not exist and the sacrament would be invalid. In fact, anyone can see that the two acts of the will – *I want ... , but I do not want ...* – are contradictory and mutually exclusive. Benedict XIV in the same document explains this doctrine at length with regard to marriage, but it applies to all the sacraments.[24]

43. Let us now apply these general principles to Anglican ordinations. We must conclude that the Anglican bishops' heresies contrary to the sacrifice of the Mass, the real presence, the sacrament of Order, etc., do not necessarily exclude the *intention of doing what the Church does*, that is, the intention of making real deacons, real priests and real bishops. Consequently these heresies do not necessarily imply the invalidity of the ordinations on account of the minister's intention. To establish that the intention is defective and the ordinations invalid, it would be necessary to prove that the Anglican bishops as they conferred orders drew on heretical doctrines *positively* to limit their intention with such words as: 'I ordain you priest, but I do not want to give you power to consecrate.' This restriction or condition does not necessarily follow from the heresy; it cannot be assumed and must be proved in the external forum. Do these proofs exist?

---

24. See my *Tractatus canonicus de matrimonio*, n. 192; and my *Tractatus canonicus de sacra ordinatione*, n. 962ff. Cf. de Lugo *De sacramentis in genere*, disp. VIII, sect. 8. However Franzelin's teaching in *De sacramentis in genere*, thesis XVII, can only be accepted with reservations, for it is not fully in conformity with numerous decisions of the Holy See.

44. In the letter which I have often quoted Cardinal Vaughan says: 'I had the assurance some time ago from a friend that, when he was ordained as an Anglican, the Bishop prefaced his ordination by warning him thus: "*Now mind this, sir, I am not going to ordain you as a sacrificing priest.*"'

45. Did this announcement point to a simple concomitant error as in the similar case connected with baptism which was put to the Holy Office (n. 40 above)? *I want to ordain you priest but I do not mean to confer on you any power to sacrifice.* In case of doubt we should presume that there was a simple error rather than a condition. If it was a question of a real condition, the ordination should be considered invalid.[25] But this can only be an isolated incident; it is not to be used in general discussion; there have even been similar happenings in Catholic ordinations.[26]

46. His Eminence goes on: ' The warning may have been unusual, but were the intention and the theory underlying it uncommon? And are there no Anglican prelates now who would declare emphatically that in ordaining they do not intend to make sacrificing priests?'

47. It is quite possible that there are Anglican prelates who can make the same declaration; but that does not establish the inadequacy of their intention, because it does not prove they actually expressed in their minds the relevant limitation. In other words, they *could have declared it*, but *did they declare it*? *Do they declare it*? If they had thought of it and if they had been questioned, the Protestants also would have declared that when they baptized they certainly had no intention of conferring grace and a character. Protestants, Jews, Greeks, pagans *would declare* that, when they married, they did not mean to form an indissoluble bond. Nevertheless their baptisms and marriages are perfectly valid. This hypothetical or interpretative will, as it is called in the schools, *could exist*, but

---

25. De Lugo, *De sacramento Eucharistiae*, disp. XIX, n. 103.

26. See my *Tractatus canonicus de sacra ordinatione*, n. 976.

in fact *does not exist*; hence there is no need to pay attention to it.

48. However, the eminent Archbishop of Westminster adds further reflections which are important from another point of view for the question we are discussing. The substance of his argument goes like this: the careful elimination from the Ordinal of all that was connected with a sacrifice, the destruction of the altars and the replacing of them with a table, the suppression of the Mass and the replacing of it with a communion service – these are clear indications that Anglican bishops could be presumed to have a positive intention not to confer in their ordination rites any power to offer a sacrifice. That is the precise point at issue in the controversy surrounding the minister's intention in Anglican ordinations. It remains to be seen whether these facts support the presumption in the external forum.

49. I suggest that the presumption is open to question. It is possible to reply that the facts are partly to be found before Queen Mary's reign; and yet neither the Queen nor Pope Paul IV questioned Anglican ordinations on the grounds of defective intention (see n. 29). Furthermore the presumption does not obtain in the case of the ordaining bishops who had no part in these sacrilegious activities. It does not even appear to obtain for the bishops who were the authors of these sacrileges. For example, from the fact that in the summer of 1552 Cranmer eliminated any mention of sacrifice from the Ordinal, how are we to conclude that at the time of his ordinations in the following year he was positively minded to exclude any power of sacrificing?

These are serious replies, especially the first, for which I have not found a satisfactory answer; but they do not remove every trace of doubt and anxiety. The following hypothesis may be helpful: suppose that in a particular country, after the Reformers had removed from their Ritual all reminders in ceremonies and prayers of the indissolubility of marriage, after they had preached in strong terms both in writing and speech against the indissolubility of marriage, in the midst of these activities one of the Reformers got married according to the expurgated Ritual. Would it be unjustified to assume that at the time of his marriage the bridegroom had the positive intention of excluding indissolubility, and as a result to regard his marriage as suspect in the external forum? This is the situation we are dealing with. It is only natural that the bishops who were responsible for these sacrileges, or who were ardent supporters of the same ideas (Barlow, for example) at the very time in Elizabeth's reign when they were conducting a more violent campaign than ever against the sacrifice – it is only natural that when they were ordaining they would have the positive desire, whether actual or virtual, not to confer the power to sacrifice. From that consideration, in my humble opinion, a shadow falls across all Anglican ordinations.

50. This shadow becomes darker still when we consult the Ordinal about the diaconate and the presbyterate. The bishop puts several questions to the future deacon, of which this is the fifth: 'It pertaineth to the Office of a Deacon, in the Church where he shall be appointed to serve, to assist the Priest in Divine Service, and especially when he ministereth the holy Communion, and to help him in the distribution thereof ... ' The *ministry of the altar* at the holy sacrifice, which is the main and essential task of the deacon, appears to be tacitly excluded. In the same way the bishop asks the future priests: 'Will you then give your faithful diligence always so to minister the Doctrine and Sacraments, and the Discipline of Christ, as the Lord hath commanded, and as this Church and *Realm hath received the same*, according to the commandments of God ... ?' I repeat: it seems to me incontestable that the Anglican Church, especially in its early days, denied at least the Eucharist as a sacrifice. Thus the rites themselves of the diaconate and the presbyterate seem to a certain extent to exclude all power concerning sacrifice. It must be presumed that the bishops, particularly those who were hostile to the notion of sacrifice, would have brought their intention in line with this exclusion, even if it was not absolute.

V
CAN THE RITE IN THE ORDINAL BE REGARDED AS SUFFICIENT?

51. Catholics today who challenge the validity of Anglican ordinations attach a measure of emphasis to Barlow's non-consecration, make much of the defective intention, and seem to recognise the ordination-rite of the Ordinal as sufficient (see n. 26). They are twofold in their error. In my humble opinion, Anglican ordinations cannot be attacked in the light of Barlow's consecration. It is easier to undermine them from the point of view of the rite than from that of the minister's intention.

52. One only needs to read the Ordinal to be convinced that the essential part of Anglican diaconal ordination consists of the imposition of hands with the words: *Take thou Authority to execute*, etc.; and in the handing over of the book of the Gospels with the words: *Take thou Authority to read*, etc. The essential part of Anglican presbyteral ordination consists of the prayer:*Almighty God* etc., the imposition of hands with the words: *Receive the Holy Ghost* etc., then the handing over of the Bible with the words: *Take thou Authority to preach* etc. Finally the essential part of episcopal consecration consists of the prayer: *Almighty God* etc., the imposition of hands with the words: *Receive the Holy Ghost* etc., and lastly the handing over of the Bible with the words: *Give heed unto reading* etc. Our question now is whether one can find in the Ordinal's rites the true matter and true form of the three ordinations.

53. To answer this question we must first find out what are the true matter and form of the three ordinations. Here above all we must take as our guide the teaching and the practice of the Church if we want to find our way through the maze of theological opinions, just as a child on a dark road holds its mother's hand for fear of getting lost.[27]

---

27. Fr Morin in the preface to his work *De sacris Ecclesiae ordinationibus* recalls that when he went to Rome in 1639 he worked on a committee of theologians which Urban VIII had set up in order to examine the Greek Ritual. It soon struck Fr Morin

54. The Council of Trent (Session VII, Canon 1) defined that Jesus Christ is the author of all the sacraments of the new law; and in Session XXIII, canon 6 defined in particular that the Saviour instituted the first three ordinations: 'If anyone says that in the Catholic Church there is not a hierarchy instituted by divine institution, consisting of bishops, presbyters and ministers, let him be anathema.' Furthermore, a theologically certain opinion supports the view that the divine institution of the sacraments in general and of the first three ordinations was *direct* and not *mediated* through the intervention of the Church, to which Jesus Christ gave the power of ordaining. If Jesus Christ instituted the first three ordinations, he must have instituted the essential elements, namely the matter and the form. To what extent did he do that? Theologians are not at one on this point.

55. Some theologians, particularly in the past, have held that the Saviour would only have instituted the essential elements of the three ordinations in a very general way, leaving to the Church the task of determining what was specific and proper to each ordination, with the power to add other accidental rites. In other words, Jesus Christ would have said in effect: 'There will be an episcopate, a priesthood and a diaconate conferred by an external sign and words which the Church will determine.' It is therefore the business of the Church, according to this opinion, to determine the external sign; for instance, the Church could decide that the external sign was the imposition of hands, or the handing over of the instruments, or the two together; that in one country it would

---

that his colleagues were simply applying *a priori* scholastic principles; they knew nothing about oriental discipline and languages. Consequently the ordinations of bishops, priests and other ministers of the Greek Church were in danger of being declared invalid. For his own part, he followed easier and safer principles: he held that schismatical Greek ordinations were valid because the Roman Church had recognised them as such, and because the rite was older than the schism. The upshot was that the ordinations were declared valid. In fact this is precisely the procedure which scholastics have followed: being men of piety no less than of erudition, they formed their theological opinions according to the known discipline of the Church, and adjusted them according to the progress of ecclesiastical scholarship. There can be no doubt that several scholastic theories on the matter and form of ordinations would have disappeared if these theologians had been able as we are to examine all the eastern and western liturgies, both ancient and modern.

be the imposition, and in another the handing over of the instruments; that in one and the same country it would be first the imposition of hands and later the handing over of the instruments. It would also be up to the Church to detemine the words which must accompany the external sign; for example, it could determine whether the words 'Receive ...' are deprecative or imperative; that in one country the words are deprecative, in another imperative; that in one and the same country they would be first deprecative and later imperative. But is it only the central government which holds this prerogative of defining the rite? Or does it also belong to heretical or schismatical bishops who have been validly ordained? When the Church chooses one rite for the East and another for the West, can she decide that the eastern rite is inadequate in the West, and *vice versa*? When changing from one rite to another in the same country, can the Church state that the old rite, which had hitherto produced valid ordinations, will henceforward be insufficient? Can the Church declare that a rite is insufficient if it is used by a minister who is heretical, schismatical or a public sinner? These are some of the questions to which the authors are far from giving the same replies. Finally, we can observe that several authors think that Jesus Christ himself instituted the imposition of hands as the matter of the three ordinations, leaving to the Church only the complete power and freedom to determine the form.

56. All these theories were formed *post factum*. These authors begin by admitting as certain that the matter of the ordinations according to the Roman Pontifical consisted in the handing over of the instruments, and the form in the imperative words. Because the Eastern Church held that the matter was the imposition of hands and the form a prayer, as did the Latin Church at least for the first twelve centuries, theologians invented the theories we have just outlined to explain the differences and the changes; these theories have no other basis. The process would have been logical if these theologians' opinion on the matter and form of the ordinations in the Roman Pontifical had been certain.

57. Progress in the study of church history gave birth to

another theory, founded on Scripture and the practice of the Church, which is most commonly accepted by modern scholars and possesses the highest degree of probability. According to this theory Jesus Christ instituted the imposition of hands as the matter of the three ordinations, and a prayer as the form. In fact we read in Acts 6.6 that the apostles, when they ordained the first deacons, 'prayed and laid hands on them'; they ordained them by means of the imposition of hands and a prayer. The same was true of the ordination of SS. Paul and Barnabas to the episcopate in Acts 13.3. The imposition of hands as the principal element in ordinations is found in other parts of Scripture: for example St Paul (2 Timothy 1.6) says: 'I remind you to rekindle the grace of God which is in you through the imposition of my hands.' In imitation of the apostles the Church has conferred the three orders in the same way, that is to say by the imposition of hands and a prayer. Thus the Eastern Church from the beginning up to the present has no other rites for the three ordinations.[28] In the Latin church up to the twelfth century the Roman and Gallican liturgies, which more or less shared the West between them, had no other essential rites for the three ordinations. It is true that later on the Western Church introduced the handing over of instruments and the imperative formulas, but it has not been proved and it is not probable that the Latin Church introduced the new elements as essential to ordination, and intended orders to be conferred by the new rites and not the old ones. It should be noted that the Roman Pontifical carefully preserved and reunited all the ancient rites of the Roman and Gallican liturgies. Thus in the ordination to the diaconate, after the preliminaries, the bishop reads the prayer in the form of a preface: 'World without end ... Lord, Holy Almighty Father, eternal God, giver of honours and distributor of orders', etc., in the middle

---

28. Some theologians felt uncomfortable and wished at any price to find the handing over of instruments in the oriental liturgy. They had recourse to fantastic explanations. 'Some other authors,' writes Billuart (*De sacramentis in communi*, dist. I, art. 5), 'insist that a handing over of instruments takes place even among the Greeks, if not by physical contact at least by moral, through the mediation of the altar to which the ordinands make a prostration.' (?!?).

of which he places his hands on the candidate as he says: 'Receive the Holy Spirit for strength to resist the devil and his temptations. In the name of the Lord'; and then come the other rites, among which there are the handing over of the book of the Gospels and the formula: 'Receive the power', etc. Now in the Roman liturgy ordination to the diaconate used to be performed by the imposition of hands and the same prayer in the form of a preface without the words: 'Receive the Holy Spirit', etc., which were added later.[29] In the same way in the ordination to the presbyterate the bishop begins by placing his hands with the priests who are present, and then he says the *Invitatorium*: 'My dear brothers, let us pray', the prayer 'Hear us', and the prayer in the form of a preface: 'World without end ... Lord, Holy Almighty Father, eternal God, author of honours', etc; then come the other rites, among which is the handing over of instruments with the formula: 'Receive the power to offer sacrifice', etc., and the final imposition of hands with the formula: 'Receive the Holy Spirit; whose sins you shall forgive', etc. Now in the Roman liturgy ordination to the presbyterate was performed by the imposition of hands and the same prayer in the form of a preface, which was the *consecratio*, that is to say the form. To conclude that the orders of deacon and presbyter are conferred today by the more recent rites, one would have to say that the Church *positively removed* the consecratory force of the ancient rites to transfer it to the new rites. Who could be made to believe that? In the consecration of a bishop in the Roman Pontifical, once the preliminaries are over, the consecrating bishop imposes his hands with the assistant bishops, saying: 'Recive the Holy Spirit'; he says the prayer 'Be propitious', the prayer in the form of a preface: 'World without end ... Lord, Holy Almighty Father, eternal God, honour of

---

29. Fr Morin (*De sacris ordinationibus*, Exerc. IX, chap. 2) explains convincingly why these words were introduced. The Roman prayer at this point in *deprecatory mode* invokes the Holy Spirit on the ordinand: 'Send forth the Holy Spirit on them, we pray, Lord', etc. To take account of the view then current in the schools that the form had to be imperative, these words were added to express the same thing in the *imperative mode*; and in order to make the moral union more evident, the consecratory canon was interrupted by the insertion of the imposition of hands.

all dignities', etc., and then the rest. The Roman liturgy consecrated bishops by the imposition of hands without the
words: 'Receive the Holy Spirit' (which were introduced
later) and a part of the same prayer in the form of a preface.[30]
Nothing compels us to follow the common opinion in saying
that the episcopal character is nowadays imprinted by the
words: 'Receive the Holy Spirit' rather than by the ancient
consecratio of the Roman liturgy. Thus the practice of the
Church, following Holy Scripture, seems to show that the
Saviour really instituted the imposition of hands as the matter
of the three ordinations, and a prayer as the form. At least
this theory seems to be very probable; it avoids many serious
difficulties. So far as I am concerned, I give it my whole-
hearted assent.

58. It follows from this theory that the imperative form:
'Receive the power', 'Receive the Holy Spirit', is not sufficient
for the validity of an ordination, because it does not qualify
as a *prayer*. Many scholastic theologians, relying on *a priori*
arguments and not knowing the practice of the Eastern
Church, or that of the Western Church in the first twelve
centuries, were certain that the form of ordinations could
only be imperative. Nugnez, quoted by Morin (*De sacris
Ecclesiae ordinationibus*, part III, Chap. 2, n. 1), goes so far
as to say: 'This pertains to the faith, and the contrary is
manifest heresy.' Progress in the study of Church history
has changed our view of the situation; today it is absolutely
certain that the form of ordinations can be deprecative,
because the Church used and continues to use deprecative
forms, and according to the theory we have expounded it
seems that the form of ordination can only be deprecative.

59. However the Saviour certainly did not intend that
prayer of no matter what sort could be a sufficient form for
ordination; for example, who would venture to say that

---

30. The Roman Pontifical's prayer in the form of a preface is the *consecratio* of the
Roman liturgy, with the interpolation however of the words 'Sint speciosi ...
omnium consequantur', which have been borrowed from the *missale Francorum*.
Perhaps the interpolated words formed part of the *consecratio* of the pure Gallican
liturgy, but it is not certain.

ordinations to the diaconate, presbyterate and episcopate were valid if conferred with the imposition of hands and the recitation of the Our Father? The only way of knowing the will of the Saviour in this question is from the practice of the Church. *A priori* arguments are useless. The prayers which the Church has used or approved of as the forms of ordinations should be considered sufficient, because the Church is the faithful guardian of her divine Founder's wishes and cannot err. All these forms used or granted approval by the Church have been brought together in Appendix III,[31] and I recommend those who want to follow this discussion to read them attentively.[32] For the same reason a new prayer can be regarded as sufficient provided it agrees *substantially* with prayers used or granted approval by the Church. Details found in particular prayers and not found in all the prayers used and approved by the Church are clearly not indispensable. For instance, the invocation of the Holy Spirit over the ordinand appears often, but not invariably; in the Maronite form for ordination to the presbyterate the Holy Spirit is not mentioned at all; and in several other rites the Holy Spirit is referred to indirectly or solely at the end in the conclusion of the prayer. Consequently a prayer without the invocation of the Holy Spirit can be sufficient for ordination. Similarly the list of the powers conferred by ordination is not found in all prayers; for example, the Roman form of ordination for bishops says nothing about the bishop's powers; the Roman and Coptic forms for presbyteral ordination say nothing about the power to consecrate and sacrifice, etc. Contrary to widespread opinion, we have to conclude that mention of the powers to be conferred – even the most important powers – does not have to be present in a prayer in order to make it sufficient as the form for ordination. On the other hand, everything that is found in all the prayers used or approved by the Church is necessary. It is in strict logic

---

31. [Unfortunately there is no room to print this Appendix here.]

32. M. Boudinhon, a professor at the Institut catholique at Paris, has published in *Canoniste contemporain* (Sept./Oct. 1895) a study of the most interesting of these prayer-forms.

true that a feature that is common to all prayers can still be accidental, but the presumption is that common features are essential, and their absence sheds doubt on the adequacy of the form. Now all the prayers used or granted approval by the Church: (1) are prayers related to ordination; (2) call down on the ordinand from God's mercy the graces he will need in his new state; (3) name in one way or another the particular ordination. In the remarkable article which I have just quoted, M. Boudinhon rightly says: 'In short, all the Catholic ordination formulae are made up according to a uniform pattern, and without much implausibility one could bring out from the variety of prayers a general and common form of ordination which I tentatively translate: "O God who ... look mercifully upon this your servant whom you have deigned to call to the diaconate (or presbyterate, episcopate, high priesthood); grant him your grace so that he may be able worthily and usefully to fulfil the duties of this order".' This prayer must be the minimum to be used as the form of ordination.

60. Now that we have stated the principles, it is time to return to the Anglican Ordinal and to investigate whether its rites contain the true matter and the true form which are sufficient for the three ordinations.

61. The opponents of the sufficiency of the Anglican rites start with a general observation. They say that ordination rites cannot be sufficient if they have not been determined by the legitimate Church authority. Pope Innocent IV, or rather the canonist Sinibaldo Fieschi, in the Decretals of Gregory IX, Book I, *De sacramentis non iterandis*, says on this subject: 'With regard to the rite of the Apostles, we read in the Epistle to Titus (*alias* Timothy) (*sic*) that they laid hands on the candidates and pronounced prayers over them, but we are not told what form of words they employed. Accordingly we believe that, unless forms were discovered later, it would be sufficient for the ordainer to say: "May you be a priest", or other words to the same effect. But later the Church laid down the forms that were observed; these forms are so necessary that if a man is ordained with

their use, what is omitted has to be supplied; if the forms are observed, the character is imprinted on the candidate's soul.' The reason for this is quite simple: the determination of rites is an act of ecclesiastical jurisdiction which could not belong to lay people, heretics or schismatics. Therefore the rites of the Anglican Ordinal having been drawn up by lay people according to the views of heretical bishops and their advisers, cannot be sufficient, regardless of their intrinsic merits.

62. Anglicans reply that the rites of the Ordinal were established by Anglican ecclesiastical authority and only confirmed by the lay power. I do not think it is necessary to discuss this historical detail; since the Anglican ecclesiastical authority was heretical or schismatical, the difficulty remains more or less the same. I stress rather the major proposition of the syllogism. Fr Le Courayer, in chapter 10 of his *Dissertation sur la validité des ordinations des Anglais*,[33] claims that in some eastern sects the form of ordination which is recognised as adequate by the Church was composed after the schism. If that were true, the observation made would immediately collapse. However Fr Le Quien in chapter II of his work *Nullité des ordinations anglicanes* replies that it has not been proved that the rites came after the schism. Moreover P. Le Courayer's arguments are hints rather than arguments. I also began this extremely difficult research, but I had to

---

33. This work, and the other by the same author, *Défense de la dissertation sur la validité des ordinations des Anglais*, were condemned by Benedict XIII because of several incidental propositions on priesthood and sacrifice; the condemnation prescinded from the question of the validity of Anglican orders. Acclaimed by Anglicans, Fr Le Courayer became obstinate in his opinions; he slipped more and more into Protestantism, and ended as a Socinian. Fr Le Quien, OP, wrote in reply two works which have some merit: *Nullité des ordinations anglicanes*, and *La même nullité de nouveau démontrée*. Fr Hardouin, SJ, also wrote two works against Le Courayer entitled *La dissertation du P. Le Courayer sur la succession des évêques anglais et sur la validité de leurs ordinations réfutée*, and *La défense des ordinations anglicanes réfutée*. Fr Hardouin knew nothing of ecclesiastical practice outside the Roman Pontifical, and was not prepared to treat of the subject. Believing that the handing over of the instruments in the West and the imposition of hands in the East were equally of divine institution, he imagined a double divine institution: one entrusted to St Peter for the West, the other to St Paul for the East. And as the liturgy of the western Church in the first twelve centuries upset this beautiful construction, he simply denied the authenticity of the documents which contained this liturgy.

abandon it. There would be a much easier area of research for those who live in Rome which would lead to the same conclusion. When they examine the value of the form of ordination in a heretical or schismatic sect, do the Roman Congregations bother about the historical origins of the form? For instance, when in 1704 the Holy Office declared that the Coptic form was sufficient, did it first carry out research and verify that the form existed before the schism? I do not think so, and it does not seem to me probable. Now if the Roman Congregations are content to examine forms in themselves, this is a clear argument to show that the form can be adequate even if it has been drawn up by heretics or schismatics. In fact this observation has no relevance to the second theory [see G 57], because if Jesus himself established the matter and the form of the ordinations both generically and specifically as the imposition of hands and an appropriate prayer, it is clear that so long as the divine institution has been respected, the rites are always adequate, even if they have been introduced by heretical or schismatical bishops or by lay people. The objection can only be grounded in the first theory [see G 55]. Indeed if one accepts this theory the difficulties that arise are serious. I have already said that the second theory is better, about which agreement should easily be possible. If the ordination rites which have been introduced by lay people or by heretical or schismatical bishops are substantially at one with the rites used or approved by the Church, one can affirm that these rites regardless of who introduced them were instituted by the Church herself; and therefore they will be sufficient. If on the contrary these rites are not substantially at one with the rites used or approved by the Church, I willingly grant that they are not sufficient.

63. Thus the rites of the Anglican Ordinal can be sufficient *a priori*, but are they in reality? I shall begin with the ordination to the diaconate.

64. When it comes to the matter and form of the diaconate in the Roman Pontifical, there are three opinions which depend on the first theory. Some think that the matter is the imposition of hands, the form being the words: 'Receive

the Holy Spirit for strength to resist the devil and his temptations. In the name of the Lord.' Others make the handing
over of the book of the Gospels the matter, the form being
the accompanying words: 'Receive the power to read the
Gospel in the Church of God both for the living and the
dead. In the name of the Lord.' Finally, several scholars
combine the two opinions, the complete matter being the
handing over of the book of the Gospels and the imposition
of hands, the complete form being the two formulae.[34]
Roman Congregations have always regarded both the first
two opinions as equally probable, even though in practice
one ought to hold the third opinion as the safest one. The
Ordinal itself contains the same rite of handing over of the
book of the Gospels with only an insignificant difference in
the words: 'Take thou Authority to read the Gospel in the
Church of God, and to preach the same, if thou be thereto
licensed by the Bishop himself.' As a result the sufficiency of
the Ordinal for the rite of ordination to the diaconate is
probable according to the judgments of the Roman
Congregations. I do not share any of the three opinions,
but it is not for me to question the probability, at least the
extrinsic probability, of the second opinion, which is recognised by such high authorities. One could add the authority of
Paul IV, who seems to have approved the rite of the Ordinal
for the diaconate and the presbyterate (see n. 17).[35]

65. At the same time we must not forget that the second
and more probable theory looks to divine institution to make
the imposition of hands the matter and the respective prayer
the form. In the Roman Pontifical this prayer is the preface,
which is the old *consecratio* of the Roman Liturgy (n. 57). It is
true that the Anglican Ordinal contains the rite of imposing
hands, but the accompanying imperative formula – 'Take
thou Authority to execute the Office of a deacon in the

---

34. See my *Tractatus canonicus de sacra ordinatione*, n. 1046 ff.

35. The Anglicans make the matter and form of their diaconal ordination consist in
the two rites taken together: the imposition of hands and the words: 'Take thou
Authority to execute', etc., and the handing over of the book of the Gospels and
the words: 'Take thou Authority to read', etc.

Church of God committed unto thee: In the name of the Father, and of the Son, and of the Holy Ghost' – is not a prayer. The inadequacy of the rite of the Ordinal is therefore more probable. It is true that the Ordinal contains two prayers which could be perfectly adequate forms, because they are quite similar to the prayers used and approved by the Church. One is at the beginning: 'Almighty God, who by thy Divine', etc.; the other is at the end: 'Almighty God, giver of all good things', etc. But these two prayers are too far apart from the imposition of hands to form a moral unity with it. These prayers therefore cannot be the form. There is a similar situation in the Roman Pontifical, where the last prayer for the ordination of a deacon: 'Holy Lord', etc. could in itself be the sufficient form since it was the *consecratio* of the ordination to the diaconate in the Gallican liturgy. But when this prayer is transferred in the Roman Pontifical it cannot be the form of the ordination, because it is too far away from the imposition of hands.

66. One has to add to these arguments the probability of nullity coming from the minister. We shall see that the Anglican episcopate is not free from criticism, either because the prayer accompanying the imposition of hands lacks a feature that is common to all the prayers used and approved by the Church, or because the Anglican presbyterate is probably invalid; and a probable opinion claims that a bishop's orders cannot be valid unless he is already a priest. For that reason all Anglican ordinations are undermined 'by virtue of the minister'. This invalidity is probable 'immediately by virtue of the minister, mediately by virtue of the rite'.

67. I pass on to Anglican ordinations to the presbyterate. In my canonical treatise *De sacra ordinatione* (n. 1074ff) I presented the opinions of numerous theologians in connection with the matter and form of ordination to the presbyterate in the Roman Pontifical. Roman Congregations consider all these opinions as probable in practice, and require reordination when something is missing to make sure that the ordination is valid; they react in this way even though it is probable that the matter only consists of the imposition of

hands and that the form consists of the preface as was the case in the old Roman liturgy (n. 57). If then the Roman Congregations in their judgments maintain that in practice it is probable that the matter and form of presbyteral ordination in the West consists of the handing over of the instruments (the chalice and the bread) with the words: 'Receive the power to offer sacrifice', etc.,[36] it follows that the rites of the 1552 Ordinal, which do not include this ceremony, must be considered in practice as probably insufficient.

68. We shall now examine the intrinsic merits of the Ordinal's rites. I shall begin by affirming that the rite of handing over the Bible with the words: 'Give heed unto reading' etc. is totally insufficient.[37] Even the Anglicans themselves seem to consider this rite merely accidental.[38]

69. The probability of the adequacy of the imposition of hands with words: 'Receive the Holy Ghost', etc., separated from the preceding prayer is also very questionable, because the words: 'Receive the Holy Ghost', etc., are not a prayer, which it ought to be according to the second and more probable theory. Even in the light of the first theory, to say that the words 'Receive the Holy Ghost', etc., were an adequate

---

36. Cf Benedict XIV, *De synodo*, Book VIII, chap. 10, n. 1; and my *Tractatus canonicus de sacra ordinatione*, n. 1083.

37. [The author has made a slip here. The words he has quoted are used at the ordination of bishops. He has given the form for presbyters correctly in the following note: 'Take thou authority to preach ...'.]

38. All Anglicans identify the matter of presbyteral ordination with the imposition of hands, but they are not agreed as to the form. Some hold that the form consists of the prayer: 'Almighty God' which precedes the imposition of hands, with or without the words which accompany it: 'Receive the Holy Ghost', etc. It seems that the first person to suggest this idea to Anglicans was Fr Le Courayer in his *Dissertation sur la validité des ordinations des Anglais*; the Anglicans themselves, even the compilers of the Ordinal, had not considered this idea. Others maintain that the form consists solely of the words: 'Receive the Holy Ghost'. This was certainly the opinion of the compilers of the Ordinal: they believed these words were the form, and for this reason they kept them. Logically the handing over of the Bible with the words: 'Take thou Authority to preach', etc., cannot be considered as an essential element of ordination, even by Anglicans. In fact the power to forgive or retain sins is deemed to be given by the imposition of hands and the formula: 'Receive the Holy Ghost: Whose sins thou dost forgive', etc. Either this power, which can only belong to priests, supposes that the power to consecrate is already given, or else the two powers are given simultaneously; consequently nothing essential remains for the handing over of the Bible and its formula.

form we would have to prove that the Saviour left full power
to determine the form of ordination if not to lay people at
least to all Catholic bishops, and even to heretical and schismatical ones. We have already seen that this assumption is
debatable (n. 55). It will not do to say that because these
words are found in the Roman Pontifical they have a
Catholic source: in the Roman Pontifical they are not
intended to grant the power to consecrate and sacrifice.[39]

70. I still have to examine the adequacy of the rite of
imposition of hands and the preceding prayer: 'Almighty
God, and heavenly Father' with or without the words:
'Receive the Holy Ghost', etc. Near the beginning of the
Ordinal there is a prayer: 'Almighty God, giver of all good
things', which could safely be called sufficient, but it is too far
away from the imposition of hands. There is another prayer
at the end: 'Most merciful Father, we beseech thee to send
upon these thy servants', but apart from its separation from
the imposition of hands, this prayer leaves something to be
desired because it makes no mention of the order involved,
namely the presbyteral order. The prayer in the Roman
Pontifical : 'God, author of all sanctification' is certainly a
sufficient form since it was the *consecratio* of the Gallican
liturgy; but in its present place in the Pontifical far removed
from the matter it cannot be the form of ordination. To
repeat, the question comes down to the rite of imposing
hands and of the prayer: 'Almighty God, and heavenly
Father', with or without the words: 'Receive the Holy
Ghost', etc.

71. To prove the inadequacy of this rite regardless of the

---

39. The Anglicans claim with some show of reason that the Holy Office's Reply of
1704 concerning Coptic ordinations in Ethiopia confirms the sufficiency of their own
rite. This Reply seemed to recognise the validity of presbyteral ordination conferred
by the imposition of hands with only these words: 'Receive the Holy Spirit'. This
Reply can be found in my work *De sacra ordinatione*, n. 1057. However, Cardinal
Patrizi, the Secretary to the Holy Office, explained in his official letter of 30 April
1875 (which I have quoted in the same work, n. 1058) that this was not the mind of
the Sacred Congregation. He seemed to imply that the decree of 1704 was not
authentic; it was however sent officially to the Vicar Apostolic for the Copts Mgr
Bel in 1860. On this difficult question see M. Boudinhon's study 'Ordinations schis-
matiques coptes et ordinations anglicanes', *Canoniste contemporain*, April/May 1895.

intrinsic merit of the prayer, the opponents of Anglican ordinations make the following comment. They say that the form must accompany or follow the matter, never come before it. And in this instance the form does come before the matter.

72. This comment is more specious than substantial. What is needed for the validity of a sacrament is the moral union between matter and form so that the form can determine the matter according to the well-known principle of St Augustine: 'Word meets element and a sacrament comes into being.' If this moral union exists, it does not matter for the validity of a sacrament whether the form comes before or after the matter. If it were true that the form which comes first can never determine the matter which does not yet exist, it would be equally true that the form, when it comes later, could not determine the matter that no longer existed. The form then would have to be always and necessarily concomitant – and that assertion is false. That is the reason why episcopal consecration in the old Gallican liturgy was certainly valid even though a complete prayer *Propitiare* came between the imposition of hands and the *consecratio*; the same arrangement is found in the Roman Pontifical. Similarly a baptism would certainly be valid if the water did not touch the child's head until the form had been pronounced.[40] In each case because of a moral unity the form determines the matter. Now there is a moral unity between the prayer: 'Almighty God' in the Ordinal, with or without the words 'Receive the Holy Ghost', etc. and the imposition of hands.

73. When I look at the inner nature of the rite I acknowledge the imposition of hands as the sufficient matter of the

---

40. In the words of Soto, *in 4, d. 3, q. unica, a. 8*: 'The term *simultaneously* should not be taken so literally, but in a moral sense, that is according to everyday usage. A person who while putting a glass to his lips says: "I drink", and proceeds at once to drink, is reckoned to speak and act simultaneously ... Simultaneously if anyone first says: "I baptize you" or "I anoint you", and proceeds at once to baptize or anoint, this is sufficient. What happens immediately afterwards by human reckoning counts as present.' Cajetan insists that matter and form must be simultaneous, but this is not a probable opinion. See St Alphonsus, *Theol. Mor.*, Book VI, n. 9; De Lugo, *Resp. Mor.*, Book 1, dub. 33.

sacrament. The question only concerns the prayer with or without the words: 'Receive the Holy Ghost', etc. Is it a sufficient form? Does it resemble substantially the prayers used or approved by the Church as the form of ordinations? Does it contain the *minimum* which is found in all the prayer-forms, and which I mentioned in n. 59 above? It is without doubt connected with ordination. But it is not a prayer *for the ordinand*, calling down on him from God's mercy the graces he will need. It is rather a formula of thanksgiving, with a prayer at the end for everyone: 'We humbly beseech thee, by the same thy blessed Son, to grant unto all, which either here or elsewhere call upon thy holy Name ... So that as well as by these thy Ministers, as by them over whom they shall be appointed thy Ministers ... ', etc. Furthermore the presbyteral order is not mentioned; the words: 'his Apostles, Prophets, Evangelists, Doctors, and Pastors' do not refer solely to priests; thus the words 'to the same Office and Ministry appointed for the salvation of mankind' are not confined to the presbyteral order. This prayer therefore leaves much to be desired; as a form it is far from being certainly sufficient.

74. The Ordinal's rite for the ordination of presbyters is better than the rite for the ordination of deacons, because it has a prayer attached to the imposition of hands, but it is not certainly sufficient. In addition, we must not forget that a certain doubt is cast over the ordination of presbyters and other Anglican ordinations by the episcopate considered as minister of the sacrament.

75. I come now to the Anglican episcopal consecration. A preliminary question comes to mind: Can a bishop be validly consecrated if he is not already a priest? To avoid overloading the discussion I shall not deal *ex professo* with this delicate controversy, which I have treated at length in an article in *Canoniste Contemporain* (Feb. 1895), and which I put before the reader in Appendix IV.[41] Both theologically and historically the probable, and even the more probable opinion, as

---

41. [Not included here.]

can be seen from that article, is that episcopate can be valid even when priesthood has not been previously received. But I cannot challenge the probability – which is at least extrinsic – of the other opinion, which has been the more common since the eleventh century; in practice this opinion has to be taken into consideration when dealing with episcopal consecration. Consequently, as the Anglican presbyterate is not above all criticism, the episcopate cannot offer every possible guarantee of validity.

76. With regard to the rite of the Ordinal the handing over of the Bible with the words: 'Give heed unto reading' could not by itself be a sufficient rite for the validity of the ordination. Anglicans themselves do not consider it as the matter and form of their episcopal consecration. The words: 'Give heed unto reading' are rather an exhortation to do good.[42]

77. The rite of laying on hands with the words 'Receive the Holy Ghost', etc. carries more weight. The imposition of hands unquestionably provides sufficient matter; we have to look at the form. The *common* opinion among Catholic theologians places the form of episcopal consecration in the Roman Pontifical solely in the words 'Receive the Holy Spirit' which accompany the imposition of hands by the consecrating bishop and the bishop assistants. Those who share this opinion have to admit that the form of the Ordinal is sufficient for the consecration of a bishop, because the form 'Receive the Holy Spirit' cannot lose its power to consecrate on account of the words 'and remember', etc. that follow in the Ordinal. Nevertheless it is as well to remember that the theory preferred by scholars today is rather the second (n. 57),

---

42. For the episcopate as for the presbyterate (n. 68, note 35) [We have corrected what appears to be a mistaken reference – Edd.], Anglicans all identify the matter of consecration with the imposition of hands, but they are not agreed about the form. Some of them hold that it consists of the prayer: 'Almighty God', coming before the laying on of hands which is accompanied by the words: 'Receive the Holy Ghost', etc. Others maintain that it consists solely of the words: 'Receive the Holy Ghost', etc. Billuart identifies the form for the Anglican episcopate with the prayer: 'Almighty God' which comes immediately before the hymn 'Come, Holy Ghost'; but he had not read the Ordinal.

which maintains that by divine right a prayer is required as the form of all ordinations; this means that in the Roman Pontifical's consecration of a bishop the form is the *consecratio* of the Roman liturgy with the addition of these words: 'May their feet be beautiful ... may they gain fruit.' Consequently the sufficiency of this form used in Anglican episcopal consecrations is not certain, even though in the common opinion among Catholic theologians it ought to be admitted; indeed its insufficiency is more probable.

78. Let us see whether the prayer: 'Almighty God, and most merciful Father', with or without the words: 'Receive the Holy Ghost', etc., provides more guarantees. It does not matter for the sufficiency of the rite whether the prayer comes before or after the imposition of hands or accompanies it. It is more a question of knowing whether this prayer fulfils all the conditions for a prayer-form and whether it conforms substantially to the prayers used or approved by the Church. The prayer: 'Almighty God, giver of all good things' would certainly be sufficient, but it is too far removed from the imposition of hands. The prayer: 'Most merciful Father, we beseech thee to send upon this thy servant', in addition to this defect, is hardly better than the prayer: 'Almighty God, and most merciful Father', which is what we need to study now.

79. We have to admit that this prayer is more in conformity with the prayers used or approved by the Church as the form of ordination than the prayers for the ordination of a presbyter are (n. 73). It refers to the ordination; it is a prayer *for the ordinand.* It has been rightly observed that parts of this prayer have been borowed, in somewhat abbreviated form, from that part of the Roman Pontifical which draws on the Gallican liturgy. [The author at this point sets out the Roman prayer *Sint speciosi* and the Anglican prayer *Grant, we beseech thee* in parallel columns.]

There is only one comment to make, but it must be made: this prayer does not make a single mention of the episcopate. One can reply that the prayer is sufficiently focused on the episcopate by the intention of the minister and the rest of the ceremony. For example, Catholic theologians who claim that the vague words: 'Receive the Holy Ghost' are the form of the episcopate say that they are attached to the episcopate by the intention of the minister and the rest of the ceremony. Similarly in marriage, surely the signs and words which express consent are referred to the marriage contract by the intentions of each partner and the whole context of the ceremony. With appropriate qualifications we can make the same statement about the form of confirmation, extreme unction and baptism.

Without wishing to challenge the seriousness of these replies, I cannot avoid repeating that there is an element in all these prayer-forms which is missing in the Ordinal's prayer. When it comes to the validity of sacraments and above all the validity of the episcopate and presbyterate, we have to follow not only the *safer* opinion but the *safest*. Moreover in a factual matter such as that of the sacraments, the example of one sacrament cannot provide a decisive argument. One has also to take account of the authority of Paul IV, who certainly regarded the rite of the Ordinal as insufficient (n. 17).

VI
CONCLUSION

80. In the course of this study, after establishing that Barlow's consecration as bishop could be considered historically certain, I believe I have shown that a defective intention in the external forum was probable without being certain. Then I maintained that the rites of the Ordinal for the diaconate are probably sufficient precisely insofar as one accepts as probable the scholastic opinion that the matter and form of ordination to the diaconate consist in the handing over of the Gospels and the corresponding words. But the defective prayer of consecration is a more probable cause of invalidity, to say nothing of doubts concerning the validity of the Anglican episcopate. With regard to the presbyterate, validity is barely possible, either because the handing over of the

instruments is missing, or above all because the prayer is defective, or finally because of doubts about the validity of their episcopate. With regard to bishops, validity is seriously probable. Now according to the juridical practice of the Roman Congregations, in dealings with the sacraments in general and ordination in particular, an ordination that is certainly valid must not be repeated either *absolutely* or *conditionally*;[43] an ordination that is certainly invalid must be repeated *absolutely*; an ordination that is probably invalid must be repeated *conditionally*. Applying this juridical practice to the subject, it follows that Anglican ordinations cannot be purely and simply accepted. They must be repeated; but in my humble opinion there might be a case for modifying the present practice and re-ordaining only conditionally the Anglican ministers, or at least the bishops, who return to the Catholic Church.

81. H. E. Cardinal Vaughan in his letter of 2 October 1894, which I have quoted several times, adds with good reason: 'The question of orders is, after all, only a side issue. Even were it proved that the Anglicans, like the Donatists, have valid orders, and even were they acknowledged by the Holy See, in the words of St Augustine it would avail them nothing "outside the unity of the Church".' Christian charity compels us to promote and hasten the return of the great English nation to Catholic unity, in the first place by the courtesy of our discussions, inspired by the respect we owe to virtue, learning and good faith, and above all by our prayers. May there be 'one flock and one shepherd'. Amen.

---

43. To discuss here and now the Church's former discipline concerning this matter would be pointless; today the juridical practice is certain and invariable. However, even in the case of an ordination which is certainly valid, if an important but inessential rite is omitted or performed wrongly, it sometimes has to be repeated. See my treatise *De sacra ordinatione*, n. 1001.

MEMORANDUM ON ANGLICAN ORDINATIONS

Mgr L. Duchesne

[1] What woman having ten silver drachmas, if she loses one of them, does not light a lamp, sweep the house, and search carefully until she finds it? (Lk 15.8).

Many voices, as serious as they are pessimistic, have been saying for a long time that the drachma which is being searched for here is well and truly lost. Those who speak in this way are inspired by sentiments worthy of the utmost respect. If they have not themselves suffered for their desperate situation, they do represent the tradition of a Church cruelly persecuted. Before contradicting them, one feels the need to salute them and to render them all the grateful homage which is due to a faith which has been conserved not out of fear or mere habit or convenience, but by sacrificing and despising such concerns.

The author of the present memorandum has prepared and drawn it up without any bias; he desires nothing so much as to see the question better treated than he has been able to do himself. Whether it is eventually settled according to his arguments or against them, he is ready to accept that solution, not doubting that it will be founded on the most serious reasons, and that it will be preceded by the fairest examination of the case produced by each side.

The books which relate to this controversy are not all easily accessible on the continent. Most of them are written in English; the best and most recent of them in any case. I have given very special attention to the work of Canon Estcourt, *The Question of Anglican Ordinations* (London, 1873). This book is considered by the opponents of

Anglican Orders as *the* classic work on the subject. In addition to this publication I have taken cognizance of many other works and collections of documents published on one side or the other. However, I have been more concerned to expound than to argue. I have confronted the facts and the texts and have pursued my path resolutely, without lingering over all the objections and quibbles which encumber this subject, but from which an intelligent student will free himself without too much effort.

[2] The exposition is set out as follows:

1. *The question of fact* – the reality of the consecration of Parker and of Barlow.
2. *The question of the rite* – the sufficiency of the Anglican Ordinal.
3. *The question of intention* – the sufficiency of the intention of those who promulgated the Ordinal and of those who use it.
4. *The question of practice* – the origin and authority of the current practice of reordaining Anglican ministers.

I
THE QUESTION OF FACT: DID PARKER AND BARLOW RECEIVE EPISCOPAL CONSECRATION?

[3] In March 1534 England severed its communion with Rome. However, King Henry VIII, the author of this rupture, would not tolerate going further than schism. Right up to his death on 28 January 1547 traditional doctrine was maintained[1], even with some rigour: no changes were made to the liturgical books.

This is not to say that all the members of the English clergy remained outside the current of heretical ideas, which for 30 years had been causing such ferment in Germany, Switzerland and France. The Archbishop of Canterbury, Thomas

---

1. This is not intended to justify the excesses committed under Henry VIII and on his orders against devotion to images and against monastic houses.

Cranmer, promoted in 1533, was a Protestant to the depth of his soul. However his installation took place in accordance with all the ordinary rules and with the approbation of Pope Clement VII. Henry VIII was succeeded by his three children: Edward VI (1547–1553), Mary (1553–1558), and Elizabeth (1558–1603), the first two legitimate and the third the daughter of Anne Boleyn. Under Edward VI and Elizabeth, Protestant influence dominated the counsels of the Crown; between these two reigns that of Mary represented a reaction, not only against the heretical régime inaugurated under Edward VI but also against the schism of Henry VIII.

Under Henry VIII and Mary bishops were ordained in accordance with the Roman Pontifical. Under Edward VI and Elizabeth there was substituted for the Pontifical a service book commonly called *The Ordinal*, annexed to *The Book of Common Prayer* or *Prayer Book*; at the accession of Mary this was put aside, but Elizabeth authorised it once again.

[4] On Sunday, 17 December 1559, Matthew Parker, chosen by this Queen to occupy the primatial see of Canterbury, was consecrated according to the Ordinal of Edward VI. Four bishops took part in this ceremony. Two of them, Barlow, who officiated as consecrator, and Hodgkin, had been elevated under Henry VIII, that is to say at the time when the Pontifical was still in use. The other two, Scory and Coverdale, had been ordained by Archbishop Cranmer according to the Ordinal of Edward VI.

Practically all the Episcopal Sees at that moment were *de facto* vacant: Parker had thus to consecrate the new nominees. On the validity of his own consecration depends therefore the validity of practically all subsequent Anglican Ordinations (episcopal or other).

[5] Parker's consecration has been contested in a number of ways. To begin with, it was argued that it never took place; later, when the fact itself had reluctantly to be conceded, it was its validity that was rejected.

The first tactic is represented by the *Nag's Head* fable, today abandoned by all English Catholics, at least by those sufficiently informed for their opinion to have any weight.

However it has retained its credit in certain theological mili-
eux; it has been used in our lifetime, and is still used outside
England, in order to justify the summary condemnation of
Anglican Orders.[2]

According to this legend, at the beginning of the reign of
Elizabeth, since the former and legitimate bishops were either
in prison or had refused to take part, the candidates
appointed to their sees met in London at a tavern called
The Nag's Head. There, at Scory's initiative, a rapid ceremony took place, at the end of which the candidates considered themselves to have been consecrated: among them was
Parker.

Such is the core of the story. As for the details, there are as
many variations as there are authors. According to one of
them, Scory ordered the candidates to kneel; then, taking
them in turn by the hand, said to them: 'Arise, my Lord
Bishop of Canterbury! Arise, my Lord Bishop of London!'
And so on. According to another narrative, Scory took a
Bible in one hand, made the candidates kneel and then
stretched out his free hand onto their heads and shoulders,
saying 'Receive authority to preach sincerely the word of
God!'

[6] These conflicting accounts appeared for the first time in
various books printed at the beginning of the 17th century.[3] It
should be noted that all of them, in spite of their lack of
uniformity, call on one and the same witness, a certain
Thomas Neale, Professor of Hebrew at Oxford, who is supposed to have been present at the scene. Thomas Neale died
in 1590, long before his recollections could be exploited in
print in the controversy.

It would be a waste of time to discuss a legend which has

2. Perrone, *De ordine*, n. 137, not. 4. Gasparri, *De sacra ordinatione*, t. II, p. 279,
nota 1 (Paris, 1894).

3. Christopher Holywood (a Sacro bosco) SS, *De investiganda vera et visib. Christi
ecclesia*, Antwerp 1604; – Parson, *Discussion if the Answere of M. Barlow, D.D. to the
judgment of a Catholique Englishman*, 1612; – Fitzsimon, *Britannomachia ministrorum*
etc., Douai, 1614; – Wadsworth, *Copies of certain letters*, etc., London, 1624 (the
letter on the ordination of Parker is of 1 April 1615); Kellison, *Examen novae refor-
mationis*, 1616; Champney, *De vocatione ministrorum*, Paris, 1618.

been discarded by all serious people and which is sufficiently disproved by what the official documents tell us about Parker's consecration.

The official record of this ceremony and of all the acts which accompanied it can be found in the *Register* of Archbishop Parker at Lambeth Palace. It has often been published. It is an extremely extensive document; it occupies no less than 34 octavo pages in what, as far as I can ascertain, is the most recent edition.[4] English Catholics have raised certain objections as to the date of the drawing up of this official record; but, since it is backed up by a large body of independent documents and other testimonies, they now accept that the consecration of Parker was celebrated as it was described in the Register.[5]

[7] But they – or, at least, some of them – still dispute whether Barlow, Parker's consecrator, had been really ordained. This question must be examined with care.

At the moment when his episcopal career began, Barlow found himself very involved in the ecclesiastical affairs of the Kingdom, in particular with the negotiations aimed at getting the King of Scotland to adopt the same position as Henry VIII. He was a priest and a monk of the Order of St Augustine. On 16 January 1536 he was elected Bishop of St Asaph. Before the royal confirmation could be given him (22 February) he left on a mission to Scotland. On 10 April he was elected to another see, that of St David's: on the 20th and 21st of that month he was in London and there received confirmation from the King and from the Archbishop. On the 26th the King put him in possession of the temporalities of his see, which normally only happens after consecration. Perhaps he was consecrated on the 23rd, Low Sunday. On the 27th he was summoned to Parliament with the other bishops;

---

4. Lee, *The Validity of the Holy Orders of the Church of England*, London, 1869, p. 391.

5. 'With regard to Parker's consecration, we have found, that as an historical fact, it is most certain that it took place on the 17th of December 1559, according to the description in the Register.' Estcourt, *The Question of Anglican Ordinations*, London, 1873, p. 371.

in the documents of his summons he is described as *episcopus Menevensis*. On 1 May he took possession of his see by proxy then left again for Scotland. Some letters of his, written during this voyage, give the title of *episcopus Menevensis*. About 11 June he was once again in London; a letter of the day after, the 12th, describes him as still Bishop elect. If this is not an error, one is obliged to admit that Barlow's consecration had been delayed until now and that the grant of the temporalities had been made, contrary to normal usage, before his consecration. This departure from the norm is sufficiently explained by the fact that, if the consecration had been put back, it was on account of the requirements of public service, that of the affairs of Scotland.

[8] From 30 June one notes the presence of Barlow in the House of Lords and from this moment the term *electus* no longer appears in any documents which concern him. He was consecrated then on one or other of the two Sundays which in 1536 occurred between 12 and 30 June, i.e. on the 18th or the 25th.

Thus Barlow was acknowledged as Bishop of St David's in the spring of the year 1536. In 1548 he was translated to the See of Bath and Wells. During the reign of Mary he left that bishopric and fled to the continent. On his return at Elizabeth's accession he obtained straight away the bishopric of Chichester, which he kept until his death in 1568.

Barlow therefore appeared before the public of his time over a period of 32 years as a bishop and as a bishop consecrated like all the other bishops. The faithful in his different dioceses considered him as such; it was the same for the clergy over whom he successively presided, and for his colleagues in the episcopate, legitimate or illegitimate, and for the sovereigns who then reigned over England. None of his contemporaries had the slightest doubt as to his ordination; nobody today or before today would ever have dreamed of disputing it if he had not been Parker's consecrator. But, since it was he who consecrated Parker, people have searched out objections. Before weighing them up we must try to appreciate the enormity of the claim thus being advanced. If these objections are admitted, it follows that Barlow was able and willing to get himself installed without consecration of any kind; that he was able and deliberately willed to keep this monstrous irregularity hidden.

[9] In fact, whatever changes were introduced in the 16th century into the English rites, it is quite clear that neither the royal authority nor Parliament nor public opinion would ever have accepted that an unconsecrated bishop should exercise any episcopal functions. This absence of consecration would have to have been hidden from Edward VI and from Elizabeth as well as from Henry VIII himself. As far as Elizabeth was concerned, dissimulation would have been very particularly necessary, for in requiring Barlow's service, the Queen and her counsellors were evidently determined that the consecration of Parker should be celebrated by a real bishop. We are not here reduced to conjecture, for we have written documents, autographs indeed,[6] well fitted to enlighten us as to the preoccupations of those who played the leading roles, Lord Cecil and Matthew Parker.

Barlow, not only as a diocesan bishop but as a member of Parliament and as a champion of Protestant ideas, had often to reckon with opponents. He was removed from the episcopate under Queen Mary; we have the acts which record the steps which had to be taken to provide his replacement. Nowhere is there any trace of the slightest doubt that he was a properly consecrated bishop. If he had never received consecration, in one form or another, this omission must have been the object of the closest of secrets.

[10] Now is such a triumph of dissimulation really plausible? Barlow was one of Henry VIII's principal ecclesiastical counsellors, one of the best known men at the court in London. His elevation to the episcopate, his mission in Scotland, his entry into Parliament drew quite special attention upon him in the spring of 1536. His acts could not remain unknown. In the world in which he moved such negligence could not have passed unnoticed. We cannot believe

---

6. Estcourt, p. 86f.

that everyone in London shared the ideas of a few advanced theologians on the uselessness of ordination. For every person who considered ordination a matter of indifference, there were 100,000 who believed it essential. And the rumours which began to circulate about these points of doctrine were of their very nature likely to provoke very special attention on the part of the orthodox. We can be sure that such attention would be even more than usually acute when it concerned people of advanced views like Barlow. For him, more than for many others, it would have been impossible to have got himself accepted as a bishop if his consecration had not rigorously fulfilled all the proper forms.

[11] But why would he have dispensed himself? Because, we are told, of his opinions. According to him ordination would not be essential for the exercise of ecclesiastical functions; it would suffice to have the royal delegation. Such was, in reality, his private conviction. In proof of it, apart from one recorded remark, whose meaning is unclear, we can bring forward Barlow's reply to the consultation document sent by the King in 1540 to the members of his episcopate. Henry VIII was then engaged in preparing the formulary entitled *A Necessary Doctrine and Erudition for any Christian Man*, commonly called *The King's Book*. To clarify his own mind in drawing up this text he had addressed various questions to his bishops on the subject of the sacraments. We have all their replies. Those of Barlow and of Cranmer, substantially the same, contest the absolute necessity of ordination.

It is a question here of individual opinions. From the fact that they were expressed by these two prelates it can in no way be deduced that they had not themselves been ordained. Cranmer certainly had been: nobody doubts it. How, on the basis of the same document and the same private opinion, could one conclude that Barlow was not or perhaps was not? We know how often Henry VIII's bishops, and these two in particular, sacrificed their personal opinions when faced with the necessity of signing royal formularies. This was precisely the case with the consultation in question. The King's Book, which resulted from it, laid down on the subject of ordination not the heretical opinion of Cranmer and Barlow but the traditional doctrine of the Catholic Church. Cranmer and Barlow complied and signed alongside the others.

[12] We are familiar with Henry VIII's temperament and with the terrible severity which he bought to the enforcement of his ordinances on religious questions. Barlow would have risked the scaffold if he had deceived the King over so serious a matter. If his attachment to heretical doctrines did not prevent him from signing official documents which clearly went against his own convictions, why would he have any difficulty in submitting to a ceremony? Did any one ever observe him hesitating, during the 32 years of his episcopate, to celebrate the rites of ordination or the other functions of his order?

[13] At this point we are told that Henry VIII himself did not believe in the necessity of ordination. This unexpected and incredible assertion is based on a document annotated in the King's own hand.[7] The document consists of a set of replies to questions addressed by Henry VIII to the bishops. In the margin the King has written several comments of his own. The consultors say: 'Making of Bishops hath two parts, appointment and ordering.' Comment by the King: *Where is this distinction found*? Appointment, the consultors continue, which 'the Apostles by necessity made by common election, and sometime by their own several assignment, could not then be done by Christian princes, because at that time they were not; and now at these days appertaineth to Christian princes and rulers.' Comment by the King: *Now since you confess that the apostles did occupate the one part, which now you confess belongeth to princes, how can you prove that ordering is only committed to you Bishops*?

It is clear that the King is here debating with his theologians, but privately and in the confidentiality of his own study. His comments are in his own hand and absolutely private. What he is observing is that his consultors have failed to indicate the proof for their assertions and distinctions. It

---

7. Estcourt, p. 70f [spelling modernised].

would be poor logic to attribute to him the contrary opinion to the one concerning which he is requesting fuller information. If there had been some uncertainty in his mind at the moment when he annotated the memorandum, that uncertainty must have disappeared before the promulgation of the official document about which he was consulting the bishops.

[14] But let us for a moment admit – not because it is at all plausible but as a mere intellectual exercise – that his definitive position was represented not by his public statement but by this ambiguous marginal note, interpreted in the sense attributed to it by our opponents. What would be the result? That the king rejected the necessity of ordination? Not at all. The result would be merely that the King attributed to himself the right and the power to celebrate it. Barlow, if he wanted to confirm his conduct to the ideas of his prince, would have had, not to refuse ordination, but to have had it conferred upon him by Henry VIII.

I am only sorry that objections of such frivolity lead me in turn to observations so lacking in seriousness.

[15] The objections raised are utterly unconvincing. The most serious argument is founded on the fact that the official record of Barlow's consecration is lacking in Archbishop Cranmer's Register. This argument would amount to something if Barlow's record were the only one missing in this Register. But we know it to be seriously incomplete; that it lacks several consecrations, in particular that of Gardiner, Bishop of Winchester and Queen Mary's Chancellor, well known for having kept throughout this troubled period an attitude more correct than most of his colleagues. Nobody has ever questioned Gardiner's ordination; nobody has ever argued against it the absence of the official record. Why should one react so differently in the case of Barlow?

We have therefore to admit as historically, that is, morally, certain the consecration of Parker's consecrator. As it took place under Henry VIII it could not have been accomplished by any other rite than that of the Roman Pontifical. There can therefore be no objection against its validity.

II
THE QUESTION OF THE RITE – IS THE ENGLISH ORDINAL SUFFICIENT?

[16] Let us now move on to the question of the rite. Is the rite, which Barlow used in ordaining Parker and which Parker himself and other consecrators after him have used and still use to this day, open to the possibility of being considered as sufficient in itself, abstracting for the moment from the intention both of those who introduced it and of those who have used and still use it?

At first sight this question has to be answered negatively, if we admit that the tradition of the instruments, with the words that accompany it in the Pontifical, belongs to the essence of the ordination rite.[8] Nobody, it is true, would make such a claim, if it were a question of a decision embracing the whole of the Church; for otherwise there would not be a single valid ordination among the Greeks and the Orientals who have kept unchanged their former usage. As far as the Latin Church is concerned, it is beyond doubt that the tradition of the instruments is an adventitious ceremony, which was unknown in the earliest times and which was only introduced gradually, spreading from neighbour to neighbour, without any intervention from the supreme authority, in the 11th or the 12th century, depending on the place. Those who claim that this ceremony, in spite of its lack of antiquity, universality and authority, is essential to the rite are obliged to admit: (i) that the Church claims the right to change the matter and the form of the Sacrament of Order; (ii) that she has exercised this right in substituting for, or in adding to, the primitive and universal right of the imposition of hands the adventitious and local rite of the tradition of the instruments. These assertions are rejected by history, for there is no evidence anywhere that the Church has ever claimed such a power over the sacraments; it looks as if the Council

---

8. The tradition of the instruments was not at first abolished: it is prescribed in the 1549 (1550) Ordinal but disappeared in the edition of 1552.

of Trent has even rejected such an idea.[9] Even if we concede that she believed herself to possess such a power, it would be strange if she had made use of it without warning the faithful. Finally, it is difficult to see any reason why she should have decided to modify substantially so ancient a ritual, whose essential features are discernible in the New Testament and which represents undeniably the usage of the apostolic period.

In the explanations which follow, therefore, no account will be taken of an opinion which has so little foundation in tradition and which besides has been generally abandoned in comtemporary theology.[10]

[17] Having put behind us this difficulty, we can proceed to compare the Anglican ceremonies with those authorized by the Roman Church and, more particularly, with those she has used or uses herself. The exposition which I now begin will only fully make sense if the reader has in front of him copies of both the Roman Pontifical and of the Anglican Ordinal. The latter is invariably to be found printed at the end of the Prayer Book. It also exists in a Latin translation, the work of two members of the Anglican clergy, W. Bright and P. Goldsmith Medd.[11]

It is necessary to give only a cursory glance at the Eastern service books in order to see that the ceremony of ordination, as they describe it, consists essentially of a public prayer accompanied by the imposition of hands.[12] The ordinand is presented to the assembled congregation which is informed of his promotion. Then the faithful are invited to join in prayer and they pray both personally and by responding to the

---

9. Sess. XXI, cap. 2 [DS 1728].

10. It must also be noted that this opinion can have no bearing on the evaluation of the rite for the consecration of bishops.

11. [*Liber precum publicarum Ecclesiae Anglicanae* (London 1887).] In my book entitled *Origines du culte chrétien*, pp. 340ff, I have reproduced and explained the early formulas of the Roman use. This book can be used for comparison with the Anglican Ordinal.

12. I cannot understand why our theologians present as the Greek form of ordination the formula *Divina gratia* etc., with which the ceremony opens. It is clearly nothing but a preamble, destined to announce to the congregation the promotion of the cleric who is to be ordained.

diaconal litany. Before and after this litany the bishop alone pronounces a prayer asking God to pour out his grace upon the ordinand.

[18] Things were not basically very different in the Latin Church in the early period of its history. To grasp this clearly it is important to go behind the present Pontifical and to distinguish what is primitive in its text from what has been added later. The ancient manuscripts which have come down to us form a series in which the oldest elements go back materially to the 7th century. In comparing these with the present text it is easy to make the necessary discernment and so to separate the ancient from the modern. From this comparison it results that we should eliminate as later additions from outside a number of ceremonies which today have a high profile: the anointings, the tradition of the instruments,[13] the formulae which accompany the vesting and the second imposition of hands on the new priests at the end of the ordination Mass. With all this eliminated, the Roman Pontifical still retains a certain complexity, the causes of which I must now try to explain.

[19] When liturgical books from Rome penetrated into Merovingian Gaul in the 7th and 8th centuries, instead of being adopted as they were, they were combined with the Gallican books in use in that country. In this way we have composite, hybrid rites such as that for the mass in the *Sacramentarium Gallicanum* of Bobbio; Gallican up to the Preface, Roman from the Preface onwards. In this way above all we have the singular mixture of Roman and Gallican ceremonies which we find in the sacramentaries called Gelasian and in the *Missale Francorum*. In the time of Charlemagne, when it would have been so easy to obtain accurate information on Roman usage and so to return to the primitive simplicity, the choice was made to stay with the contamination now already familiar. Little by little this hybrid ordinal was substituted for the Gallican ordinal; it

---

13. It must be understood that in this study we are concerned only with the three highest orders; the diaconate, the presbyterate and the episcopate.

was even introduced into Italy and in time it came to replace the former Roman rite in Rome itself.[14]

[20] As it happens, we are able to compare with these complex books the primitive Roman book, as it has been conserved in the Leonine and Gregorian Sacramentaries as well as in the earliest *Ordines Romani*. These genuine and officially authorized texts give us clear information as to the rites and formulae in use in Rome from the 6th to the 10th century at the very least. If we keep exclusively to them, we are able to reconstitute what was in fact a very simple ceremony. The ordinands – deacons, priests, bishops – are presented to the officiating bishop, who invites the faithful to pray for them: *Oremus, dilectissimi nobis*, etc. The faithful do so obediently, associating themselves with the singing of the litany; then the celebrant sums up their petitions in the words of a collect. When this corporate prayer has been concluded, he begins another prayer of a eucharistic kind in the form of a thanksgiving, inflected in a specially solemn tone and preceded by the invitations *Sursum corda* and *Gratias agamus*, like the Preface of the Canon of the Mass. This 'eucharistic' prayer is what the *Ordines Romani* call *the* prayer, the benediction of the diaconate, the priesthood, the episcopate. It is in any case the last prayer. Once it is over the mystery is accomplished and the *ordinands* are now the *ordained*. This they were not when the prayer began. In fact in one of the ordination rites, that for priests, the collect which immediately precedes this prayer clearly assumes that the consecration is still to come; it is still here a question of those to be ordained: *Quos tuae pietatis aspectibus offerimus consecrandos* ('whom we offer to be consecrated ... ').

Thus, a prayer for the ordinands, instigated, led and summed up by the officiant, constitutes the first part of the ceremony. A consecratory prayer, pronounced by the consecrating bishop alone, using the most solemn of intonations and following a eucharistic model, constitutes the second

---

14. It is to this circumstance that we owe the introduction into the Roman ordination rite of the Gallican ceremony of anointing.

part. The first is but a preparation, the second is operative. At the end of the first the candidate is not yet ordained; at the end of the second he clearly is.

[21] The Leonine and Gregorian Sacramentaries contain no formula other than those just mentioned. They do not mention the imposition of hands; this should not however surprise us, for in books of this kind the words are the principal concern and the accompanying ceremonies almost always taken for granted. But the 'rituals' in the strict sense, the *Ordines*, also omit the imposition of hands, not invariably but fairly frequently.[15] It is in any case clear from other evidence that this ceremony was always practised. If it has left so few traces, this, I believe, is because formerly it was not accompanied by any special formula or, perhaps, because it could take place at a number of points during the prayers described above.

[22] Today the imposition of hands takes place for deacons during the 'eucharistic' prayer: for priests before the prayer of the faithful; for bishops at the end of the litany. For priests it is not accompanied by any formula; for bishops the phrase is simply: *Accipe Spiritum sanctum*; for deacons there are a few added words: *Accipe Spiritum sanctum ad robur, ad resistendum diabolo et tentationibus eius* ('Receive the Holy Spirit for strength, for resisting the Devil and his temptations'). In this last formula there is clearly nothing which characterizes either the functions of the ordinand or any kind of power of order.

[23] We have therefore, in the critical analysis which concerns us here, to put to one side these imperative formulae which have no credentials in antiquity and which only have the importance sometimes attributed to them if they had been found uniformly in the three rites relating to deacons, priests and bishops. This being the case, we have to take into

---

15. It is lacking in the *Ordo* of the St Amand manuscript, published for the first time after my book *Les origines du culte chrétien*; it is lacking also in Mabillon's *Ordo VIII. Ordo IX* makes a point of including it in the case of deacons, priests and bishops, but not in the case of the Pope. It is not found either in the Small Ritual for the consecration of the Pope which is included among the formulae of the *Liber diurnus*.

consideration the imposition of hands alone, whether or not it is accompanied by special words, whether or not these words are more or less expressive of its meaning.

Thus, the primitive Roman rite, at the very least the oldest that we can reach and which, in the time of Charlemagne, had already been in use for several centuries and was still in use, without the addition of extraneous ceremonies, for about one or two centuries more, consisted of (1) public prayer for the ordained and (2) the laying on of hands. If this rite was sufficient at that time, then any rite equally complete and equally expressive must, considered in itself and objectively, be a sufficient rite.

[24] Let us now examine the Anglican Ordinal. It derives quite evidently from the Roman Pontifical, not from the very ancient Pontifical represented by the ninth-century texts, but from the Pontifical at about the same stage of development as that found in editions currently in use. For each of the three hierarchical orders we find the presentation of the candidates by the archdeacon, his testimony in their favour, the questioning of the congregation as to possible impediments, the litany, the examination of the candidates, the bishop's exhortation, the *Veni Creator* and the imposition of hands, preceded in the case of priests and bishops by a solemn consecratory prayer. The laying on of hands has a particularly important place; it is accompanied by an imperative and declaratory formula. For priests and bishops this formula begins with the words *Accipe Spiritum sanctum* (Receive the Holy Ghost). This is not so for deacons; in their case they are simply addressed with the words: *Accipe potestatem exsequendi officium diaconi* ... (Take thou authority to execute the office of a Deacon ...).

[25] This is the first difference. There is another, which is much more serious: the consecratory prayer is absent in the ordination of deacons. This fact would lead to the conclusion, if we follow the principles enunciated earlier, that the Anglican rite is insufficient for the ordination of deacons.

The question in the case of the ordination of priests and bishops is a different one. Here we have a solemn prayer with the same meaning and the same style as the Roman prayer. At times even the same language has been conserved. This solemn prayer immediately precedes the imposition of hands; the link between the two is as strongly emphasized as in the Roman Pontifical. The most important difference is that in the Pontifical the laying on of hands precedes the bishop's prayer, whereas here it follows it. This divergence does not seem to have much importance. In both cases there is both an imposition of hands and a solemn prayer for those being ordained.

[26] Let us now compare the content of this prayer in the two liturgies. If the Anglican formula is found to be as expressive as the Roman it will be clear that the Anglican ordination – on this count, let it be understood – raises no insoluble objection.

Let us turn first of all to the Roman text. In the prayer at the ordination of priests the following ideas can be found. God is the sovereign distributor of all honours and dignities, and their hierarchical arrangement has no other *raison d'être* than in the general order which proceeds from him. In the Old Testament both Moses, for the government of the people, and Aaron, for the priesthood, had auxiliaries who formed a second order under them. In the New Testament there were Teachers to help the Apostles spread the preaching of the Gospel. In the same way Christian pontiffs (*pontifices summi*) need helpers of the second rank. God is asked to grant to these his servants (those who are presented before him) the *presbyteral* dignity and also the virtues necessary for its worthy execution.

That is all. There is no more precise reference to the powers conferred, no other definition of the function of the order bestowed.

[27] In the Anglican prayer[16] there is no reference to the relationship between priest and bishop; the Old Testament examples are omitted, that of Moses as well as that of Aaron; but there is an explicit reference to the ecclesiastical

---

16. 'Almighty God, and heavenly Father, etc.'

leaders of the New Testament, to Apostles, Prophets, Evangelists, Doctors and Pastors. It is made clear that the ordinands have been called to the same office and ministry appointed for the salvation of mankind, and the divine help is invoked as well upon the ordinands as upon the faithful confided to their ministry.

This prayer is undoubtedly lacking in precision; but is not the same true of the Roman prayer? This uses neither sacerdotal nor sacrificial language, except with reference to the priests of the Old Law. The Eucharist is not alluded to at any point; the presbyteral functions are only described here in the most general terms. It is exactly the same – neither more nor less – in the Anglican Ordinal.

[28] Let us move on to the formula for episcopal consecration. In the Roman Pontifical this begins with a long disquisition on the vestments of the Levitical priesthood and on the teaching which can be deduced therefrom. God is then asked to pour out his grace on those presented before him, called to the high priesthood. There follows a long series of requests for these persons. The functions which the new bishops are called upon to exercise are hardly characterized at all; however, mention is made of preaching, of the power of keys, of the general government of the Church confided to their care. Of sacrifice and of the Eucharist not a word is said.

The Anglican prayer[17] once again removes any reference to the Old Testament. It recalls the fact that our Redeemer instituted for the needs of his Church Apostles, Prophets, Evangelists, Doctors and Pastors. It then asks God to give grace to the candidate to fulfil the duties of his ministry. These duties are not enumerated in any greater detail than in the Roman formula – or in any less; preaching and the power of the keys are mentioned in the same terms: at this point the Anglican text borrows from the Pontifical. There is only one difference between the two texts worth noting; the Anglican text does not use the word priesthood (*sacerdotium*) which occurs twice in the Roman text: *Et idcirco his famulis*

---

17. 'Almighty God, and most merciful Father, etc.'

*tuis quos ad summi sacerdotii ministerium delegisti ... Comple
in sacerdotibus tuis mysterii tui summam ...* (' ... these your
servants whom you have chosen for the ministry of the high
priesthood ... Bring this mystery to completion in your
priests').

[29] It remains to be determined whether the use of this
term, which as it happens receives very little attention in the
rest of the text, should be considered as essential. If that were
the case, we would have to go on to ask why the mention of
priesthood (*sacerdotium*) is essential in the ordination of
bishops when it does not appear to be so in that of priests.
The two orders however are not distinguished from each
other in any strict sense by the sacerdotal power. We could
also ask why, in the prayer for bishops, that power which
most clearly characterizes their order, that of propagating
the hierarchy through ordination, is not the subject of even
the faintest allusion.

It is thus more natural to believe that in these formulae of
prayer only one thing needs to be considered, that is the
prayer itself, the appeal to the grace of God for the ordinands
and for their ministry. From the moment that that appeal is
given expression the prayer is sufficient. As for the definition
of functions and powers, the primitive rites of the Roman
Church refrain from indicating them in the consecratory
prayer. It is not reasonable to demand more of the
Anglican rite.

[30] These somewhat cursory considerations, based on the
text of the essential prayer contained in the Roman Pontifical,
allow us to dismiss a whole host of objections, specious rather
than solid, which have been pressed into service in this
debate. Some of those who admit, as I do here, that the
form of the Sacrament of Order must be looked for in the
consecratory prayers and not elsewhere have advanced *a
priori* claims as to what these prayers should or should not
indicate. They have argued that they should indicate, at least
in summary form, the nature and functions of the order being
conferred; they have demanded allusions to sacrifice and to
the power of ordaining; they have – in a word – set out a

complete programme which the Church should have followed in using the power which, it is claimed, has been left to her of determining the form of the sacrament. They argue also that, once this form has been definitively laid down by the Church, no inferior authority can alter it in any noteworthy way without this alteration affecting the validity of the sacrament.

All this is quite extraodinary. What need have we to reason *a priori* as to what the consecratory prayer should or should not contain in order to be sufficient? Do we not possess texts officially adopted by the Church, and, in particular, the most authoritative of them all, the Roman text? We have seen how lacking in precision it is and how little concerned its author has been to incorporate in it any definition – or even the most cursory mention – of the essential functions of priest and bishop.

[31] On the other hand – and here I reply to the second objection – it is not exact to say that the Church has constituted the *form* of the Sacrament of Order. We must not confuse form and formula. In every country the competent ecclesiastical authority has drawn up the text of a prayer, has adopted it and has more less imposed it as obligatory. But it is not the content of this text which is the *form* of the sacrament. In fact, as soon as you have a prayer for the ordinand, you have the form of the sacrament. This prayer, as we can establish from Scripture and liturgical tradition, has been in use since the time of the Apostles; it goes back as far as ordination itself. There is absolutely no need to imagine that the Church had to institute it; to do so indeed runs contrary to history.

As to the wording of this prayer, that is the responsibility of the liturgical authority. In drawing up a text, in imposing it, in forbidding any others which do not conform to it, the Church, as far as I can see, does not intend to go beyond her ordinary prerogatives by invoking some kind of extraordinary power of delegation which would allow her to control the essence of the sacramental rites and so to prescribe what is of divine law. The historical study of the texts of the liturgy give no justification for any such intention or any such claim.

[32] It follows from this that it would be quite useless to look in the consecratory prayers for any phrase to which one could attach a special power of the kind that belongs to the baptismal formula or to the words of consecration in the Eucharist. In the ordination prayers no specific phrase, no particular word, is essential. That which is essential and which constitutes the form of the sacrament is the prayer itself, determined by its general sense alone and by the context of the whole ceremony, independently of any particular choice of words.

We are ceaselessly told in this discussion that the sacraments are sensible signs of invisible grace and on this basis attempts are made to quantify the expressive properties of acceptable formulae. In acting in this way we can forget that the sensible sign is neither the form alone nor the matter alone but the sacrament in its entirety. Moreover, the sign in itself may be more or less clear; its power of signification derives both from the teaching of the Church, which instructs us as to what meaning to attach to one symbol or another, and also from the ceremonies and other circumstances which accompany the sacramental rite and which help us to get a clearer idea of its effect.

In the administration of the Sacrament of Order – as, incidentally, in the administration of all the sacraments – the minister and the subject are factors in the determination of the meaning of the rite. That is too evident for me to have to develop any further.

[33] Up to this point I have only considered and compared the consecratory prayers. Let us now cast a glance at the others. As far as the Roman rite is concerned the only one left to study is the collect which precedes the *Vere dignum*. It is remarkable that, both for bishops and for priests, this prayer mentions sacerdotal grace, *gratiae sacerdotalis virtutem* or *cornu*. In the Anglican Ordinal the collect which follows the litany contains nothing similar, but this is excluded by the fact that the same prayer is common to the ordination of deacons, of priests and of bishops. However there is reference to priesthood in the collect of the Mass at the ordination

of priests: 'Mercifully behold these thy servants now called to the office of Priesthood'; the same term is repeated in other formulae and also in the rubrics.

[34] Here it is important to note that, unlike Greek, Latin and other Romance languages, English does not possess two distinct words corresponding to the two ideas of presbyterate and *sacerdotium*. The word *priest* is used to translate both the Latin *presbyter* and the Greek *presbuteros*, and also the Latin *sacerdos* and the Greek *hiereus*. Similarly, the word *priesthood* is the equivalent of both *presbyterium* (*presbuterion*) and *sacerdotium* (*hierateia*). The proof that it includes two meanings is that the Latin translation of the Ordinal made by Anglicans commonly renders *priest* and *priesthood* as *sacerdos* and *sacerdotium*.[18]

We must not in any case attribute too much importance to the presence or absence of these latter words in the formulae of ordination. In the first place, *sacerdos*, unlike *presbyter*, does not have the advantage of antiquity. *Sacerdos* is not biblical; *presbyter* or *episcopus* are the words used in the New Testament and by authors in the primitive Church up to the end of the second century. *Sacerdos* and *hiereus* do not appear before Tertullian and Origen. Moreover, in the context of ordination these words are ambiguous; they characterize neither a particular order nor even order in its generic sense but, rather, a function common to the two highest orders. It is therefore more natural to employ here the terms *presbyter* and *episcopus*, which are clearer, more characteristic and more ancient.

[35] And this is precisely the case in the Roman formulae. These are the terms which appear in the most significant phrases of the consecratory prayers: *Da, quaesumus, in hos famulos tuos presbyterii dignitatem ... Tribuas eis, Domine, cathedram episcopalem*. Even if the Anglicans were excluding,

---

18. This is how the translators (p. vi) explain the basis of their choice: Verbum PRIEST visum est verbo PRESBYTER eis in locis reddere ubi de ordine eorum ageretur qui in ministerio Christi inter episcopos et diaconos locum habent; ubi autem de ipsa ministerii eorum executione, verbo SACERDOS [Bright and Medd, op. cit., p. vi]

which is not the case, any sacerdotal interpretation of the official word *Priesthood*, this would not constitute an objection to the sufficiency of their formulae.

In the Anglican Ordinal the words which accompany the imposition of hands, 'Receive the Holy Ghost etc.', are highly expressive. It is possible that those who drew up the Ordinal believed that this formula was the essential one. In this they were deceived, as were so many Catholic theologians who looked for the matter of the Sacrament of Order elsewhere than in the laying on of hands and for its form elsewhere than in the thanksgiving prayer. I do not need therefore to investigate the formulae used at the laying on of hands, either in their original version or in the version that was modified in 1662, for the ordination of bishops. This modification, as it happens, only clarifies the distinction between priest and bishop.

III
QUESTIONS OF INTENTION

[36] From what has been set out it follows that the ordinations of priests and of bishops are celebrated in the Anglican Church according to a rite which is objectively sufficient for the validity of these orders.

It is no less certain that this rite does not have a legitimate origin. We are told that it has the authority of the leaders of the Anglican Church, of the Primate of Canterbury in particular; we are further told that at the time when it was authorized the Holy See had not yet officially imposed any particular text or edition of the Pontifical. But the English Church was at the time in a state of rupture with the Roman Church; what is more, the changes which she introduced into the ordination rites, as into the liturgy of the Mass, clearly went far beyond what any bishops who had remained faithful to the Holy See would have allowed. Finally, these changes were in many cases inspired by Protestant views of the sacraments, the sacrifice of the Mass and the Christian priesthood.

[37] The dubious origins of the Anglican Ordinal do not however necessarily entail its insufficiency so far as validity is concerned. To the theological reasons which could be advanced but which it is not my concern to evaluate here, to the considerations which I have just examined in discussing the form of ordination and its relationship with the formulae employed and the use of the words *sacerdos* and *sacerdotium*, I am content to add one observation. The Holy See accepts as valid the ordinations performed in the Monophysite and Nestorian Churches separated from Catholic unity since the sixth or even fifth century. Certain fractions of these heretical groups have returned to communion with the Roman Church, which has allowed them to retain their liturgical rites. The ceremonies and the formulae of ordination are the same for the Uniate Chaldeans as for the Nestorians, for the Uniate Syrians as for the Jacobites, for the Uniate Copts as for the heretical Copts. Upon what is this acceptance based? On the inspection of their liturgical books, on the content of their formulae, on the knowledge of the rites and ceremonies to which these bear witness. Was there ever any question of setting up an enquiry to discover whether these formulae clearly predated the schism, whether they might have had as their author some learned heretic, whether they might have been promulgated by some patriarch in revolt against legitimate authority? It would in any case be very difficult to ascertain.

[38] At this point it will be argued against me that the cases are not the same; that the Christological heresies of the East left intact the old beliefs in the sacrifice, in the hierarchy and in the Eucharist, whereas the Protestant errors which inspired the reformers of the English ritual have a direct bearing on questions of worship and the sacraments. I agree. But does the Ordinal give any indication of suppressing all hierarchy, of confusing the degrees of deacon, of priest and of bishop, of abolishing any rite of ordination? Not at all. It indicates precisely the opposite. Here is the Preface in which, from the beginning, the intention of those who promulgated the Ordinal has been formulated:

It is evident unto all men diligently reading holy Scripture and ancient Authors, that from the Apostles' time there have been these Orders of Ministers in Christ's Church; Bishops, Priests, and Deacons. Which offices were evermore had in such reverend estimation, that no man might presume to execute any of them, except he were first called, tried, examined, and known to have such qualities as are requisite for the same; and also by publick Prayer, with Imposition of Hands, were approved and admitted thereunto by lawful authority. And therefore, to the intent that these Orders may be continued, and reverently used and esteemed, in the Church of England; No man shall be accounted or taken to be a lawful Bishop, Priest, or Deacon in the Church of England, or suffered to execute any of the said functions, except he be called, tried, examined, and admitted thereunto, according to the Form hereafter following, or hath had formerly Episcopal Consecration or Ordination.[19]

[39] In this way it was willed to conserve both the ancient orders and ordination. In the ordination rites it was thought necessary to introduce changes and a choice was made from among the formulae and ceremonies then in use. Public prayer and the laying on of hands were not only retained but expressly indicated as necessary. Various other actions and various other formulae were also retained. In short, the ancient orders, those of which Scripture and the early Christian writers testify as having existed in the apostolic age, those which the Church had maintained up to the sixteenth century, up to the moment when the rites were changed, were maintained and this was very clearly stated. All this was said to a nation strongly attached to the former liturgical tradition. It is possible that, among those who drew up the Preface and the Ordinal, there were some whose personal opinions went much further. but we are not concerned with

---

19. [The author failed to note that the last eight words were not added until 1662.]

such personal opinions; we have only to take account of those expressed in the public and official document. And such a consideration retains all its force when we turn from the intention of the compilers of the Ordinal to the intention of those who have used it and still use it. What is an Anglican bishop intending to do when he celebrates the ordination of priests? Evidently he intends to make priests, priests such as existed from the time of the Apostles and later times right up to the sixteenth century at least. That is the essential element in his intention, which in this respect is no different from the intention of a Roman Catholic bishop, or of a Greek or some other schismatic bishop. That he might profess, on his own behalf or even on account of the more or less official teaching of his Church, some doctrine or other as to the nature of the powers transmitted in ordination from the Apostles' time, cannot impair the effect of the sacred action. The teaching of our theologians is quite clear on this point. Mgr Gasparri gives a very good résumé of it[20] in his recent treatise on Ordination:

> It follows from what has been said that an ordination is valid if the minister, while intending to do what Christ's Church does, nevertheless THINKS that the rite is not a sacrament, is not a sacred rite, confers no power, or that the Church of Rome is not the true Church of Christ, provided HE DOES NOT SAY BY A POSITIVE ACT OF THE WILL: It is not my will to administer a sacrament, to perform a sacred rite, to do what the Church of Rome does, etc.

[40] Thus, as long as there is only a single act of the will, with the intention of performing by means of the rite what the Church does and has done from the time of the Apostles up to the present, the opinion, private or publicly expressed, of the ordaining minister is of little relevance. Now, in the case under consideration, how can one judge the *intention* of the ordaining minister? Evidently, by his external actions. He

---

20. Op. cit. (cf note 2 supra), volume II, p. 193.

celebrates the traditional rite of ordination; this must mean that he intends to ordain. The situation is the same in the case of an Anglican bishop and of a Catholic bishop.

Such is the normal situation, the only one which we need to take into consideration here. If, in any particular case, on precise and conclusive evidence, a positive intention which contradicts that which the external action itself implies can be adduced, then we can discuss that case. But, as long as all is done as the Anglican Ordinal lays down, we will have to admit that the intention is sufficient.

IV
THE QUESTION OF PRACTICE: THE GENESIS OF THE PRESENT DISCIPLINE

[41] That is all very well, someone will say. In that case how has it come about that Anglican ordinations have for so long been considered by us to be invalid? How can we admit that a practice of reordination, which involves the reiteration of genuine sacraments, has been able to establish itself with the tolerance and even the approbation of the Holy See? Do we not have here a precedent which is fatal to any attempt to rehabilitate Anglican Orders?

It is not for me to advance any theoretical considerations by way of reply to such questions. I shall content myself with citing some facts, which cannot be, and have not been, contested and which could perhaps shed some light on the present situation.

[42] There cannot be the slightest doubt about the fact that valid sacraments have been reiterated in the Catholic Church and that this has taken place not under improper conditions but in response to directions given or tolerated by legitimate authority.

In the third century the baptism of heretics was proclaimed valid by Pope Stephen but invalid by the African Church under the influence of St Cyprian. The latter's position was maintained after Stephen's death and up to the Council of Arles in 314 by the whole of the African Church, without the popes believing that they were bound to maintain the same rigour with which they had at first backed up their protest. Throughout the whole of the fourth century the Churches of Syria and Cappadocia continued to rebaptize heretics, although Rome required no such repetition.

[43] At Rome itself and throughout the whole Church, Eastern and Western, there was maintained through all the centuries of antiquity and of the high Middle Ages a form for the reconciliation of heretics which can only be considered as a reiteration of the Sacrament of Confirmation. Heretics can baptize validly; they cannot confer the Holy Spirit. That is the principle, proclaimed a hundred times in theory and constantly applied in practice.

As far as ordination is concerned, although practice underwent less changes, it did undergo some important ones. The problem arose above all when it was a question of resolving the situation of certain bodies of dissident clergy. To halt the progress of disobedience by energetic measures or to lead back into unity well-disposed schismatics; here we have two perfectly legitimate strategies, but they cannot be put into execution by the same means. To the second of these two belong the theories and the more merciful measures applied to the Novatians, the Donatists and the Monophysites; these theories and practices bear witness to the currently received doctrine of the indelibility of the character conferred by ordination.

[44] But there are facts which point in the opposite direction. In 769 the Roman Council, summoned to deal with the litigious situations created by the irregular episcopate of Constantine II, decided that all the ordinations conferred by this pope or antipope should be considered as null. His successor, Stephen II, who presided over the synod, refused to repeat the promotion of the deacons and priests ordained by Constantine although he had been authorised to do so; but he caused to be re-elected with all due legal form the eight bishops consecrated by his predecessor and solemnly reconsecrated them.

Ordinations conferred by Photius in the next century were

declared null both by Popes Nicholas and Hadrian II and also by the 8th Ecumenical Council (canon 4).[21] However, since the ecclesiastical authorities opposed any promotion or rehabilitation in the case of the clergy so condemned, it is not easy to record any clear case of rehabilitation.[22] What can be proved is that, in the person of John IX, the Roman Church passed a final judgement on these quarrels and consigned to oblivion all the irregularities against which several popes had raised the liveliest objections.

[45] The ordinations of Formosus offer an even more famous case than the previous ones. They were, as is only too well known, solemnly condemned and rigorously repeated under Popes Sergius II and John X. These popes, it must be admitted, are not among those who adorned their see by the splendour of their sanctity; but it cannot be denied that they were as legitimate as their contemporary colleagues. Over these they had the advantage of duration; they occupied the Apostolic See long enough to be able to ensure the sustained execution of their decrees. It is even noteworthy that if they were able, in the eyes of the Canon Law of the time, to get themselves recognised as legitimate popes, this was precisely because they chose to treat as null the episcopal consecrations of Pope Formosus. In fact, like that hapless pontiff, and like the appalling Stephen VI, who caused Formosus' corpse to be dug up and brought before a conciliar tribunal, Sergius III and John X had been bishops before their elevation to the papacy. Their only way of proving that they had not contravened the legislation prohibiting translations was to declare null their previous episcopal consecration by annulling all the acts of the Pope from whom they had received it.

[46] We know that Pope St Leo IX had great difficulty in convincing himself that ordinations conferred by simoniac bishops ought not to be reiterated. The *Liber Gratissimus* of

---

21. [I.e. the Fourth Council of Constantinople, AD 869–70. See N. Tanner, *Decrees of the Ecumenical Councils* (London and Washington, 1990), p. 169.]

22. This assertion cannot be found in any of the current manuals of church history; it will shortly be proved by a learned Father of the Society of Jesus.

St Peter Damian is devoted to this question. He resolves it in favour of validity; but he refers explicitly to the anxieties of Leo IX and to the numerous reordinations celebrated by other bishops.

All this is sufficient to establish that, if the practice of reordination were to be abandoned by the Church in the case of Anglican ministers, this change could claim the most serious precedents.

[47] But now we need to discover what in fact is the origin of the present discipline. It cannot be said that it proceeds from a Roman decision taken with full cognizance of all the facts. Before the year 1704 the Roman Congregations were not involved in this affair; by that time reordination had been the practice for nearly 150 years. The decision pronounced in 1704 in the case of Bishop Gordon was inspired and motivated by very suspect documents; it was based, more particularly, on the Nag's Head legend. There is therefore no need to view it as an authoritative solution or as a significant event from which the practice of reordination takes its origin.

Whence then does this practice take its origin? It comes from the seminaries or English colleges established on the continent at Douai, at Reims and at Rome. It is in these establishments, colonies of a Catholicism which was being persecuted in England, that we find the first cases dating from 1570.[23] To all intents and purposes it was only in such places that they could take place. In England itself the legal position of Catholics would hardly have allowed of such reordinations; what is more, until the nomination of the first Vicar Apostolic in 1623 there was no longer any Catholic bishop there to celebrate them.

[48] But it is quite clear that the principles applied on the continent were imported from England. The adversaries of Anglican Ordinations have no difficulty in establishing that this was the position held in those English ecclesiastical circles in which, under the direction of the Jesuits, fidelity to the Holy See was maintained. What they are not however able

---

23. See the list drawn up by Estcourt, op. cit., pp. 133ff.

to make clear is the reason for this judgement.[24] In the contested ordinations so many irregularities were accumulated – irregularities of rite, of canonical form, even of legal form – that they could be rejected for very different reasons. Catholic controversialists readily pursued their adversaries over the terrain of legal forms; nowhere do they emphasize with any special force an objection drawn from the insufficiency of the rite. Before the death of Elizabeth they never advanced the absolute defect of Parker's consecration; the Nag's Head legend had not yet acquired credibility. It was even later that any doubt was raised as to Barlow's consecration.

From this account of the facts it follows that, in the English ecclesiastical world of the reign of Elizabeth, we should not look for any precise information, any official enquiry or any authentic judgement on the validity of Anglican ordinations. Neither the imprisoned or exiled bishops, whom death soon took from the scene, nor any local representative of the Holy See would seem to us to have handled this question and to have brought it to a solution which could be called official. We remain confronted by a practice of obscure origin, for which nobody assumes responsibility.

[49] If we move from the reign of Elizabeth back to that of Mary, we ought to be able to find more precise information. At that time the Sovereign was a Catholic, religious affairs were under the direction of the Papal Legate Cardinal Pole, and the bishops in office were all in communion with the Holy See. The question of the Ordinal was already posed, for the new rite had been in force for four or five years before it was repealed.

We cannot however point to any official declaration on the subject which concerns us. The Ordinal was eliminated from use and the Pontifical resumed its place; that is about all we can really say. We can add that, in a royal edict of March 1554, it is laid down that 'touching such persons as were heretofore promoted to any orders, after the new sort and fashion of orders; [considering they were not ordered in

---

24. Estcourt is quite clear on this point, op. cit., pp. 117, 133.

very deed,] the bishop of the diocese, finding otherwise sufficiency and ability in these men, may supply that thing which
wanted in them before'.[25] This would seem to indicate the
supplying of non-essential ceremonies rather than the reiteration of ordination.

[50] In a Brief of 8 March 1554 addressed to Cardinal Pole,
Pope Julius III enumerates the dispensing powers he is
according to his Legate. To this enumeration belongs the
following passage:

> ... also with regard to Orders which they never received,
> or received badly, and the gift of consecration which was
> conferred on them by other bishops or archbishops, even
> heretics and schismatics, or otherwise less rightly and
> without the customary form of the Church being main-
> tained ...

The Pope is here aiming, among other cases, at that of
bishops consecrated outside the form in common use in the
Church. It in no way emerges from the context that he is
accepting these consecrations as valid or authorizing his
Legate to declare them to be so. But neither is it clear that
he has specially in view the Ordinal of Edward VI and that he
is declaring null consecrations celebrated according to this
rite.

It is certain, in any case, that none of the bishops so consecrated remained in office during the reign of Mary. The
question therefore as to whether they ought to be ordained
simply did not arise.

[51] As for the lower clergy, Cardinal Pole delegated to the
ordinaries the power to rehabilitate them. He authorized
them to restore to the exercise of their orders even those
who had received them 'from heretical and schismatic
bishops, even less rightly, provided that in their ordination
the form and intention of the Church was maintained.'[26] In

---

25. [The text is quoted in Estcourt, p. 29, and E. C. Messenger, *The Reformation, the
Mass and the Priesthood* (London, 1936–7), vol. II, p. 52. Duchesne omits the clause
in square brackets.]

26. Estcourt: Appendix XVIII, p. xlvii; Burnet, vol. VI, p. 361.

bringing the wording of this restriction close to that of the Papal Brief one could be tempted to believe that the Legate did not believe that he ought to use all his powers. But, here again, there is nothing to prove either that Julius III had given permission to his Legate to dispense from the forms in common use in the Church or that either he or the Legate was passing judgement on the insufficiency of the rite of Edward VI.

[52] No conclusions can therefore be drawn from these official documents. The ordination registers kept in the different episcopal palaces of England have been studied to see whether they might contain any evidence for reordination. They have revealed none; yet it seems morally impossible that, if reordination had been prescribed as a general measure, there would not have been found somewhere or other some note to the effect that the ordinand in question had previously undergone the same ceremony, which had been declared null on the grounds of insufficiency.

Outside these documents and some observations of a general nature, the adversaries of Anglican ordinations have introduced into the debate some particular occurrences and some more or less public remarks. Several of them prove absolutely nothing; the most significant, when they are well attested, do not allow us to draw any conclusion other than that they are particular judgements on particular cases of which the details almost always escape us. We must also allow examples of excess of zeal.

We have therefore no proof that from the reign of Mary the Ordinal was ever the object of an enquiry or of a judgement with regard to its sufficiency.

[53] What is quite clear is that this Ordinal, and above all the Prayer Book as a whole, of which since 1552 the Ordinal was a part, had against them the feeling of a large part of the nation. The English people did not regard their government's breach with the Holy See as a crime. Henry VIII was allowed a free hand on that score. But when Edward VI tampered with the rites with which they were familiar, when they saw prayers in the vernacular substituted for the old Latin

prayers, when the ceremonies of the Mass were altered so profoundly, then their disapproval made itself felt and some formidable insurrections took place. These were put down, but not without difficulty; from this point, however, opposition to the Reformers had found its focus.

When this opposition took control of the government, its first target was the Prayer Book. From the accession of Queen Mary it was on this point that conservatives and Reformers eyed each other with the closest attention. The first actions of Mary, private at first and then public, related above all to this question. She began by re-establishing the Latin Mass; she then proscribed the liturgical innovations of Edward VI; she then restored all matters of worship to the position in which they had been left by Henry VIII. Only later, and with much less support from public opinion, was she able to reverse the schism itself and restore obedience to Rome.

[54] It is not suprising, given such a state of opinion, that a movement of very strong feeling against ordinations celebrated according to the new rite should have appeared. That this movement could have been contained within reasonable limits, that spirits so offended and so excited could have been able to distinguish clearly between what was simply irregular and what was prejudicial to the very essence of the sacraments, is more than we have any right to expect.

Even had these been less burning questions, even had there been on the scene theologians capable of a calm and serene comparison of the age-long and venerable Pontifical with the new rite so recently devised by Archbishop Cranmer, even had these theologians succeeded in getting a hearing from a public so overcome with emotion, it is difficult to believe that this public would have heard them express any other verdict than that formulated today by the adversaries of Anglican ordinations. These theologians, to be sure, imbued with the ideas of their time, would not have failed to claim as essential elements the tradition of the instruments, the anointing, and the imperative formulae: 'Take thou authority ... Receive the Holy Ghost.' At that time they were very far from the expert evaluation and comparison of rites and of texts which later would come to shed so much light on these delicate points. On the contrary, they still lived within the scholastic tradition; they had before their eyes the Decree of Eugenius IV to the Armenians, hardly a century old. One of the most celebrated theologians of the time, Dominic Soto, who came in fact to England in the reign of Mary, argues quite emphatically against the sufficiency of the laying on of hands.

[55] It is therefore only natural that from the time of Queen Mary a very strong current of opinion hostile to the validity of Anglican ordinations should have been formed. But it was only a current of opinion; it did not derive from an ecclesiastical judgement pronounced after a full examination of the question. It cannot even be proved that it was inspired by a practice recommended explicitly by Cardinal Pole.

It is right also to take note of the opposite opinion. On the accession of Elizabeth there were 9,400 priests in England; of these 200 refused to accept the new ecclesiastical changes. These were the ancestors of the present Catholic clergy. As for the 9,200 others, it is clear that they demonstrated very little attachment to the Holy See. In this they continued the tradition of the clergy, even of the episcopate, of the time of Henry VIII. But can we really believe that they could treat their ordination so lightly? Clearly the majority of them must have held as equally sufficient ordinations celebrated according to the Pontifical and those celebrated according to the Anglican Ordinal.

[56] To this assessment, which must not lightly be dismissed, should be added that of a great number of experts, strangers both to the nationality and to the religious divisions of the English. The oldest we can cite is that of an Italian prelate, Daniele Barbaro, Coadjutor to the Patriarch of Aquileia, who, in a report addressed to his government, deals explicity with the Ordinal of Edward VI which had just been published: 'In 1549-50,' he writes, 'another book was published by royal authority and confirmed by Parliament; this book contains a rite for the conferring of Holy Orders. These Ordinations only differ from those in the Roman Catholic religion on one point, namely that in

England an oath has to be taken to renounce the doctrine and authority of the Pope.'[27] This judgement, coming as it does from a bishop, is not without value. It is true that in this earliest period the tradition of the instruments remained, together with the tradition of the Bible, in the ordination of priests; but the formula *Accipe potestatem offerre sacrificium* (Receive authority to offer sacrifice) etc, had already disappeared.

[57] One could, if one were to give credence to certain Anglican assertions, single out one very serious factor in favour of validity. Pope Pius IV, it is claimed, made an offer to Queen Elizabeth to authorize the use of the Prayer Book, which by that time included the Ordinal. The result of scrutinizing the evidence available up till now is that this proposition was treated as a reality in the official entourage of Queen Elizabeth and that her Ambassadors in France, Throckmorton and Walsingham, treated it very seriously.

But, in this kind of question, it is difficult to build anything on a document of which we do not have the text and on an initiative known to us only through witnesses who, though no doubt serious, are hardly disinterested.

I believe that, as far as this fact and others which are brought into this debate are concerned, further light could be forthcoming from archival material, notably from the correspondence of the Papal Nuncios in France and the Low Countries.

[58] However that may be, it is beyond all doubt that, from the 16th century to the present day, the practice of reordination has been subject to ceaseless criticism from Catholic authors – not so much in itself but in the assessment on which it is based and which leads to the conclusion that Anglican orders are radically null. Such criticisms have come for the most part from the continent; but even in England there are several cases of well-instructed Catholics who on this point differ from their co-religionists. Much is made of those Anglican ministers who have submitted to

---

27. *Archivio Veneto*, vol. V, p. 3.

reordination; but there are also those who have not felt able to do so and have preferred, once received into the bosom of the Roman Church, to abstain from any ecclesiastical function rather than to appear to despise the ordination they received in the Anglican schism.

So, when all is said and done, the jury is still out.

L. DUCHESNE

CONCERNING THE VALIDITY OF ANGLICAN ORDERS

E. M. De Augustinis, SJ

[1] To make a sound judgement on the validity or nullity of Anglican episcopal and priestly ordinations, from the time of Queen Elizabeth of England down to our own day, one must investigate, first of all, whether or not there has been a doctrinal decision by the Holy See on this matter. If there has been no such decision, then one should see if, from the acts of the Roman Pontiffs who lived when the new ordinations began, it can be seen that they held these ordinations to be valid or null.

After this first investigation, if there has been no pontifical decision declaring them null, and if it does not appear from the acts of the Pontiffs that they were held from the beginning to be such, further inquiries must be made concerning Anglican ordinations:

1. The ministers who performed them,
2. The rite that they used,
3. The intention they had when performing the rite.

If this inquiry shows that Anglican ordinations were carried out by ministers who had supernatural power to ordain, since they were true bishops, that they performed them according to a valid rite and with the intention of doing what the Church does, they should be held to be certainly valid. If any of these three things, which are absolutely necessary for a valid ordination, is seen to be lacking in Anglican ordinations, then they must be declared certainly null.

We will, therefore, divide this inquiry into two parts. In the first part, we shall see if the Holy See has ever made any doctrinal pronouncement about the validity of these ordinations; or if, with regard to these ordinations, the Holy See has from the beginning acted in such a way that they were held either to be valid or to be null. In the second part, we shall investigate the validity of these ordinations, examining the minister, the rite and the intention.

PART ONE

JUDGMENT OF THE HOLY SEE ON ANGLICAN ORDINATIONS

[2] The ordinations of ministers of the Anglican Church began with the consecration of Matthew Parker as Archbishop of Canterbury in the year 1559, the first year of the reign of Queen Elizabeth, because it is from that consecration that all the other ordinations of the Anglican clergy are derived.

One hundred and twenty-five years after the consecration of Parker, in 1684, the question concerning the validity of Anglican orders was examined in Rome by the sacred Congregation of the Holy Office. After appropriate inquiries had been made and the matter had been seriously examined, on 21 August 1685 the eminent cardinals of the Congregation decided that a decision on the matter should be deferred to a later date; so they declared the problem 'deferred'. Therefore, the question concerning the validity or nullity of Anglican ordinations had not been decided in Rome before 1684, nor was a decision taken in 1685.

[3] In 1704 John Clement Gordon, who had been consecrated Bishop of Galloway according to the Anglican rite, became a Catholic and asked His Holiness Pope Clement XI if he would declare null the orders that he had received when he was an Anglican. Having heard the views of the most eminent Cardinals of the sacred Congregation of the Holy Office, His Holiness, on 17 April of that same year, decreed

as follows: 'the aforesaid petitioner John Clement Gordon should be promoted afresh to all the orders, including holy orders and the order of the presbyterate.'

Was this a doctrinal decision that declared null all the ordinations that had been performed according to the Anglican rite up to that time, and was it a statement that all ordinations performed according to that same rite would not be valid? Certainly not. The Decree of 17 April 1704 was issued for one particular case and concerned that case alone. In the Decree it is not stated that the Orders should be conferred *ex integro* on Gordon because the Orders that are conferred by Anglican ministers according to the Anglican rite are null. The motives put forward by Gordon in his petition to the Supreme Pontiff to have the orders he had received declared null *are not the motives of the Decree*, since there is not a single word in the Decree that approves of these motives or which makes even the slightest reference to them. On the other hand, those motives are false *in fact* and erroneous *in law*, as will be clear further on. So even then the question about Anglican orders remained undecided. And so it has remained right up to our own day, because after that Decree there has been no other issued concerning Anglican Orders.

[4] But someone will say perhaps: if the Holy See has not formally declared Anglican Orders null, it has nevertheless let it be clearly understood by its acts that it held these Orders to be invalid. Let us see if this assertion can stand up to factual proof.

It should be noted above all that if the Holy See had considered as null all Anglican ordinations and had let this be understood from its acts, it would certainly have pronounced the nullity of those ordinations by solemn Decree when the question was raised in 1684, and would not have suspended judgement concerning them, as in fact it did, after a prolonged study, in 1685.

Moreover, if in fact there had been pontifical acts which let it be understood that the Orders conferred according to the new Anglican rite should be considered null, why were these acts not even hinted at in the discussions of 1684, 1685, and 1704?

[5] Prescinding from all this, what are these pontifical acts that are now being put forward as decisive in the controversy concerning Anglican Orders? They are as follows: – In a Bull of 20 June 1555 Pope Paul IV, speaking of those ordained in England, makes this statement: 'If some were promoted to ecclesiastical orders, whether sacred or not sacred, by someone other than a bishop rightly and correctly (*rite et recte*) ordained, they are bound to receive the same orders again from their Ordinary, nor can they exercise those orders in the interim.' – And in a Brief of October 30th of that same year the same Pontiff declared: 'Bishops and Archbishops can be said not to have been rightly and correctly ordained only if they were not ordained and consecrated in the form of the Church.'

Now these documents do not prove the nullity of Anglican ordinations. In the words quoted, the Supreme Pontiff declared that those Ordinations were invalid which had not been conferred by Bishops or Archbishops *rightly and correctly ordained*; he also declared that those who had been ordained *in the form of the Church* were not in this category; but he does not say, either explicitly or implicitly, that *the Ordinations of the Bishops or Archbishops who ordained the Anglican Ministers* were not performed *rightly and correctly*, because they were not conferred *in the form of the Church*: meaning to speak of the *essential form* which makes the ordination valid, and without which it is null. – So it is clear that the words *rightly and correctly* as well as *in the form of the Church* must be understood as meaning the *essential form* for the validity of Ordinations, because only in this case would the Ordinations be null by reason of the rite; and only in this case could it be said, as Pope Paul IV said in the above mentioned documents, that since the Orders had not been conferred, they have to be received *again*.

[6] Here it is useful to point out that there is another document of the same Supreme Pontiff, Paul IV, of the same year 1555, which rather makes one suppose that Anglican

Ordinations were held by the Holy See to be valid, whatever changes had been made in the ancient Catholic form. The proof of this is as follows. The principal author of such changes had been the Archbishop of Canterbury, Thomas Cranmer. Against him on 4 December 1555 Paul IV pronounced a sentence of excommunication, depriving him of the Archbishopric and of every office and benefice, and handing him over into the hands of the civil power. His crimes are clearly listed in the sentence, among which are those with regard to the sacraments of the Holy Eucharist and of Orders: but there is not a word that suggests that he had made any changes in the essential form of sacred ordinations, or that by doing so he had brought to an end in the Anglican Church the sacred hierarchy that is of divine institution.

Now if Rome had believed that Anglican ordinations were invalid, and they were invalid because in their conferral the *new form* introduced by Cranmer had been used, a form that must be held to be not only *illicit* but also *null*, then Cranmer would certainly have been pronounced guilty of this most serious crime. In fact this accusation was not made. The Pope's words were: 'We pronounce, judge, determine and declare that the said Thomas, then Archbishop of Canterbury, heedless of the salvation of his soul, by THINKING AND TEACHING contrary to the preaching and observance of Holy Mother Church, against the rules and dogmas of the Church and the Holy Fathers, the Traditions of the Apostolic Roman Church and the Holy Councils, and the rites of the Christian religion which have been heretofore customary in the Church, especially with regard to the Sacraments of the Body and Blood of Our Lord Jesus Christ and Holy Order ... ' (V. Post. Ann. Raynaldi t. 2, ad an. 1555, n. 30).

There is complete agreement between this sentence of the Supreme Pontiff and the acts of the judicial process against Cranmer, in which he is accused of *having promoted bishops and priests without permission from the Holy See*, and one can read the evidence that bears out this accusation, while there is no statement that he changed the essential form of sacred ordinations in such a way as to render them null.

[7] Moreover, Cardinal Pole came to England as Papal Legate in the reign of Mary Tudor (who had succeeded Edward VI and had brought back the English nation to the Catholic faith) and reconciled the ecclesiastics who had been guilty during the schism; far from annulling the ordinations and the consecrations that had been conferred in the *new form*, that is with the *Ordinal* of Edward VI, he held them to be valid, admitting those who had been ordained according to that new rite to the exercise of the orders they had received. Here are the words of Cardinal Pole: 'All those ecclesiastical persons, whether seculars or regulars of whatever orders, who have, by the alleged authority of the supremacy of the Anglican Church, received various grants, dispensations, concessions and indults, and *Orders* as well as ecclesiastical benefices, or other spiritual goods, once they have sincerely returned to the unity of the Church, shall be mercifully *received in their orders* and benefices either by ourselves or by those deputed for this by us, as indeed *many have already been received*, and we shall take these steps in due time in the Lord.' (V. Stat. Philippi et Mariae, c. 8.) In this way it came about that Bishops Thirlby, Warton, Aldrich and King were reconciled but not consecrated for a second time; so also those who during the three year period had been ordained priests according to the *new rite* were not again ordained. There is not a single instance of a new priestly ordination.

[8] The following points have, therefore, been demonstrated:

  – there has never been a Pontifical doctrinal decision which declared the nullity of Anglican ordinations;
  – nor was there any act of the Holy See which even implicitly affirmed this nullity in the first years of the new rite;
  – on the contrary, there are documents which lead one to believe that the ordinations were held to be valid *at that time*.

Later, that is from perhaps the first half of the 18th century, these ordinations were considered *from a practical point of view* to be invalid, since the ordinations of Anglican ministers, who were converted to the Catholic faith, were repeated unconditionally. Many reasons were commonly proposed by Catholics to prove that these ordinations were in fact invalid.

These reasons will be dealt with in the second part of this inquiry.

PART TWO

THE VALIDITY OF ANGLICAN ORDINATIONS

§1
Parker is consecrated Archbishop of Canterbury

[9] To provide a clear proof of the nullity of Anglican Orders one begins by denying the fact of the episcopal consecration of Parker. It is said that in 1559, at the beginning of the reign of Elizabeth in England, those whom she had named to initiate the new hierarchy met in a London tavern called 'The Nag's Head' and there, without any other ritual, apart from a ridiculous indication of the office, were constituted the bishops of the premier sees of the Kingdom. In this way Scory, a religious become apostate, made them all kneel down in front of him, and then took the hand of Matthew Parker and said to him: 'Arise, Bishop of Canterbury'; then in the same way he turned to Grindal and said: 'Arise, Bishop of London'; he continued in the same way with the other two, Horne and Sandys.

This fable about the nomination of Parker as Archbishop of Canterbury, carried out in 'The Nag's Head' tavern, was recounted for the first time in John Holywood's book, *De investigatione verae et visibilis Christi Ecclesiae*, printed at Antwerp in 1604. It has been repeated from that time right down to our own day as if it were a historical fact. Nowadays, however, it has been shown quite clearly to be false.

[10] Published 45 years after the consecration of Parker as Archbishop, the story relies entirely on one *alleged* eye-witness account by a person who had already been dead for 14 years when the account was first spoken of and who during his life had never made the slightest allusion in any of his writings to the alleged scene that took place in the 'Nag's Head' tavern.

Moreover, those who recounted the tale were not in agreement about how it happened. Some told the story in the version that we have just given above, while others described Scory as placing the bible on the head of each of the designated bishops, saying to each one: 'Receive the power to preach sincerely the word of God.' Nor were they in agreement in their designation of the persons promoted to the English episcopal sees.

And then the story, in whatever form it was told, went contrary to so many other circumstances of fact, which are absolutely certain, that, for anyone who wanted to investigate it fully, there could be no doubt about its being a complete fabrication.

[11] It was not very long before it was directly demonstrated to be a fable by 'Parker's Register', kept in Lambeth Palace. In that Register it is recorded that Parker was consecrated 'in the Chapel below his Palace in Lambeth on Sunday, 17 December, AD 1559.' William Barlow, John Scory, Miles Coverdale and John Hodgekyn were consecrated bishops. The rite used was that of the *Ordinal* of Edward VI, and *all four* bishops placed their hands on the head of the ordinand and pronounced the words of ordination.

It was claimed that this part of the Register, which contained the episcopal consecration of Parker, had been falsified; but it was examined from every angle and found to be authentic since it was impossible to find any trace of fraud. On the other hand, the arguments drawn from the Register taken as a whole and from the impossibility of a fraudulent insertion of all that refers to Parker, confirm the truth of what is to be found there. The same thing is demonstrated by other documents kept in the public archives which speak of Parker's consecration. It would be folly to think that these had been falsified. Parker was, therefore, consecrated Archbishop of Canterbury according to the new Anglican rite.

But was he validly consecrated? Was he consecrated by one who had the power validly to consecrate him? Was he consecrated according to a valid rite? Did the Minister who consecrated him have the intention that is required for a valid consecration? These are the serious questions that must be examined separately in the paragraphs which follow.

§2
Parker was consecrated by one who had the power validly to do so

[12] To demonstrate the nullity of Parker's consecration, on the grounds that it was not performed by one who alone had the power to effect it, the argument runs as follows:

The consecration of a bishop can only be validly performed by someone who is a bishop; the consecration of Parker, therefore, will have to be declared null if it was carried out by someone who in his turn had not been validly consecrated as a bishop. Now it is said that Parker was consecrated bishop by William Barlow, and Barlow was never consecrated bishop. Therefore the episcopal consecration of Parker was certainly null.

Before replying to this argument by proving that Barlow was truly consecrated bishop and was so consecrated before he consecrated Parker, it should be noted that he was not the only one to consecrate Parker; along with him three other bishops took part in the consecration, John Hodgekyn, John Scory and Miles Coverdale. These three, along with Barlow, performed the imposition of hands on Parker and pronounced the form of episcopal consecration. Since, then, there were, besides Barlow, three other ministers involved in the consecration of Parker, the validity of this consecration does not depend *solely* on the episcopal character of Barlow, but rather on the episcopal character of each one of the consecrators. For this reason, even supposing that Barlow was not a bishop, if the other consecrators were, or one of them was, Parker could have been validly consecrated by him, and as far as the minister of the rite is concerned, the episcopal character of Parker cannot be denied.

[13] Very well. Scory and Coverdale were, it is true, consecrated according to the *Ordinal* of Edward VI and the validity of their episcopal consecration depends on the validity of this rite. It is, however, an indisputable fact that Hodgekyn was consecrated on 9 December 1537 by three bishops according to *the Catholic rite* of the Sarum Pontifical, and so it is an indisputable fact that he had truly been consecrated a bishop. It was by him, a true bishop, that Parker was consecrated bishop, with his imposition of hands together with the pronunciation of the essential form of episcopal consecration, as we shall see.

[14] But let us examine also the consecration of Barlow. Can this be denied? Or at least, can it be called into doubt *for serious reasons?* Certainly not. It is true that the consecration of Barlow is not to be found in the Archiepiscopal Register of Cranmer, but this argument against its validity is, in this case, of no value. This register consists of sheets of parchment in an uneven and disordered condition, collected together in one volume, from which many things are missing. It is therefore not suprising that sheet should be missing on which the consecration of Barlow was registered.

On the other hand, it is clear from authentic records that Barlow was personally *enthroned* in his episcopal see of Menevia; in directing that see he had controversies with his chapter which, however, always *recognized* him as a consecrated bishop. It is clear too that he received donations and entered into contracts as bishop, and that as such took part in the consecration of other bishops during the reign of Henry VIII. It should be added that Barlow not only had a seat in Parliament, in his capacity as bishop, but also had precedence there over other bishops who were certainly consecrated validly. It is a known fact that the English bishops, after the Prelates of the five privileged sees, took their place in parliament according to the date of their consecration. Moreover, Barlow intervened in provincial synods, convoked by the metropolitan, and he put his signature to the acts of these synods, where all the bishops sign according to the order of their episcopal consecration. Finally, Barlow's name is to be found in the same order in the list of bishops deputed for the funeral of Henry VIII: his name appears between Thomas Goodrich, consecrated bishop on 19 April 1534, and Henry Holbeach, consecrated on 24 March 1538. These and other proofs demonstrate without any doubt that Barlow was consecrated a bishop before the year of 1538, that is, more than 21 years before the consecration of Parker.

The validity, therefore, of Parker's episcopal consecration cannot reasonably be denied on account of the lack of episcopal character in Barlow, his consecrator.

§III
Parker was consecrated bishop with a valid rite
The Anglican rite for priestly ordinations is also valid

However, the episcopal character of the consecrating bishop is not enough to bring about the validity of the episcopal consecration carried out by him: it is essential that there should be used that rite alone which can confer the consecration: that is to say, valid matter and form must be used, which constitute the sacramental sign instituted by our Lord Jesus Christ to confer grace and the episcopal character. Was the rite used for the consecration of Parker a valid rite?

The problem arises because Parker, as we have already said, was consecrated with the *new* rite, the rite in the *Ordinal* of Edward VI, which was very different from the Catholic rite that had until then been used in the Church of England. One must, therefore, investigate whether or not the new Anglican rite, used for the consecration of Parker, and then used always from that time onwards, with very slight modifications in 1662, retained what is essential for a valid episcopal consecration. The same investigation must also be carried out to see if the new Anglican rite has kept the essential matter and the form required for a valid presbyteral ordination.

[16] Perhaps, at first, it could appear obvious that the rite has not preserved the essential matter and form of hierarchical ordinations, since it has altered the ancient Catholic rite even to the extent of abolishing the 'Tradition of Instruments'; for this reason it is not a valid rite, and cannot be validly used for the consecration of bishops or for the ordination of priests and deacons.

This, however, is a false conclusion. The 'Tradition of Instruments' in the ordinations to major orders, that is, to the diaconate, to the simple priesthood and to the episcopate, does not constitute either wholly or in part the *sacramental sign* of ordination, but it is only a *declaration* of the effects. It does not confer the power of Orders, but it shows the right to exercise the power *that has already been received*. In a word, the Tradition of Instruments is not an essential requirement for the conferral of Orders and so is not an essential part of ordination; it is only a declarative ceremony of ordination.

This is the doctrine that is most commonly taught nowadays by theologians and is most certain. It is based on Scripture, which does not speak of the Tradition of Instruments, but of the imposition of hands along with the corresponding prayer of the minister, as the sacramental sign that confers the grace of the Order. It is based on the very clear and constant teaching of the Fathers which states that hierarchical Orders are conferred through this sign of the imposition of hands. It is based on the constant usage of the Greek Church, which does not use any Tradition of Instruments, and by the same usage of the Latin Church in which the usage of the Tradition of Instruments only began in the eleventh century. Finally, it is based upon the explicit statements of most learned ecclesiastical Latin writers, *contemporaneous* with the introduction of that rite of the

Tradition who state that it is used to *declare, not to confer*, the power of Orders.

[17] Here it is relevant to point out that at that very same time when, from the changes made in the ancient rite, the Tradition of Instruments ceased to be used in England for Anglican ordinations, and the only sign used was that of the imposition of hands with the corresponding form, the Council of Mainz (1549), expounding the Catholic doctrine on the sacrament of Orders, declared that the sacramental sign for major Orders was the imposition of hands: 'In the conferring of Orders, *which is administered with the imposition of hands as a visible sign*, they should teach that to those who have been rightly ordained God gives the grace by which they are made fit and competent to fulfil their ecclesiastical functions rightly and usefully.' The Council of Trent, in 1563, four years after the consecration of Parker, in its teaching that Ordination is a true sacrament, demonstrates this with the words of the Apostle to Timothy where he speaks of the grace of episcopal consecration conferred on him by the imposition of his hands: 'I remind you to rekindle the gift of God that is within you through the laying on of my hands' (2 Timothy 1.6).

So the fact that the tradition of the instruments is missing from Anglican ordinations does not make them invalid. The sacramental sign that is necessary and sufficient for their validity is present, that is, the imposition of hands and the corresponding sacramental formulas.

[18] What we have said so far, however, is not enough to prove this conclusion. The sacramental sign of ordination must signify the Order that it confers, and so in the ordinations of bishops and priests, while the matter, i.e. the imposition of hands, remains the same, the form, i.e. the words that correspond to the matter, and along with the matter constitute the sacramental sign, must in each ordination, – of bishop and of priest – be such that clearly signifies the Order and the spiritual power that is being conferred through this sign. Is this form so clearly determined in the *Ordinal* of Edward VI?

To this question some Catholic doctors have replied in the

negative and so have judged the form used in Anglican ordinations to be invalid. However, in giving this reply, they have
only studied the imperative words said by the bishop at the
end of the ordination. In fact, the reply ought to be different if
one considers not only these words, but also the prayer that
precedes them and of which they are a sort of conclusion. It is
in this prayer that in fact the sacramental form of Orders is to
be found, according to the teaching of Scripture and
Tradition. 'They were ordained with the laying on of hands
and prayer: *for it is in this that ordination consists*' (S. John
Chrysostom, Hom. 14 in Act. Ap. n. 3).[1]

[19] To begin with episcopal consecration: in the Anglican
ritual, after the presentation of the Elect to the consecrating
archbishop with these words: 'Most Reverend Father in God,
we present unto you this godly and well-learned man to be
Ordained and Consecrated Bishop', there follows the consecrator's exhortation to pray, and then there are the litanies in
which he says: 'That it may please thee to bless this our
Brother elected, and to send thy grace upon him, that he
may duly execute the Office whereunto he is called, to the
edifying of thy Church, and to the honour, praise and glory
of thy name.' At the end of the litanies the consecrator prays
as follows: 'Almighty God, giver of all good things, who by
thy Holy Spirit hast appointed divers Orders of Ministers in
thy Church; Mercifully behold this thy servant now called to
the Work and Ministry of a Bishop; and replenish him so with
the truth of thy doctrine, and adorn him with innocency of
life, that, both by word and deed, he may faithfully serve thee
in this Office, to the glory of thy Name, and the edifying and
well-governing of thy Church; through the merits of our
Saviour Jesus Christ, who liveth and reigneth with thee and
the Holy Ghost, world without end.' Then some interrogations are put to the candidate by the Archbishop, who then
continues with the prayer, asking: 'Grant, we beseech thee, to
this thy servant such grace, that he may evermore be ready to
spread abroad thy Gospel, the glad tidings of reconciliation

---

1. [PG 60, 116 – Rambaldi.]

with thee, and use the authority given him, not to destruction, but to salvation; not to hurt, but to help; so that as a wise and faithful servant, giving to thy family their portion in due season, he may at last be received into everlasting joy; through Jesus Christ, etc.' At the end of the prayer the consecrator places his hands on the candidate and says: 'Receive the Holy Ghost, and remember that thou stir up the grace of God which is given thee by this Imposition of our hands; for God hath not given us the spirit of fear, but of power, and love, and soberness.'[2]

[20] In this episcopal consecration, faithfully reported by us as it stands in the Ordinal of Edward VI, it appears very clear that the sacramental sign, constituted by the matter and the sacramental form, that is by the imposition of hands and the prayers accompanying it, is *determined in no uncertain manner*. Over the person presented *to be consecrated bishop* the prayer asks that the grace from heaven will come down on him so that *as a bishop* in the Church of God and according to the divine institution he may serve faithfully to the glory of the divine name and the good of the Church itself. It is *for this* that he receives the Holy Spirit and his grace by the imposition of the hands of the consecrator, and those words are addressed to him which the Apostle Paul addressed to Bishop Timothy who had been consecrated by him.

The words alone: 'for God hath not given us the spirit of fear, but of power, and love, and soberness', would already be enough by themselves to render sufficiently determined the meaning of the others which immediately precede them: 'Receive the Holy Ghost, and remember that thou stir up the grace of God which is given thee by this Imposition of our hands.' These indicate what kind of imposition of hands is being dealt with, that is to say the imposition of hands that is used in the consecration of a bishop, mentioned by St Paul to Timothy in the words quoted above. They indicate the nature of the grace that is conferred by this imposition of

---

2. [The author has given the 1552 form, before the addition of the clause 'for the Office and Work of a Bishop ...']

hands, the grace that a bishop is given in order to carry out his ministry, the grace of which Paul speaks in those same words (2 Timothy 1.6-7).

[21] Now if the meaning of the formula 'Receive the Holy Ghost', along with what follows, right up to the word 'soberness', is clearly and sufficiently determined to indicate an episcopal consecration, this becomes crystal clear and such as to be incapable of any other application when it is put alongside the *prayer* that precedes it and to which it is joined, from which it cannot be separated and of which it is only the final expression.

In confirmation of what has been said so far to prove the validity of episcopal consecration conferred with the *new rite* of Edward VI, we shall refer to what the illustrious Professor Gasparri teaches in his book *De Sacra Ordinatione* (vol. 2 c. 5 n. 1109). He writes: 'Now among all the rites which the Roman Pontifical prescribes for episcopal consecration, it is the commonly held opinion that the matter is the laying on of the hands of the consecrating bishop (or rather, bishops), and the form is the associated words: "Receive the Holy Ghost". It is our opinion that, in accordance with the criterion expounded in n. 988, a hypothetical consecration would be valid – as it was in the ancient liturgy – if it were conferred with the laying on of the bishop's hands with only the *Preface* and without the words "Receive the Holy Ghost". For how can you prove that the Church has withdrawn the consecratory power from this eucharistic prayer? Similarly, on the hypothesis that the bishop lays on his hands *with only the words "Receive the Holy Ghost"* and without the *Preface*, we admit *with the commonly held opinion* that the ordination would be valid; for although the *words, taken by themselves*, are indeterminate, and are insufficient as expressions of the conferring of the episcopal order, they are given *sufficient determination*, not only by the *Preface*, but even by *the ceremonies themselves without the Preface*.'

Certainly, if the words 'Receive the Holy Ghost', taken by themselves, are enough for the essential form of episcopal ordination, they are more than sufficient when they are *deter-*

mined in the same sentence by the words of the Apostle which concern the grace of the episcopate, and when, in addition to this, they are *even more clearly determined by the consecratory prayer* which precedes them.

[22] In the same way Anglican priestly ordination conferred according to the *Ordinal* of Edward VI should be declared valid. In this ordination the candidates for ordination are presented to the Bishop with these words: 'Reverend Father in God, I present unto you these persons present, to be admitted to the *Order of Priesthood*.' Then the Bishop says: 'Good people, these are they whom we purpose, God willing, to receive this day unto the holy *Office of Priesthood*.' He then prays as follows: 'Almighty God, giver of all good things, who by thy Holy Spirit hast appointed divers Orders of Ministers in the Church; Mercifully behold these thy servants now called to the *Office of Priesthood*; and replenish them so with the truth of thy doctrine, and adorn them with innocency of life, that, both by word and good example, they may faithfully serve thee in this Office, to the glory of thy Name, and the edification of thy Church; through the merits of our Saviour J. C., who liveth and reigneth with thee and the Holy Ghost, world without end. Amen.' There follows an exhortation and some interrogations. Then the Bishop offers another prayer which concludes with the imposition of hands on each of the persons to be ordained, accompanied by these words: 'Receive the Holy Ghost; whose sins thou dost forgive, they are forgiven; and whose sins thou dost retain, they are retained. And be thou a faithful Dispenser of the Word of God, and of his holy Sacraments; in the name of the Father, and of the Son, and of the Holy Ghost. Amen.'[3]

In this rite there is the imposition of hands by the bishop along with the corresponding form for the priesthood, and so there is present the sacramental sign for the Order of priest. This sign is *determined*, because in the last formula, which has just been quoted above, those same words are said with which

---

3. [De Augustinis is quoting the 1552 form, without the later addition of the clause: 'For the Office and Work of a Priest in the Church of God'.]

Jesus Christ gave to priests the power to forgive sins, and there is given the power to be a 'dispenser of the Sacraments of God' (St Paul says: 'dispensers of the mysteries of God' (1 Corinthiaus 4. 1)). Moreover, the determination of those final words of the ordination is made *even clearer by their being joined to the preceding prayer and to the other parts of the ceremony*, in which it is said repeatedly that what is being dealt with is the ordination of a *sacerdos*, a *priest*.

[23] As far as the rite is concerned, the validity of Anglican ordinations is challenged because it is objected that the rite was drawn up and approved by those who denied that the Mass was a true sacrifice and did not believe in the real presence of Jesus Christ in the Sacrament of the Altar. It was also objected that in the compilation of the new rite they had expressly corrupted the ancient form of ordinations, in order to remove from them the idea of the sacrifice that is to be offered by true priests in the consecration of the Holy Eucharist. They say that if, along with the authors of the Anglican rite, those who make use of it do not believe that there are true priests in the Church, how can they make priests by that rite, and consecrate bishops, who cannot be bishops if they are not priests?

This objection, which is the most specious argument by which the nullity of Anglican ordinations is supported, can concern *either the intention of the minister* of these ordinations, *in the sense* that his intention cannot be the kind of intention that is required for the validity of the act – and we will speak about this in the next paragraph – or it can concern *the rite itself, in the sense* that it cannot be declared valid because it was introduced by one who did not believe, and is used by one who does not believe either in the real presence of Jesus Christ in the Most Holy Eucharist or in the Holy Sacrifice of the Mass.

[24] The objection proposed in this second sense is easily resolved by recalling the Catholic doctrine about the faith that is required in the minister of the sacrament. According to this, when the matter and form of the sacrament are such as to constitute the *sacramental sign*, substantially and inte-

grally, as this is required according to its divine institution, then neither the lack of probity in the minister nor his lack of faith can make the sacrament null.

Certainly, the Arians committed a most serious error in faith when they denied the divinity of the Word of God. Through such heretical impiety they denied the *true meaning* of the form of Baptism which signifies the Most Holy Trinity of three divine Persons, Father, Son and Holy Spirit, in the unity of the divine nature. And yet the Baptism conferred by them was valid because the words used in it were those that constitute the form of Baptism; and Pope St Siricius, in his First Letter to Himerius (ch. 1) wrote: 'At the beginning of your letter you have written that very many people who were baptized by the impious Arians are hastening to the Catholic faith, and that some of our brethen want to rebaptize them. This is not lawful, since the Apostle forbids this practice and the canons contradict it.'

Then St Thomas (3, q. 64, a. 9), when he is discussing the general question for all the sacraments: 'Whether the faith of the Minister is necessary for a sacrament?', replies: 'Because the Minister acts as an instrument in the sacraments, he does not act by his own power but by the power of Christ. Now, just as a man's *charity* pertains to *his own power*, so too does his *faith*. Therefore just as it is not required for the performance of a sacrament that the Minister be in charity, but even sinners can confer sacraments, as we have said; so too his *faith* is *not required* for the performance of a sacrament, but an unbeliever can perform a true sacrament, provided that the other conditions which are necessary for the sacrament are not lacking.'

[25] Since, therefore, the validity of the sacramental sign used in Anglican ordinations has already been demonstrated, this validity is in no way destroyed by the errors about the Most Holy Eucharist which were held and are held by the ministers of such ordinations. These men act not 'by their own power' but 'by the power of Christ', who confers the sacramental character of Orders, presuming always, that is, that his minister performs the external sacramental sign of

ordination (*sacramentum tantum*) in the way that this was instituted by Him and is used in his Church.

Nor can it be said that with the Anglicans the sacramental sign, that is, the sacred rite of ordination, is no longer that instituted by Jesus Christ and used in his Church, because the ancient Catholic rite that was used in England, has to a great extent been altered and changed in the new Anglican rite. Such changes and alterations have been made, and they are many. However, these concern accidental parts of the rite, not the essence itself, since in the *Ordinal* of Edward VI there is preserved substantially intact that sacramental form that constitutes, along with the imposition of hands by the bishop, the valid sacramental sign for the conferral of Orders.

From all this it follows that, notwithstanding the changes made by the Anglicans in the ancient Catholic rite, and notwithstanding the fact that these changes were made by heretics, and with the scope of spreading heretical doctrines about the Eucharist and the Holy Sacrifice of the Mass, since in the new rite the sacramental sign has remained substantially valid, the ordinations are valid as far as the rite is concerned.

[26] To take away the force of this conclusion, it would be pointless to quote what St Thomas teaches in that same third part of the *Summa Theologica* (q. 60, a. 7. ad 3): 'One who pronounces the sacramental words in a corrupt form does not seem to be intending to do what the Church does if he does this deliberately; consequently it seems that the sacrament is not performed.' The argument drawn from these words runs as follows: the Anglicans have corrupted the rite with which the sacrament of Orders is conferred. Therefore they no longer confer the sacrament.

This argument, however, does not hold water. The teaching of the Angelic Doctor in the words just quoted in no way touches Anglican ordinations. This appears clearly from these words of St Thomas themselves: he speaks of the person who 'pronounces *the sacramental words* in a corrupt form', that is to say, he is speaking of someone who alters and corrupts *the form* of the sacrament. Now it has already been demonstrated above that the *form* of the sacrament has not been corrupted in the Anglican ritual, the 'words of the sacrament' have not been corrupted. This is the case because in the *Ordinal* of Edward VI the words which constitute the valid *form* of ordination have been conserved.

[27] In confirmation of what we are saying about the meaning to be given to the words of St Thomas, one should study the article from which these words have been taken and pay careful attention to the objection to which the Holy Doctor is replying.

The question examined in article 7 is this: 'Whether determined words are required in the sacraments'. It is clear that it is a question here, not of all the words that are used during the ceremony of the administration of a sacrament, but only of those that constitute the sacramental *form*. This is confirmed by the conclusion of the article, which runs as follows: 'The Lord pronounced determined words in the *consecration* of the sacrament of the Eucharist, saying: "This is my body" (Matthew 26. 26). In the same way he enjoined the disciples to *baptize with a determined form of words*, when he said: "Go, make disciples of all nations, baptizing them in the name of the Father and of the Son and of the Holy Spirit" (Matthew 28. 19).' This comes across even more clearly from the argument that St Thomas puts forward in this same article: 'I reply that one should say just as we said above (art. 6, ad 2) that in the sacraments the words serve as the form, and so too the sensible objects serve as the matter. Now in everything which is made up of matter and form, the determining principle is the form, which is, so to speak, the purpose and end of the matter; therefore the determined form is a more fundamental requirement *for the existence* of anything than the determined matter; for it is required of the determined matter that it be appropriate for the determined form. Therefore since sacraments require determined sensible objects which act in sacraments as the matter, they require much more a determined form.'

So St Thomas is dealing with those words which are the sacramental *form*, and are necessary *for the existence of anything*. So, in the third objection, he talks of the corruption of the words that constitute this form; replying to his objections, he gives as examples of changes in the *form* of baptism those changes in which instead of *in nomine Patris*, one were to say *in nomine matris*, and instead of *in nomine Patris et Filii* one were to say *in nomine patrias et filios*.

There can be no doubt that St Thomas is speaking here always and exclusively of the corruption of the 'essential form' of the sacrament; but such an alteration of the essential form of the sacrament of Orders is not to be found in the Anglican *Ordinal*, as we have demonstrated above.

§4
The intention of the Minister in Anglican Ordinations is the intention that is required for their validity

[28] For the validity of Anglican ordinations, it is not enough that they be carried out by a bishop and that a valid rite for the conferral of Orders be used; it is also required that in using this rite the minister, the bishop, that is, have the intention of wanting to do what the Church does. Was such an intention present at the consecration of Parker? Was it present in subsequent Anglican ordinations in such a way that these can be considered valid? It is claimed that this intention was absent from the beginning, that it never could have been present, because the men who used the *Ordinal* of Edward VI, namely Barlow, the consecrator of Parker, and the others who carried on the Anglican ordinations, did not have, and could not have had, the intention of consecrating bishops or of ordaining priests, since these men denied the true and proper sacrifice of the Eucharist.

This problem calls for careful investigation; to provide a clear solution we shall, first of all, consider *that which is not required* necessarily in the minister for him to have the intention of *doing what the Church does*. We shall then look at what is absolutely required in the minister for him to have this intention. In other words, we shall see what this intention really consists of.

[29] Beginning, then, with the intention that is not required in the minister, we call attention to the fact that it is the common teaching of theologians that the minister is not required to intend the *purpose* of the sacrament or the *effect* that it produces. So that a heretical minister, who thinks that a sacrament does not confer grace or does not imprint a character on the soul, – while divine faith teaches the opposite – in spite of this, can have a true intention of conferring the sacrament, and with this intention he validly confers it.[4]

St Thomas in Part Three of the *Summa Theologica* (q. 64 a. 9 ad 1) says: 'If the minister suffers from a lack of faith concerning the very sacrament which he is performing, even if he believes that there is *no* interior effect consequent upon the exterior action, he still knows that the Catholic Church intends to perform a sacrament by this external action: *therefore despite his lack of faith he can intend to do what the Church does, even if he judges that this is nothing.* An intention of this nature is sufficient for the sacrament: for, as we said above (a. 8 ad 2), the minister of a sacrament *acts in the person of the whole Church, the faith of which supplies for what is lacking to the faith of the minister.*' St Thomas again, in the article which follows (a. 10 ad 3), notes that 'a perverted intention perverts the work of the intender, and not the work of another. Therefore the perverse intention of the minister perverts what he does in the sacraments, *insofar as it is his own work, not insofar as it is the work of Christ*, whose minister he is: the same is true if a man's agent had an evil

---

4. It should be noted that if a heretical minister in conferring a sacrament intends to do what is done by his co-religionists, believing that they belong to the Church of Jesus Christ, and does not intend to do what is done in the Church of Rome, the sacrament is not, because of this, invalid. 'You will ask,' says Cardinal Bellarmine (de Sacr. in gen. L. 1 c. 27), 'what if someone intends to do what some particular, *false* Church, such as the Church of Geneva, does, and *intends not to do* what the Church of Rome does? I reply, even this is sufficient ... For what destroys the efficacy of a sacrament is not the minister's error about the Church, but the lack of intention' – De Augustinis. [R. Bellarmine, *De controversiis christianae fidei* III (Naples 1858), p. 76 – Rambaldi.]

intention in giving alms to the poor when his master had a good intention in ordering that they should be given.'

[30] Bellarmine, too, in his refutation of Tilman and Kemnitius, makes the correct observation that this same teaching was defined by the Council of Trent, and that it is according to this teaching, and in no other way, that canon 11 of Session 7 must be understood. 'Both authors,' says Bellarmine, 'in the passages we have quoted say that the Council of Trent defined that a sacrament is not performed unless the minister intends not only the *act* but also the *end* of the sacrament, i.e. unless he intends the purpose for which the sacrament was instituted – which is certainly very different from my own opinion. However this is simply a lie. For the Council does not mention the end of the sacrament anywhere in canon 11; nor does it say, as these authors seem to believe, that the minister must intend to do what the Church intends, but what the Church does. Now "what the Church does" does not refer to the *end* but to the *action*. In fact, the Church's practice proves this point. For the early Church did not rebaptize people who had been baptized by Pelagians, and we do not rebaptize people who have been baptized by Zwinglians and Calvinists, although we know that all such people baptize without intending the true end of baptism, which is to remove original sin.'

[31] From what has been said up to this point concerning the intention required in the minister of the sacraments for their validity, it is clear that no solid argument can be put forward against the validity of Anglican ordinations that is based on the errors of the Anglicans with regard to the Holy Eucharist. It is claimed that the minister, who denies that a priest has the power to 'transubstantiate' the bread and wine into the body and blood of Our Lord Jesus Christ, or that he has the power to offer a true propitiatory sacrifice in the Holy Mass, cannot have the intention of ordaining priests. But, in making this assertion, it is presumed that the minister who ordains a priest, for the validity of the act, as well as having the internal intention with regard to ordination, must also have the intention with regard to the *purpose* and the *effect*

of ordination. Now this presupposition has been shown to be false. *It is not required of the minister that he intend what the Church intends*, but only *that he intend what the Church does*. ' "What the Church does" does not refer to the end but to the action.'

[32] Cases of Anglican ordinations are brought up, in which the ordaining minister declares publicly, before a priestly ordination, that he does not intend to ordain a priest who offers sacrifice in the true sense of that word. This declaration does not deprive the minister of the intention of wanting to ordain a priest, or of doing what the Church does in the ordination of priests. Therefore, in spite of his declaration, he who really wants to and intends to ordain a priest, ordains the priest in accordance with the power that has been divinely conferred upon him, a priest, that is, who can offer the divine Sacrifice in the Eucharist. This is a certain conclusion, and it is confirmed by the following Decree of the Holy Office of 18 December 1872.

The Decree runs as follows:

> In certain places some (heretics) use the required matter and form simultaneously in baptism, but *warn* the candidates *expressly* against believing that baptism has any effect on the soul, saying that it is a merely external sign of initiation into their sect. For this reason they are accustomed to mock Catholics for their belief concerning the effects of baptism, calling it superstitious.
>
> The questions are these:
> 1. Is baptism administered by these heretics *of doubtful validity on account of the lack of the intention* of doing what Christ wished if the minister declares explicitly before baptizing that baptism has no effect on the soul?
> 2. Is baptism conferred in this way of doubtful validity if the declaration we have described is not made explicitly immediately before baptism is administered, but if the minister has often made the declaration at other times, and *this doctrine is preached publicly within the sect*?

Reply:
To 1. *No; for despite the error as to the effect of baptism the intention of doing what the Church does is not excluded.*
To 2. *The answer follows from 1.*[5]

Therefore in Anglican ordinations the fact that the minister did not believe in the real presence of Jesus in the Sacrament or in the Sacrifice of the Altar would not imply that his intention was lacking; the intention was not lacking even when the minister expressly declared that he did not intend to ordain priests who could offer true sacrifice. So this is not a reason for declaring Anglican ordinations null.

[33] But did the ministers of these ordinations have that intention that is absolutely necessary for their validity, the intention, that is, with regard to the *act*, which is the intention of *doing* what the Church *does*? When it is a question of ordaining bishops, priests and deacons, this intention is always present when there is the intention of constituting these ecclesiastical ministers with a sacred rite, and of doing what has been done right from the beginning of Christian society, as this appears from the writings of the New Testament and from Church history.

Now it is perfectly plain that the ministers of Anglican ordinations did have this intention. To be reassured on this point it is enough to take a look at the *Ordinal* of Edward VI, in which the rite for these ordinations is to be found. Here are the opening words of the 'Preface:' 'It is evident unto all men diligently reading the holy Scripture and ancient Authors, that from the Apostles' time there have been these Orders of Ministers in Christ's Church; Bishops, Priests, and Deacons ... . And therefore, to the intent that these Orders may be continued, and reverently used and esteemed in the Church of England; no man shall be accounted or taken to be a lawful Bishop, Priest, or Deacon ... or suffered to execute

---

5. [A fuller text of the Response can be read in DS 3102.]

any of the said Functions, except he be called, tried, examined and admitted thereunto according to the form hereafter following, or hath had formerly Episcopal Consecration, or Ordination.' Thereafter in the rite for the ordination of deacons and of priests, and for the consecration of bishops, there is frequent mention of their sacred ministry in the Church of Jesus Christ and of the wish, by means of this rite, to confer these Orders.

[34] For the sake of brevity we will just take a glance at this. In the ordination of priests the bishop prays: 'Almighty God, giver of all good things, who by thy Holy Spirit hast appointed divers Orders of Ministers in the Church; Mercifully behold these thy servants now called to the Office of Priesthood, etc.' Then in his exhortation to those who are to be ordained he says: 'You have heard, Brethren, as well in your private examination, as in the exhortation which was now made to you, and in the holy Lessons taken out of the Gospel, and the writings of the Apostles, of what dignity, and of how great importance this Office is, whereunto ye are called. And now again we exhort you, in the Name of our Lord Jesus Christ, that you have in remembrance, into how high a Dignity, and how weighty an Office and Charge ye are called: that is to say, to be Messengers, Watchmen, and Stewards of the Lord' etc.

[35] With regard to episcopal consecration, the candidate is first presented to the consecrating bishop with these words: 'Most Reverend Father in God, we present unto you this godly and well-learned man to be ordained and Consecrated Bishop.' Then the people is exhorted by the consecrating bishop to pray, with these words: 'Brethren, it is written in the Gospel of Saint Luke, That our Saviour Christ continued the whole night in prayer, before he did choose and send forth his twelve Apostles. It is written also in the acts of the Apostles, That the Disciples who were at Antioch did fast and pray, before they laid hands on Paul and Barnabas, and sent them forth. Let us therefore, following the example of our Saviour Christ, and his Apostles, first fall to prayer, before we admit, and send forth this person presented

unto to us, to the work whereunto we trust the Holy Spirit hath called him.'

It has been demonstrated, therefore, that the ministers of Anglican ordinations in ordaining bishops and priests intend to do what the Church does; for this reason their intention is sufficient for the validity of the act.

We conclude: Anglican ordinations, about which the Holy See has not yet given a doctrinal judgment, are valid because they have been carried out by a suitable minister, with a valid rite and with the intention of doing what the Church does.

August 1895   *Emilio M. De Augustinis* SJ

[37]   **POSTSCRIPT**

1. The two documents of Pope Paul IV, referred to in the newspaper, *La Vérité*, and published by the English Benedictine, P. Gasquet, were known to me.
2. I deal with these specially in Part One of my study and I show that they *do not in any way imply* the nullity of those Anglican ordinations that were conferred according to the *Ordinal* of Edward VI. In these documents the Pope simply declares that the orders are null if they are conferred by a bishop who was not ordained 'rightly and correctly' (*rite et recte*); and he states that the person was not ordained 'rightly and correctly' if he was not ordained 'in the form of the Church'.

   However, the upholders of the validity of Anglican ordinations prove that these Orders were conferred by bishops who had been ordained 'in the form of the Church', because *this form*, i.e. the form which is sufficient for the validity of the act, was maintained in the *Ordinal* of Edward VI, and this was always used in Anglican ordinations.

[38] 3. The Brief of Pope Julius III to Cardinal Pole, dated March 8 1554, was also known to me. This grants to Cardinal Pole, who was Legate in England, ample faculties of which I have spoken in my study. I argued from this

that, far from declaring Anglican ordinations null, the Holy See held at that time that they were valid.

In the brief of Julius III, cited above, special attention should be given to the words which concern those who had been consecrated bishops according to the Anglican rite; there can be no doubt that reference is made to this rite and that it is held to be valid, because these bishops are allowed to exercise the Orders they had received: 'They received the gift of consecration which was conferred on them by other bishops or archbishops, even heretics and schismatics, or otherwise *less rightly (minus rite) and without the customary form of the Church being maintained.*'

It should also be noted that in relation to ordination carried out with the *Ordinal* of Edward VI – which had a valid form, but had been introduced unlawfully, since it had changed the ancient rite of the English Church – the Pope says explicitly: 'without the CUSTOMARY form of the Church being maintained'; whereas Paul IV, speaking not of this or that particular rite, but of the *essential form* for ordination, says 'not in the form of the Church'.

The decision of Paul IV is the same as that of his predecessor, Julius III.

Julius III maintains that the ordination is valid if it is carried out according to the *form that is essential* for the conferral of Orders in the Church, even though this was done with a form that is *inessentially* different from the ancient one, and unlawful, 'without the customary form of the Church being maintained'.

Paul IV maintains that the ordination is valid when it has been carried out according to the *form that is essential* for the conferral of Orders in the Church; he therefore declares the nullity of the Ordination that was not carried out 'in the form of the Church'.

ANGLICAN ORDERS. A HISTORICAL AND THEOLOGICAL EXPOSITION

James Moyes, Aidan Gasquet, OSB, and D. Fleming, OSF

PROLOGUE[1]

[1] Moved and touched as we are with the sense of the greatest and deepest reverence towards the supreme authority of the Apostolic See, we wish in all humility to set out the following points as an *introduction* to our report.

1. Although the whole question of the validity of Anglican orders has only recently been raised and submitted to the examination and judgment of the Apostolic See, it cannot in any sense be described as a *new* question, as it has been investigated, weighed and settled by the Holy See with great precision on several occasions in the past. It is worthy of careful note that on every occasion when the question was submitted to examination and judgment, the Holy See's verdict was always the same, with no shadow of hesitation or variation, namely that these orders were to be held indubitably null and altogether invalid. Thus, according to a document kept in the Archive of the Holy Office, the Holy See submitted this question to mature deliberation and minute examination on no less than **eight distinct occasions, and each time without hesitation an unambiguous judgment was pronounced against the validity of these orders**.

[2] (a) The very first judgment, which by any standard

---

1. [Where possible we retain the typographical devices to be found in the original printed version. However we have taken the liberty of removing some of the synonyms and epithets – honorific or otherwise – which can sound intolerably verbose in English. We have not been able to include all the appended documentation from Westminster.]

carries the greatest weight, and lays the foundation for the original and invariable practice of requiring that all Anglican ministers received into the bosom of the Church should be ordained **absolutely and de novo** is found in Paul IV's Bull and Brief of 1555, in which he conveyed practical directions to Cardinal Pole, the Apostolic Legate for England, and instructed him that all who were ordained by bishops who had not been consecrated 'in the form of the Church' should be ordained DE NOVO. The Cardinal, being well acquainted with the Pope's mind, explained that in this clause the phrase 'form of the Church' should be taken to mean the form contained in the Roman Pontifical.[2]

This judgment was followed by several others to exactly the same effect. The best known and most important are the three following:

[3] (1) 13 August 1685. In the case of a certain French Calvinist who had been ordained according to the *revised and augmented 1662 form* of the Ritual of Edward VI, the Consultors of the Holy Office, on the basis of a very careful comparison between the Anglican Ritual and various ordination rites of the Church in both the West and the East, 'gave a unanimous response in **favour of the invalidity of the ordination in question**'. It is evident from the Holy Office's Register that Innocent XI passed and promulgated this decision only after the opinions of many theologians from Italy, Belgium, France and England had been heard. Moreover, this verdict is all the more significant and decisive insofar as it decrees the invalidity of an ordination performed according to the revised and augmented Anglican Ordinal of 1662, which contains a fuller and more specifically determined form than the one in use from about the middle of the preceding century. It follows *a fortiori* that this verdict clearly tells against the sufficiency of the Anglican Ordinal of 1552 before it was revised and corrected in 1662. Now all Anglican orders without exception for more than a century were conferred according to the unamended Ordinal.

---

2. [The authors refer to an Appendix showing how Cardinal Pole's treatment of those who had been ordained under Edward VI varied from case to case.]

It also deserves notice that in the 1685 case (according to the evidence of Genetti in the case of 1704) this conclusion and verdict was reached *adequate et unice*, **i.e. paying attention** *only* **to the defect of the intention and form employed by Anglican heretics in the ordination of presbyters**, and taking no account of any doubt concerning the *fact* of Parker's consecration, which on the strength of historical evidence had been judged 'somewhat confused and complicated'.

[4] (2) **In 1704** there occurred the well known case of the conversion of John Clement Gordon, the Bishop of Galloway, to the Catholic faith. This case too was submitted to the Holy See for examination and judgment. The records of the preceding case of 1685 were re-examined, and in addition to the many *vota* which had already been delivered in the 1685 case, three more were obtained, the most important of which was submitted by Joseph F. Genetti on 16 April 1704. This *votum* carries all the greater authority because of Genetti's great thoroughness in obtaining reliable information. To that end he visited England together with the Nuncio, the Very Reverend (later Cardinal) Dr Adda, where, as the Register shows, the issue was seen to carry such important practical consequences that a meeting was held of seven or eight highly qualified priests (Genetti describes them as doctors of the Sorbonne or of Douai, and all distinguished scholars, including the Very Reverend Dr Gifford), under the *chairmanship* of the celebrated Dr Leyburne, the learned President of Douai College. There the matter was examined and discussed for fifteen days on end, at the end of which the meeting was dissolved; after sufficient time had been allowed for maturer consideration of the question, all **declared unanimously against the validity of Anglican orders**. At the same time it should be noted that the certainty of the *votum* submitted by Genetti and supported by all these means of inquiry **did not in any way depend upon merely historical questions, much less on the so called 'Nag's Head fable', but rather, in Genetti's own words, on 'the defect of the intention and the defect of form employed by the Anglican heretics in the conferring of the order of**

presbyterate. For they did not have either the *will* or the *power* to make true priests who would possess power over Christ's physical Body, which they do not even believe to be present in the Eucharist'. When account was taken of this *votum* and of others to the same effect, and when they were all compared carefully with the *vota* which had been submitted in the earlier case of 1685, it became at once evident that in both cases theologians 'attached most weight to the DEFECT OF FORM and of the meaning required for the conferring of the power of the priesthood' (The Bishop of Castoria, the Vicar Apostolic of Holland, in his letters of 20 December 1684 and 2 February 1685. J.F. Genetti, 16 April 1704).

It follows, as is evident from the Archive of the Holy Office, that all doubtful historical considerations were set aside, so that the conclusion is based solely on theological principles, namely **defect of form**. It was agreed unanimously that Anglican ministers who returned to the Church, both presbyters and bishops, were to be treated as mere laymen. This is what was done thereafter without further discussion (See the Acts of the Archive of the Holy Office, fol. 776).

[5] When Pope Clement XI gave judgment against the validity of the Anglican orders conferred on John Clement Gordon, he gave this judgment, as Cardinal Franzelin showed, 'on the matter of fact in the individual case proposed, *and indirectly on the general principle of invalidity*' (cf. Cardinal Franzelin's *votum* of 25 February 1875).

Similarly when in 1844 Dr Nardi, a Professor of Canon Law in the University of Padua, published a work entitled: *Elementi di diritto Ecclesiastico*, (Elements of Canon Law), containing the proposition, 'Anglican ordinations are doubtful', and sent the work to Rome to be examined, Gregory XVI entrusted the examination of the book to a commission of learned theologians and canonists, which included Dr Ludovicus Ferrari, the Prefect of Ceremonies in the Vatican Basilica, who was one of the most erudite canonists of his day. These theologians and canonists judged that 'Anglican ordinations are not *doubtful* but absolutely invalid'. Accordingly the proposition we have quoted was omitted from the second edition of the work in 1854, to be replaced by the following: 'On the contrary the ordinations of Protestants are of no worth, even among those who have retained the external appearance of episcopacy, as in England, Denmark, Sweden and Norway, because the consecration of bishops has been invalidated by a breach in the succession, and the rite has been changed in its essentials, so that the idea of priesthood and Christian sacrifice has been altogether lost' (Vol. 2, p. 97). The same case is mentioned in a work by Maziere Brady entitled 'Episcopal Succession', vol. iii, p. 3.

[6] (3) The third special case in which the Holy Office examined this question with mature deliberation occurred in 1875, when Cardinal Manning sought a response to the question whether the decision allegedly given in **the case of the Abyssinians** had any implications favourable to the recognition of the sufficiency of the form employed by Anglicans in their ordinations. This case deserves all the greater attention because of the *votum* given by Fr (later Cardinal) John Baptist Franzelin, SJ, at that time Professor of Dogmatic Theology at the Gregorian University. In his close examination of the whole question, Franzelin investigated all previous relevant documents and submitted them to careful and painstaking analysis.

At the end of his acute examination of all the factors concerned, this learned theologian reached the following clear and distinct conclusion:

Prescinding totally from the fact of Parker's consecration, and thus saying nothing about such matters as the consecration in the Nag's Head tavern, he reached the following conclusion: '**From the Edwardine form itself and from its origin and history, it is certain that the orders of this sect are simply null and void**'. Moreover, since the words 'Receive the Holy Ghost, etc' in the Anglican rite were chosen in order to replace and suppress the ancient Catholic rite, they are to be understood 'not to retain but expressly to exclude the sense that the priesthood is conferred'. In accordance with this solid and well-founded conclusion, the Holy Office on 30 April went on to declare that its previous decisions concerning Anglican orders had not been changed in any way by anything contained explicitly or implicitly in the decree for the Abyssinians of 1704.

[7] Thus the mind of the Apostolic See on this practical and important question can be clearly deduced from the series of eight decisions beginning with Cardinal Pole's question of 1555, and ending with Cardinal Manning's request in 1875.

From this series of totally congruous decisions, giving no hint of variation, and from the uniform and completely consistent practice, three facts stand out very clearly:

(a) All these decisions were taken only after most careful examination and precise research into all aspects of the question, and after a comparison had been made between the Anglican form and **the forms** in use **in both West and East**. In addition, the most learned theologians of the age assisted the process by shedding on the question the light of theological and liturgical scholarship. Finally we have the evidence of Genetti that the most learned and qualified priests and bishops in England were also consulted.

(b) The arguments on which these decisions were based indubitably give the lie to the suggestion that the judgments and their promulgation were due to ignorance or distortion of certain historical facts, or because the Nag's Head fable concerning Parker's consecration had been accepted uncritically. The decisions themselves show clearly that they were taken independently of such reasons and motives; it is made absolutely plain that they were reached on account of **the defect of form and intention**, which according to solid theological principles, makes Anglican orders altogether null and void without recourse to any other reasons.

(c) Since from the time of the so-called 'Reformation' to the present day it has been the constant practice of the Catholic Church in England to obey these pontifical decisions with complete fidelity, it is as clear as day that this method of proceeding was derived from

directives coming from the Holy See itself, and was introduced by its authority. This practice, indubitably based
as it is on so many unambiguous papal decisions, cannot
be in any way changed or even modified without the
most serious consequences. The reverence in which the
wisdom and prudence of the Apostolic See are held in
England would be gravely weakened, with disastrous
consequences for the genuine reconciliation and union
of Christians.

[8] To conclude, the Apostolic See's practice in this matter
accords with the continuous tradition which prevailed in
England from the earliest days among Catholic writers,
both bishops and presbyters, who without hesitation unanimously rejected these orders as invalid; it also accords with
the conclusions which in our own times the most learned
Catholic historians have drawn after thorough, precise and
scientific research. Consequently, a very brief reply can be
given to those who argue that, if the Apostolic See wished
to take the indulgent line and recognise Anglican orders, such
a procedure would smooth the way for the return of the
whole Anglican sect into the bosom of the Church: we can
categorically and unambiguously state our deep conviction
that a judgment recognising the authenticity of Anglican
orders or favouring them in any way – as is called for by
some who are in total ignorance of the historical facts and
the present state of the Anglican sect – could not be given
without a radical change to a custom which from the first was
introduced into England by the unquestionably valid decisions and commands of the Apostolic See, and which was
most scrupulously observed there up to our own times.
Such a change would without any doubt produce the following consequences which would be utterly disastrous to
Catholic interests:

[9] (1) In the judgment of many, nothing could be conceived which would add greater plausibility to the absurd
claim of the Anglican heresy in its modern form that the
Anglican Church is an integral part or 'branch' of the

Catholic Church, the sole Bride of Christ, just as much as is the Greek Church. Thus they say the Church is divided into three integral parts, the Roman, the Greek or Oriental, and the Anglican. They realise that nothing will undermine such an inherently heretical claim so much as the fact that their orders are not recognised as valid and genuine in the Catholic sense.

(2) The bishops, presbyters and faithful in England, Scotland and Ireland, and in the far-flung regions in which English is spoken, agree almost unanimously that such a decision would be a great obstacle to the conversion of non-Catholics to the Church. Moreover, it would encourage Anglicans in claiming and maintaining the alleged rights of their sect.

(3) Above all, it would weaken confidence in the wisdom and prudence of the Apostolic See. Adversaries would be encouraged to assert, as they are already only too ready to assert, that an authority **could not be accounted reliable and infallible** if it had been so gravely mistaken in defining which sacramental conditions are sufficient, if it had recognised its error only after three centuries during which it imposed a custom and practice which involved the *material* sacrilege of repeating ordination, and if it was now at last *compelled* to amend its own decrees. One should certainly expect that other errors needing correction, even in doctrine, would also be discovered, errors which until now the aforesaid authority had mistakenly believed should be numbered among the truths of revelation.

Such allegations, for all their falsity and injustice, would certainly be passionately repeated with great eloquence and show of scholarship, and would be published and taught everywhere by Anglicans and Nonconformists alike. As a result Catholics would experience great distress that an avoidable cause or occasion had occurred which might seem to the general public to confirm the heretics' allegations and arguments, or to give some hint of justification or soundness to their claims

and alleged rights. This would certainly create great confusion and thus prove a great obstacle to conversions to
the Catholic faith.

Consequently all considerations of utility or so-called
expedience should be kept distinct and excluded from the
question: Are Anglican orders valid or not? We are very
anxious that the Apostolic See should have only one
thing in view, namely the truth of the matter.
Accordingly we urgently request that, prescinding from
all other considerations, the inquiry should be concentrated on this single question on its own merits, so that it
can be answered solely according to the dictates of truth
and justice.

[10] Any modification in the practice which has so far been
enjoined by the Apostolic See would be all the more deplorable in that the increasingly stringent inspection to which the
whole issue is being subjected – involving as it does the scru-
tiny and evaluation of all the historical facts and the relevant
theological principles which are intrinsically connected with
the question – makes it more and more easy to recognise the
wisdom and meticulousness of the series of decisions outlined
above which have been taken by the Holy See over three
centuries, and to acknowledge the Apostolic See's remarkable prudence and shrewdness in solving this question.
This we shall try to show in the following two chapters.
In the *first* we recount the relevant **historical facts**; in the
second we set out the **theological arguments** from which a
clear and unquestionable solution can be derived.

HISTORICAL PART
I. EXPOSITION OF THE RELEVANT FACTS

I
The Context at the time of the So-Called Reformation

[11] 1. The **Reformers**, under Cranmer, the Archbishop
of Canterbury, exercised the greatest and most **decisive**

influence in the composition of the Edwardine Ritual and Liturgy.[3]

2. In pursuing this work of composition they agree at many points with the Lutheran and Zwinglian Reformers of Germany and Switzerland, and were in continuous correspondence with them. They received advice and help from well-known members of the sects, such as John de Alasco, Bucer, Peter Martyr and Bullinger, as their 'Original Letters' on the Reformation show. Indeed, Bucer and Peter Martyr were given chairs of Theology in the two English universities.

[12] 3. Although the English Reformers retained episcopacy as the most appropriate form of ecclesiastical government, their own writings show that they borrowed from the Lutherans and Zwinglians the following doctrinal principles:[4]

(1) No holy order should be considered a sacrament in the Catholic sense, as imparting an inner indelible character.

(2) Ordination is no different from the installation of a civic official in the matter of the conferring of grace.

(3) For bishops or presbyters no ordination or **consecration is necessarily required** for validity, but only an institution, even though ceremonies are retained for decency's sake.

(4) **Every Christian is a priest**. The only difference between the presbyteral and lay states arises from the external nature of the Church, so that only those who as public ministers have been entrusted with the duty of dispensing the Lord's Supper to others are to be accounted presbyters.[5]

(5) Christ's sacrifice, together with his self-offering on the cross, has **altogether ceased**. Consequently the Eucharist **is not a sacrifice**, except in the sense that it is

---

3. [The authors justified this point in an Appendix.]

4. [The authors substantiated this point in an Appendix collecting quotations from the English Reformers.]

5. It should be noted that there is no reason why such an extrinsic and even temporary ministry should not be held to be of divine or apostolic institution.

a 'sacrifice of praise' or a **commemoration** of the sacrifice Christ offered once for all on the cross. It follows that the Mass, taken as a propitiatory sacrifice, is a 'blasphemy' and an insult to Christ.

(6) **Only Christ is a sacrificing priest**; besides him, no one is a priest, except in the sense that all Christians are called priests. Accordingly there does not exist any priesthood for the performance of sacrifice.

(7) Christ is not **objectively** present in the Eucharist. There is no other presence of Christ in the Eucharist apart from his real presence **by grace in the soul of the receiver**.

(8) The power of forgiving sins which Christ granted to his Apostles does not apply to the sacrament of penance, but was only the power of condoning sins by the sacrament of baptism or of declaring the remission of sins through the preaching of the Gospel, which promises the condoning of all sins to all who repent and believe. The power of the keys, i.e. of retaining or remitting, refers only to the Church's authority in the external forum.

(9) Justification is by faith alone, excluding good works.

(10) Sacraments do not produce their effect *ex opere operato*, but by arousing faith in the soul, as signs which are the most vivid representation of Christ's Passion. Hence no **intention** is required in the minister.

[13] 4. Unquestionably the **essential reason** for the changes made in the subsequent conduct of the liturgy in England was to propagate these heretical tenets throughout the Anglican institution, and (since the *law of prayer is the law of belief*) to impart them to every member of every parish, keeping the people in ignorance of the ancient Catholic liturgy which expressed sound doctrine opposed to the heretical teachings.

[14] 5. The Anglican liturgy itself shows that this was indeed the authors' intention. Thus in the liturgy for the celebration of the Lord's Supper, in no less than **sixteen**

passages they systematically removed all reference, implicit as well as explicit, to the propitiatory sacrifice and the real and objective presence of Christ, and **substituted words compatible with Reformed doctrine**. Similarly in the composition of the *Edwardine Ordinal* all reference to a priesthood conferred for **sacrificing**, or for the power of offering and consecrating, was rejected and deleted; the only ceremonies retained were those which signified nothing more than the ministry of a commemorative sacrament, and the ministry of preaching the word of God and declaring the remission of sins which forms part of that word.[6]

[15] 6. This removal of any trace of the Catholic doctrine concerning the sacrificial nature of the Catholic priesthood and the Mass was carried out under the pretext of a return to the purity of the early Church, since the Reformers maintained that in the primitive Church no form existed of the propitiatory sacrifice of the Mass or of a sacrificing priesthood or of a sacrament of penance. It would be utterly false to suggest that in this liturgical revision the Reformers desired nothing but a return to the primitive Church, the removal from the liturgy of the insertions made, as they claimed, in the middle ages, and the retention of the early, Catholic elements. It becomes readily apparent how erroneous these claims are if one examines the prayers which were substituted for the Catholic rite, which are for the most part essentially **new, of recent composition, and derived from the writings of the German Reformers**.

[16] The Reformers' intention is most clearly revealed in the composition of the form for presbyteral ordination: omitting the handing over of the instruments and the accompanying words, since they imply a sacrifice, they retain the words 'Receive the Holy Ghost', since they can be taken in the heretical sense expounded above, even though they are not part of the primitive form, but just as much of recent origin as the words the authors have removed.

---

6. [To illustrate this point the authors refer to an Appendix setting out the Catholic and 1552 Anglican ordination rites in parallel columns.]

Similarly in the form for episcopal consecration, they change and mutilate the eucharistic Preface, which is truly ancient, and displace it from its proper position, because it refers to *priesthood*. At the same time they retain the words 'Receive the Holy Ghost', which can hardly be found in the ancient Pontificals in use in England, and were added to the form of episcopal consecration no earlier than the middle ages.

[17] Thus it is evident that the intention of the revisors of the Anglican liturgy was that it should unambiguously express the **denial of priesthood and sacrifice in the Catholic sense**, and the substitution of (a) an external, **non-sacrificial ministry** (called presbyterate in the etymological sense of *seniority*); (b) a commemorative sacrament, in which Christ is not present or received *objectively* but only through the faith of the receiver, and which cannot be called a sacrifice, except in the sense of the 'remembering of a sacrifice' or 'a sacrifice of praise or thanksgiving'; and (c) the power of remitting sins, but only in the sense of the power to confer baptism or to declare the divine sentence of the remission of sins, which is promised abundantly in the Gospel to all who repent and believe. The Articles of Religion and the Homilies approved by the Anglican Church give unquestionable proof of this and provide irrefutable evidence of the doctrine and intention of the authors of the Edwardine Ritual and liturgy.

II
The Context since the Reformation

[18] These heretical dogmas were promulgated so effectively everywhere and became so deeply rooted in everyone's mind that for three centuries after the Reformation no other, or scarcely any other, form of teaching came to the ears of Anglicans.

The following well-known historical facts clearly confirm this assertion:

(1) **Altars were destroyed** and replaced by **tables**. (Often the consecrated stones were placed at the church doors

so that the act of walking over them would gradually teach people to hold them in contempt.)

(2) The Eucharist, which had been a daily sacrifice, was not even celebrated every Sunday, but ordinarily only **once a month** or **three or four times a year**.

(3) When there was a celebration, only those who intended to communicate were allowed to be present. Moreover it was laid down that the eucharistic elements of bread and wine which were left over after the celebration of the Lord's Supper belonged to the incumbent so that he and his wife and children could consume them at the family meal. This fact shows clearly how far the mind of the Anglican sect had departed from the doctrine of the real presence of Christ in the Eucharist.[7]

(4) All signs of **eucharistic devotion** were suppressed. There were no genuflexions, all indications of *presence* were removed, and candles, incense and sacrificial vestments were discarded. The only vestments retained were non-sacrificial: alb, surplice, stole and cope.

(5) The custom of hearing confessions became more or less extinct. At the most, there remained the custom of *inviting* a person preparing for death or communion whose conscience was seriously burdened to relieve their conscience, if it so prompted them, by revealing their sin to a minister so as to receive absolution. However, sacramental confession for adults in good health fell into desuetude, and was vehemently denounced by bishops and incumbents everywhere as a corrupt abuse and a blasphemous usurpation of power.

(6) By the civil laws of England the celebration of Holy Mass and the Catholic administration of the sacraments became liable to the **charge of high treason**. The English statutes show plainly that priests were hanged and quartered if they dared to celebrate these rites. Women suffered a cruel death for offering hospitality to priests who

---

7. [In an Appendix the authors printed a number of quotations from 'documents concerning the profane use of the eucharistic elements'.]

celebrated Mass or heard Catholics' confessions. These laws were passed with the approval and under the initiative of the Anglican sect, through their bishops who were their legislative representatives in the House of Lords.

(7) The obliteration of Catholic doctrine and practice within the Anglican sect was carried out so effectively that for about three centuries it is difficult, if not impossible, to find in the theological works (and they were many and lengthy) brought out by bishops and other ecclesiastics a single clear affirmation or hint that **the priesthood is to be understood in the Catholic sense** as signifying an intrinsic power of offering sacrifice and remitting sins: a power which is conferred by grace, which imprints a character, and which can be validly conferred only through ordination by a bishop. To be sure, throughout these works priesthood or presbyterate is maintained and defended, but only in the sense of the Reformers; priesthood however in the Catholic sense, signifying a 'priest who sacrifices' or 'says Mass' ('*Massing-priests*') is fiercely attacked and derided.

[19] It is true that passages to the opposite effect can be quoted from a small number of untypical writers such as Laud, who stray unsystematically in the direction of neo-Anglican teaching; however these passages carry no weight, as they speak of sacrifice in the commemorative sense, or in the sense of a sacrifice of praise. Indeed, when these quotations are examined in their context, they are seen to be poles apart from Catholic teaching, and to be like occasional 'sheltered bays in the vast ocean' of the turbulent and muddy doctrine of the Protestant Reformers.

It is an easy task for anyone with a smattering of historical knowledge to prove this for himself by browsing among the public records, the works connected with the Reformation published by the Parker Society, and the writings of the leading bishops and other ecclesiastics which appeared in the 16th, 17th and 18th centuries.

III
The Context Today

[20] The tenets of the Reformers, including the denial of priesthood and of sacrifice, have long been thoroughly assimilated and are still held tenaciously by the great majority of Anglicans, including a significant proportion of ecclesiastics. Prominent among their advocates are many leading bishops, such as the Anglican Bishop of *Liverpool*, the Bishop of *Worcester* (who in a recent address when so far as to assert that no consecration or ordination by a bishop was necessary for a valid ministry), and the Bishop of *Sodor* (who before a large audience in *Exeter* Hall in London maintained that the Anglican liturgy had been composed expressly to exclude totally the doctrines of eucharistic sacrifice and priestly absolution). All the works of the Bishop of *Liverpool* take the same line. The Bishop of *Exeter*, replying to the Pope's *Letter to the English*, declares that the Roman Church is a 'fallen' Church and the 'Babylon' of the Apocalypse.[8]

[21] However in about the last fifty years, since the beginning of the well-known 'Oxford Movement', **Neo-Anglicanism** has come into existence, first with the name 'Puseyism', then 'Ritualism' or the '**Anglo-Catholic Renewal**'.

The principal doctrines of this school are these:

(1) There exists a visible Catholic Church to which all ought to belong;

(2) This Church consists of all the baptized who accept the canonical scriptures and the creeds (i.e. the Apostles', Nicene and Athanasian creeds), even though they are understood and expounded in various ways, who possess a valid ministry and sacraments, and who accept the first

---

8. Among the Anglican bishops of the nineteenth century none has been more eminent or learned or distinguished than Lightfoot, the Bishop of Durham, who died a few years ago. This important witness teaches openly that 'the Church of England has *no priestly system* and does not set up a *priestly tribe* between God and mankind'. [We have made the best of what seems to be a garbled text.]

four or six general councils (i.e. the councils of the undivided Church).

(3) This Church consists equally not only of the
Roman Catholic, the Greek and the Oriental Churches,
but also the Anglican Church.

(4) Therefore the Anglican Church, both in England
and in territories under British rule, is **an integral part of
the Catholic Church**, with no less right and truth than the
Roman and Greek Churches, and is their equal.

(5) By divine institution all **bishops are equal and independent**, although for the sake of convenience the dioceses in each nation are gathered under a single primatial
authority, and placed under metropolitans. A national
church is not subject to any external authority, and the
Bishop of Rome has no jurisdiction over it.

[22] (6) The Anglican Church welcomes the benefits of
the Reformation. However, while it is grateful to the
Reformers for liberation from the Roman Church and
for the removal of the spurious additions and corrupt
superstitions introduced in the middle ages, it claims as
its own the whole body of doctrine which is known with
certainty to have been handed on by the undivided
Catholic Church (in the sense explained above), and
therefore claims to possess a priesthood empowered to
absolve sins and offer sacrifice. It wishes to revive all the
dogmas and customs which are common to the Western
and Eastern Churches, but it is no less prepared to maintain strenuously and absolutely its proper independence
from the Roman See. It rejects the primacy of jurisdiction and the infallibility of the Roman Pontiff. It repudi-
ates the Lateran Councils, the Councils of Florence and
Trent, the Vatican Council, and the Dogmatic Decree on
the Immaculate Conception. The Anglican bishops'
Responses to the Pope's *Letter to the English* vigorously
and categorically repudiate all these authorities as
'innovations'.

The Neo-Anglicans hope that these ideas and actions
will lead to the restoration of the doctrine and practice of

eucharistic sacrifice and sacramental confession, and the recovery of the privileged name of 'Catholic'; they hope too that by imitating the beauty and splendour of Catholic liturgy they will exercise a greater attraction and influence over people's souls. Above all they do everything they can to gain the reputation for a venerable antiquity, they constantly assert that their church today is in every way the same as the church which St Augustine founded in England, and consequently lay claim to all the achievements and glories of the ancient Church of England.

[23] (7)[9] In support of their claim of *continuity*, they maintain that the Church founded by St Augustine was altogether exempt from the authority and jurisdiction of the Roman Pontiff, and that St Gregory himself renounced any such jurisdiction; it was only later in the middle ages that the Roman Pontiffs craftily and despotically usurped power over the Church of England. Consequently, they maintain, when Henry VIII and the Reformers rejected the authority of the pope they were doing no more than **restore the Church in England to its original independence** (Cf the addresses of the Bishops of *Peterborough* and *Stepney*.)

(8) To lend credibility to this assertion and maintain the Anglican church's singular claim that it is the associate and equal of the Roman and Oriental Churches, and that it possesses equal rights with them while remaining completely independent, it is essential that they enjoy a **valid ministry**. For this reason they make every effort to have **the validity of their orders recognised**.

[24] (9) Consequently neo-Anglicans (or 'Anglo-Catholics', as they like to call themselves) leave no stone unturned increasingly to obscure the actions and intentions of the English Reformers and consign them to oblivion. They employ every conceivable subtlety, and

---

9. [The paragraph numbering, which has gone awry in the original, has been corrected here.]

even – *at least in appearance* – a degree of pious subter-
fuge, to explain the 'Articles' and liturgy in a Catholic
sense. They assert erroneously and without proof that
the changes were not introduced to eradicate Catholic
doctrine, but – God help us – to eliminate the widespread
abuses and superstitions of the age!

Clearly such a denial of the pernicious effects of the
Reformation in England is at variance with the obvious
interpretation of well-known facts and with the documents which come from that sad epoch.[10]

[25] (10) Although the Neo-Anglican party has not
won the adherence of the majority of Anglicans, several
bishops and ecclesiastics give it qualified support, though
with some reservations, and it enjoys a considerable following among the laity. National pride and vanity is
flattered by the idea of a national, ancient, Catholic,
English church independent of the Roman See, easily
outshining the Roman church, and altogether superior
to it in doctrine, wealth and learning: a church pre-eminent among all the Christian churches, just as the British
Empire is pre-eminent among nations.

The Bishop of *Salisbury* expounded this future super-
iority and pre-eminence of the Anglican church with
clarity and vigour before his diocesan synod in May
1895.

This is the reason why the question of the validity of
Anglican orders has been recently revived. The Neo-
Anglican party, with its strenuous advocacy of something resembling the Catholic understanding of eucharistic sacrifice and priesthood, deserves the credit of
making it *possible* for Catholics to discuss the question
with them, whereas it had been impossible to discuss it
with the old Anglicans. For they held that the question
'was not their problem', and their conception of priest-

---

10. [The authors refer to appendices containing quotations from the English
Reformers and analysing the Anglican liturgy.]

hood, holy orders and apostolic succession was far removed from ours.

II. HISTORICAL ACCOUNT

I

Chronological Account of the Events
during the Reformation in England
which bear on the question of Anglican orders

[26] We now proceed to a short, straightforward narration of what happened at the time of the Reformation in England. Our aim is to provide a clear and informed understanding of the perverse tendency and heretical nature of the doctrinal and liturgical changes which are directly relevant to the question of Anglican orders.

I. The first point to note concerning the unhappy secession of England from the Apostolic See is that the *organic, constitutional* separation and rejection of papal authority was above all the work of Henry VIII and his council; the *doctrinal* and *liturgical* separation, i.e. the rejection of Catholic doctrine and liturgy, took place only after Henry's death in 1547, and must be put down to the Anglican church under Edward VI, and in essentials to Archbishop Cranmer and his associates in the deplorable work of the Reformation.

II. In **November 1534** Henry VIII put an end to papal jurisdiction in England, and set himself up as Supreme Head of the English church (cf. *Act of Supremacy*, 26 Henry VIII, c. 1,2,3).

III. Shortly before this declaration Henry VIII had secured the primatial see of Canterbury for **Thomas Cranmer**, a priest who had given full support to the king's lamentable aspiration after papal powers. Cranmer had spent some years in Germany, where he had become infected with the errors of Protestantism, and, though he was already a priest, had secretly married the niece of Osiander, a Lutheran pastor.

[26] IV. Henry VIII retained Catholic doctrine almost in its entirety, save for the supreme authority of the pope; no significant change was made to Catholic worship and liturgy.

Archbishop Cranmer however secretly encouraged **preachers** dedicated to the *Reformation*, and arranged for several zealous *Reformers*, such as **Latimer, Holbeach, Hilsey** and **Shaxton**, to be made bishops in England. As early as 1536 Henry VIII gave his approval to the formulation of the Articles, which cast some doubt on the sacramental nature of Holy Order; for while Baptism, Eucharist and Penance are included among the sacraments of the New Law, in accordance with Reformation theology nothing is said about Order and the other sacraments.[11] Cranmer had advocated this step, as an extant *votum* of his shows. Later, in 1540, he formulated further questions which he put to the bishops, concerning among other subjects the sacrament of Order; again we have his own *votum*, in which he unambiguously and strenuously denies the sacramental nature of Holy Orders. Thus, although no doctrinal or liturgical errors were directly and definitively introduced during the reign of Henry VIII, nonetheless Protestantism had already been propagated and gained a number of supporters among the English clergy and laity.

[28] V. When Henry VIII died in January **1547**, the Duke of *Somerset* acquired supreme political power as the Protector of King Edward VI, who was only nine years old. *Somerset* and his council were zealous **Reformers** and followed the teachings of Zwingli. Thus Cranmer at last gained a free hand to promulgate his heresies and to give effect to his plan of distorting the liturgy – a plan which he had been cherishing secretly for some time.

His aim was:

1. To remove from the Liturgy every trace of Catholic doctrine which was opposed to his heresy;

---

11. In an address to the Synod of 1536, Cranmer said: 'There be weighty controversies ... whether the ceremony of confirmation, of orders, and of annealing, and such other (which cannot be proved to be institute of Christ, nor have any word in them to certify as of remission of sins,) ought to be called sacraments, and to be compared with baptism and the supper of the Lord, or no.' In resolving this question, the Synod followed Cranmer's ideas as closely as the circumstances allowed, and drew up the 'X Articles of Faith', which included only Baptism, Eucharist and Penance among the sacraments. (See Wilkins, Councils, iii. p. 817f; Cranmer's Works (Parker Society), 24.79).

2. To make the Liturgy express the errors of the Reformers;

3. To compose a Liturgy in English.

It is undeniable that the lead in the composition of these rites was taken by Cranmer.

Cranmer's method was to take the Sarum Missal, Breviary and Ritual as his basic source, selecting only what was consistent with the Reformers' teachings, and adding other elements from the German Reformers' liturgical books, especially those of Luther and Bucer. He justified these aberrations on the grounds of acknowledged purity and antiquity, assuming that the *Reformed* doctrine corresponded exactly to that of the primitive Church of the *time of the Apostles*.

[29] VI. In December 1547 a law was passed requiring communion to be distributed to the people under both kinds. In March 1548[12] an 'Order' in English for the distribution of communion was inserted into the Mass.

VII. In the composition and publication of this book the lead and direction was taken by Cranmer, according to the heretical principles which he had set out in his book *On the True Doctrine of the Sacrament*.

VIII. Cranmer's beliefs, which had originally been generally Lutheran (though he retained episcopacy as a more convenient form of church government), now became generally Zwinglian or Calvinistic, as his own writings fully show.[13]

Cranmer took great satisfaction from his regular correspondence with the *Reformed* churches of Frankfurt and Geneva, and welcomed *Reformed* preachers when they came to England. **John de Alasco, Bucer, A. Hales and Bullinger**, all dedicated *Reformers* of the Calvinistic school, became his intimate friends and advisers. Bucer was appointed Regius Professor of Theology at Cambridge University, while Peter Martyr was entrusted with the same office at the University of

---

12. [The authors' date of 1848 must be a misprint.]

13. [Here and in paragraph IX the authors refer to an appendix on Cranmer's theology.]

Oxford. Such zealous Protestants as **Hooper**, **Ridley** and **Ferrar**, all of whom had embraced the *Reformed* doctrine of justification by faith alone, were made bishops.

[30] IX. Cranmer's writings at this time contain a bold defence of several heretical doctrines, as the following five negative propositions clearly show:

> 1. He denies the doctrine of the invocation and intercession of the saints.
> 2. He denies the doctrine of Purgatory and of suffrages for the souls detained there.
> 3. He denies that the Mass is a **propitiatory sacrifice** for the living and the dead, and affirms that the only sacrifice in the Lord's Supper is one of 'prayer and praise' on the part of those who receive Holy Communion, and the communicants' sacrifice of themselves.
> 4. He denies **Christ's real and objective presence** in the Eucharist, i.e. a presence independent of the faith of the communicants, or distinct from the grace of Christ which is poured into the soul.
> 5. He denies that a **priesthood** for the offering of sacrifice was instituted in the New Law, except in the sense that every Christian is a priest.

Thus Cranmer took pains to assert and constantly repeat his teaching that the one and **only sacrifice and offering of the New Law was the unrepeatable one which was accomplished once for all on the cross**. Consequently the Eucharist is essentially a **sacrament** and not a **sacrifice**, indeed a merely **commemorative** sacrament of the one sacrifice of Calvary. The heretic followed the other Reformers in maligning the doctrine held by the whole Church in communion with the Apostolic See concerning the sacrifice of the Mass and priesthood divinely instituted to offer sacrifice, calling this doctrine 'idolatrous', 'blasphemous', and 'detracting from the sacrifice and priesthood of Christ, the one Mediator on the cross'.[14]

---

14. [The authors refer to an Appendix proving these assertions by means of quotations from the works of Cranmer and his associates.]

[31] X. Hence it is no surprise that the new liturgical book of 1549 composed by Cranmer and his associates exemplified all these heresies. Even a cursory reading suffices to make this evident. For:

1. In the first part, which corresponds to the Breviary, and contains a very short office to be recited daily by the clergy, the invocation of saints is totally omitted and every trace of intercession has been removed. In the collects for the feasts of saints which are retained in the Calendar, reference is made to their *example*, but not a word is said about their merits or intercession.

2. Similarly all mention of relief for the souls in Purgatory granted through the suffrages of the faithful has been removed.

3. In the section which replaces the Mass and the liturgy of the Eucharist, all mention of 'victim', 'offering' and 'sacrifice' (except a 'sacrifice of praise' which is totally consistent with the Reformers' heresy) is deliberately and wilfully excluded.

4. Every indication of the real and objective presence, and all rubrics relating to the worship of the Host, such as the elevation, the joining of the fingers and the ablution, etc., were changed or removed.

5. The celebrant was directed to ensure that the people could hear his words and see his actions. This directive corresponds exactly to the Zwinglian heresy, which holds that communion is *ex opere operantis*, not *ex opere operato*, and that grace is conferred and faith aroused by the sight of the representation of the Lord's passion and death. In order to add force to this heretical teaching that the Eucharist is no longer to be regarded as a sacrifice, only those who were intending to receive communion were allowed to remain during the celebration; the rest were dismissed before the beginning of the new canon.[15]

[32] XI. This new liturgy combining the heretical mutila-

---

15. [To support this statement the authors refer to an Appendix containing extracts from the new liturgical books.]

tion of Catholic forms with the expression of *Reformed* doctrine was called '*The First Prayer-Book of Edward VI*'. It is
said that all the English bishops, with the one exception of
Day, the Bishop of Chichester, subscribed to this liturgy,
though one of them, namely Thirlby of Westminster, later
protested publicly in Parliament that the bishops had never
given their assent to the doctrine contained in the book, and
that the book had been corrupted and the word '**oblation**'
removed from it after they had signed their names. Several
bishops also argued strenuously against Cranmer and his
followers in Parliament in defence of the Catholic doctrine
concerning the Eucharist and sacrifice.

XII. Although the Reformers, with the aid of the Protector
and his Council, gradually gained the upper hand, and several
of them acquired the principal episcopal sees, vigorous resis-
tance continued to be offered to the Prayer-Book.
Nevertheless it was approved, and on 15 January 1549 a
law was passed prescribing its exclusive use and the suppression of the Catholic Missal and Breviary throughout the
realm.

The Edwardine Ordinal

[33] XIII. Thereupon Cranmer at once set himself to replace
the Catholic Pontifical with a new Ordinal. Although he
retained the three orders of Bishops, Presbyters and
Deacons, claiming to be following the pattern of the primitive
Church, his own writings show beyond question that he held
and advocated the Reformers' teachings concerning the
merely extrinsic character of ministry – teachings which
were altogether in accordance with his own denial of sacrifice
and a sacrificing priesthood. He cleverly maintained that consecration or ordination should be preserved solely as 'fitting
ceremonies' and were not essential, so that mere institution or
nomination would suffice (see his Response: Stillingfleet MSS
1108, Lambeth). Grace was not conferred in the imparting of
ecclesiastical office any more than in civil. According to him a
'Presbyter' was a minister of word and sacraments in the same
sense as a Lutheran pastor; a 'Bishop' was the chief pastor of

a diocese in the same extrinsic sense as a Lutheran 'Superintendent'. The truth of the foregoing statement is shown by the fact that five parts out of six of the form for the ordination of presbyters correspond almost word for word with the form of ordination composed by the Lutheran Martin Bucer. The chief difference is that Cranmer gives three distinct forms for the three orders of Bishops, Presbyters and Deacons, mentioned expressly in Scripture, while Bucer gives only one; but there is not a single word concerning the character, still less of sacrifice. The Ordinal, like the communion service, was composed through-out in accordance with Cranmer's heretical views; just as every mention of propitiatory sacrifice and the real and objec-tive presence was removed from the communion service, so too every indication of a sacrificing priesthood in the Catholic sense was deliberately and systematically excluded from the Ordinal.[16]

This Ordinal composed by Cranmer and his associates was approved in advance by a law of January 1550, and was published in the March of the same year.

The Second Prayer-Book

[34] XIV. As the influence of Cranmer and his followers increased the request was made that the Prayer-Book should be re-examined in the light of Calvinist teaching and brought completely into line with it. This was done. In the first Prayer-Book, despite the heretical intentions of the authors concern-ing sacrifice, there remained some ten passages which showed a slight resemblance to the liturgy of the Missal, though they were not inconsistent with the denial of sacrifice;[17] these points, however, concerned only the *order of the parts* and of the prayers, not essential doctrine. Even this tenuous resemblance to the old Mass was removed from the second Prayer-Book. One should never forget that this **second**

---

16. [For proof of their statement the authors refer to an appendix comparing the Pontifical with the Ordinal.]

17. [In support of this assertion the authors refer to a note which we have not been able to find in the printed text.]

Prayer-Book, which was thoroughly heretical and Protest-ant in form, was adopted by Queen Elizabeth with a few trivial alterations,[18] and expressly preferred to the earlier book. This second book, with one or two trifling additions, is still in use among Anglicans today.

To make the heretical doctrine of the second Prayer-Book even clearer and reinforce its message, a decree was promulgated, signed by Cranmer and Goodrich with Ridley's approval – all of whom were authors of the book – ordering the **destruction of all altars in churches** and replacing them with common, movable tables.

[35] XV. In 1552 Cranmer and others of the same complexion drew up a profession of faith called the 'Articles of Religion', which were sanctioned by the King and imposed on all ecclesiastics in the realm. These articles state:

'And because (as holy scripture doth teach) Christ was taken up into heaven, and there shall continue unto the end of the world, a faithful man ought not either to believe or openly confess the real and bodily presence (as they term it) of Christ's flesh and blood in the sacrament of the Lord's Supper.'

'The offering of Christ, made once for ever, is the perfect redemption, the pacifying of God's displeasure, and satisfaction for all the sins of the whole world, both original and actual, and there is none other satisfaction for sin but that alone.'

'Wherefore the sacrifices of Masses, in the which it was commonly said, that the priests did offer Christ for the quick and the dead, to have remission of pain or sin, were forged fables, and dangerous deceits.'

These articles were composed in order to destroy the doctrines of the Real Presence in the Catholic sense and of the sacrifice of the Mass. It is not true that the intention was only to exclude a *corporal* and *local* presence or the false and

---

18. The chief modifications are: first, a conflation or combination of the new and the old formulas for the distribution of communion; secondly, the omission of the Black Rubric.

superstitious opinions attributed to Catherinus and others, as some disingenuously claim.[19]

Moreover the Articles approved of the 'Book of Homilies' as containing sound doctrine, and recommended the people to read it carefully. Now these homilies mount a vehement attack on the sacrifice of the Mass and deny the sacramental nature of Holy Orders. The articles, though corrupted by the heresies we have noted above, were adopted by Queen Elizabeth and the members of the Anglican sect, and every Anglican bishop and ecclesiastic continues to subscribe to them up to the present day.

[36] XVI. All these changes were put into effect by Cranmer and the *Reformers*. With the support of the government they took upon themselves supreme authority in England over ecclesiastical affairs. A few, such as Gardiner, Bonner and some other Catholic-minded bishops, who resisted these changes, or rather, perversions, were imprisoned or removed from their sees.

The restoration of religion under Queen Mary

[37] XVII. When Edward VI died in July 1553 the Catholic faith was restored, and through the efforts of Cardinal Pole, the Papal Legate, the English Church was reconciled on 30 November 1554.

Cardinal Pole's most noteworthy achievements during his period as Legate were the following:

1. All heretical bishops were expelled from their dioceses.
2. Those bishops who had been consecrated during the schism according to the rite of the Pontifical, and who repented of their schism, were restored to their sees.
3. **No bishop consecrated according to the form contained in the Ritual of Edward VI was restored**. On the contrary, Taylor, who had been consecrated Bishop of Lincoln according to the Edwardine rite, was expelled from his see *'because of the nullity of his consecration'*.

---

19. [The authors develop this point in an Appendix.]

[38] 4. Pole treated *priests* in a similar way. The great majority of them had been ordained before 1550 according to the rite of the *Pontifical*; once they repented, they were reconciled and restored 'in their orders', as Cardinal Pole explained in setting out the nature of his faculties and their extent. No **single case has yet been found** in which it can be proved that Cardinal Pole or any bishop under his authority recognised the validity or sufficiency of the form of the Ordinal of Edward VI by restoring without reordination any priest ordained according to that form.

5. On the contrary, there are several documents which prove clearly that the bishops who passed judgment on the heretical ministers of the time were careful to ascertain whether they had been ordained after the introduction of the new Ordinal. If the bishops were assured that this was the case, they decided not to submit them to a removal from their grade, because they had not received a valid priesthood from which they could be degraded.[20]

[39] 6. **Cardinal Pole** sent Bishop Thirlby to Rome to obtain guidance from Pope Paul IV with regard to the reconciliation of the Church in England. Thirlby returned with the Bull '*Praeclara Charissimi*' dated 21 June 1555, in which the pope gave Cardinal Pole authority to restore English ecclesiastics who repented, on this important condition:

'... in such a way that if some were promoted to ecclesiastical orders, whether sacred or not sacred, by someone other than a bishop or archbishop **rightly and correctly (*rite et recte*) ordained, they are bound to receive the same orders again,**[21] **nor can they exercise those orders in the interim.**'

Moreover, when clarification was asked about the precise identity of the archbishops or bishops who were 'not

---

20. [The authors refer to an Appendix in which they set out the evidence.]

21. [The Westminster authors have omitted the words: 'from their Ordinary'.]

rightly and correctly ordained', the Apostolic See published an Explanatory Brief in the October of the same year which contained the following definition: 'Bishops and archbishops can be said not to have been rightly and correctly ordained only if they were not ordained and consecrated IN THE FORM OF THE CHURCH. Consequently those who were promoted to orders by them **did not receive the orders in question**, and are **obliged to receive** the orders **over again** from their Ordinary, according to the contents and meaning of our letters.'

[40] 7. On receiving the Bull and the Brief, Cardinal Pole held a synod and [published] his Legatine Constitutions, in which he defined the nature of the sacraments, and declared that the form of Holy Orders was that contained in the Roman Pontifical and, with some trivial differences, in the old English Pontificals.

8. It is therefore clear from the decisions of the Holy See (which had been kept fully informed by the English bishops at Rome) and from the whole method of proceeding of Cardinal Pole (who had indubitably been instructed 'according to the mind of the Pontiff') that orders conferred according to the form of the Anglican Ordinal were to be held *invalid*. It is clear too that this invalidity was judged to be the consequence of the **insufficiency of that form**, long before the spread of the 'Nag's Head fable', which not was published (or rather invented) for another fifty years.

XVIII. **The Restoration of the Reformation under Queen Elizabeth**

[41] When Queen Mary died, she was succeeded in November 1558 by Elizabeth, who from her earliest years had been brought up according to the Reformed doctrine. During her reign the Reformers regained complete power in ecclesiastical matters. Anglican documents prove beyond doubt that, long before a reply could have been received from the Pope by any channel, Elizabeth and her council had worked out a com-

plete programme of legislation for obliterating papal authority and restoring the Reformed religion, and had received the
congratulations of the Protestant rulers on that account.[22]
From this it is clear that **responsibility for the separation
belongs to the Queen, and not to the Pope**, as Anglicans
maintain.

Elizabeth and her Council passed a series of laws abrogat-
ing papal authority in the realm, revoking the laws passed
under Mary, and re-establishing Protestantism. One of these
laws enjoined the use of a slightly modified version of the
second Prayer-Book of Edward VI – i.e. the one most tainted
with Protestantism – in all churches throughout the realm.
Severe penalties were imposed on all who refused to conform
to the Prayer-Book.

[42] XIX. All the diocesan bishops openly and strenuously
resisted these innovations in Parliament. The English presbyters in Convocation publicly professed fidelity towards
the Pope and the Catholic doctrine concerning the
sacrifice of the Mass. Nevertheless the Protestant party,
aided by the Queen, prevailed everywhere. With a single
exception, the bishops were expelled from their sees and
imprisoned. Presbyters who refused to conform were
deprived of their office, and others were appointed in their
place.

XX. Elizabeth's first concern was to appoint to the see of
Canterbury a man who was a convinced and determined
supporter of the Reformers' heresies, and who shared her
own inclinations. She chose her own chaplain **Matthew
Parker**. The English Catholic bishops, however, categorically
refused to consecrate him as bishop. When all else failed, the
Queen imposed this duty on a few schismatical and heretical
bishops who had conformed under Henry VIII or Edward VI,
and who, after being deprived and exiled under Queen Mary,
had now returned eager to assist the restoration of
Protestantism under Elizabeth.

---

22. See the public archives: Calendar of State Papers, Elizabeth, vol. 1, Letter from
the Queen of Denmark. Device for alteration of religion, Brit. Mus., Cotton MS,
Julius, F. 6.

[43] XXI. They were: (1) **William Barlow**, a religious who, after leaving his order in 1536, had been named to the sees of St Asaph and St David's (Menevia), and had later been translated to the diocese of Bath and Wells. He was a dedicated Reformer and a strenuous advocate of Protestant doctrine; (2) **Miles Coverdale** and (3) **John Scory**, both zealous Protestants, who had been imposed on the sees of *Exeter* and *Chichester* under Edward VI; (4) **John Hodgkins**, the suffragan Bishop of Bedford, who after being consecrated under Henry VIII had adopted the teachings of the Reformers under Edward VI. It should be observed that, of the four above named who performed Parker's consecration, John Hodgkins is the only one who was certainly ordained bishop according to the Catholic rite. Scory and Coverdale were consecrated under Edward VI, not according to the Catholic rite but the newly fabricated Anglican Ordinal. As to Barlow's consecration, we shall show later that no record of it has ever been found, and that for several reasons it is highly questionable.

XXII. According to the Lambeth Register – and we have no reason to doubt the substantial accuracy of its account of the facts – **Matthew Parker** was consecrated by the four men named above in Lambeth Palace on 17 December 1559 according to the form of the **Ritual of Edward VI**. The bishops laid their hands on him, saying in English: '**Receive the Holy Ghost, and remember that thou stir up the grace of God which is given thee by this imposition of our hands; for God hath not given us the Spirit of fear, but of power and love and soberness.**'

[44] XXIII. The origin of all Anglican orders can be traced back to **Matthew Parker**, whose ordination we have described. For the arguments put forward to prove that not all Anglican orders have come down from that one source depend upon the premise that other validly consecrated bishops, such as **de Dominis**, took part in Anglican consecrations as *assistants*. However, even if (for the sake of argument) assistant bishops are co-consecrators according to the Roman rite, this could not be maintained of the Anglican rite,

in which the Archbishop or principal consecrator alone says 'Receive etc'; the assistants do not pronounce this form as ministers or in any other way, nor do they speak any prayer similar to the prayer 'Almighty God', or any eucharistic Preface, as assistants do in the Roman rite.

[45] XXIV. **William Barlow's** own consecration is historically very doubtful. The doubt is well founded, and depends on two factors above all.

(1) Barlow[23] himself, his Metropolitan Cranmer, and Cromwell, who was the King's Vicegerent in all ecclesiastical affairs, openly and publicly declared that Orders are not a sacrament, that episcopal consecration is not necessary, and that mere nomination or installation is sufficient. Consequently, when men of great influence in Church and state did not believe in the necessity of consecration, no weight can be allowed to the argument that since Barlow lived and acted like a bishop he must necessarily have been consecrated. To be sure, such a presumption would have force in Catholic regions where those with authority in Church and state believe in the necessity of consecration and certainly insist on it; but the presumption is groundless in a region where such authorities openly and notoriously reject any such belief.

[46] (2)[24] Despite the most thorough research, no reference in writing to Barlow's consecration has ever been found in the registers, public records or other documents. It should be observed that there is no truth in the argument that, if we deny Parker's[25] consecration on the grounds that no record of it can be found in *Cranmer's Register*, the same is true of several other consecrations. This line of argument is false. The reason why we deny, or have serious doubts about,

---

23. In a public sermon Barlow denied the necessity of episcopal consecration and asserted that it was sufficient to be nominated by the King. He stated this in 1536, the very year in which the King promoted him to the see of St Asaph.

24. [We have corrected the numbering of the paragraphs again.]

25. [There must have occurred two slips of the pen here. Para. XXII concedes the existence of a written record of Parker's consecration; it is *Barlow's* consecration which the authors are contesting.]

Parker's consecration is that, while according to regular procedure a record or mention of this consecration *should be found in four other sources* besides Cranmer's Register, none of these contains any trace of it. Consequently Barlow's case is absolutely *unique, since he is the only diocesan bishop of the sixteenth century for whose consecration no record of any form can be traced anywhere.*[26]

According to the common procedure for the appointment of bishops in England at that time, in each case no less than **fourteen** public instruments had to be drawn up and preserved in the public Archives. Of these fourteen documents **nine concerned nomination and five consecration**.

The nine documents relating to Barlow's nomination *are extant*; *the five relating to his* **consecration** *are nowhere to be found.*

For these reasons, taking account also of the declaration made by Barlow himself, his Metropolitan Cranmer, and Cromwell, the King's Vicar General, that *consecration was superfluous and nomination alone was sufficient*, we are justified in concluding that there are solid reasons for doubting Barlow's consecration. This doubt precludes the moral certainty which Catholics require concerning the episcopal character of the one from whom the succession of orders is said to be derived.[27]

---

26. Of the hundreds of bishops of the period there are only four of whose consecrations no records are to be found anywhere, namely *Barlow, Goldwell, Pates and King*. *Goldwell* and *Pates* were appointed under Queen Mary, and were probably consecrated in Italy before returning to England; consequently the record of their consecration probably awaits discovery in Rome or in some other Italian city. King was not a diocesan bishop but a suffragan with the title Rheonensis *in partibus*; the record of his citing can be read in the Consistorial Acts of 7 January 1527. The mention of his episcopal dignity at a time when Catholicism was still in force is sufficient proof of his consecration, since an unconsecrated suffragan bishop *in partibus* is a contradiction in terms. Thus Barlow's case is singular and absolutely *unique*.

27. [The authors refer to an Appendix countering arguments which had been put forward in favour of Barlow's consecration.]

CONCLUSIONS

[47] XXV. The foregoing account of the history of the *Reformation* in England points consistently to the following conclusions.

A. The complete overthrow of the Catholic religion in England was carried through to its sad conclusion on the initiative and under the direction of Cranmer, Ridley, Goodrich and the whole coterie of English Reformers, who maintained continual friendly contacts with their continental counterparts, and constantly received from them advice and help.

B. These *Reformers* strenuously denied (a) **the Real and Objective Presence**; (b) **the propitiatory sacrifice of the Mass**; and (c) the sacrificing **priesthood**; while they taught just as persistently that the Presence is *through faith* or grace, that the Eucharist is the *mere commemoration* of the sacrifice Christ offered and accomplished once for all, and that priesthood is an *extrinsic ministry* by which the laity are represented, and which is conferred or taken away essentially by nomination, or *ceremonially* by the rites of ordination.

[48] C. These heretical denials provided the *motive* for the radical changes made in the liturgy. The 'Prayer-Book', the Ritual (called the 'Ordinal') of Edward VI, the 'Articles' and the 'Homilies' were composed with the **express intention** of propagating these heresies. In every part of these works it is impossible to conceive any other way in which this motive could have been made more plain.

D. These denials and heresies, which essentially pervert and destroy the notion of priesthood and of sacrifice, which is its function, formally constitute the '**Intention of the Rite**' contained in the Ritual or Ordinal of Edward VI, i.e. they constitute what the Ordinal was designed to express. In the theological section of this essay we have spoken of the rite as *formally* considered when we view it in the light of its formal motive, according to the demands of common sense and unquestionable theological principles.

[49] E. When one has regard to this essential character of

the Anglican rite as it can be clearly inferred from its history, its formal motive and its origin, no importance whatever should be attached to any slight and remote analogy it may have with the ancient Greek and Oriental rites, whose *formal* motive and structure is clearly in accordance with orthodox doctrine. If any lack of clarity or precision can be detected in these rites, it should generally be put down to their antiquity or to incomplete liturgical development. By contrast, the lack of precision in the modern Anglican rite (i.e. that of 1552) is undoubtedly due to **the heretical and systematic denial of priesthood and sacrifice**, and to the proclaimed intention of mutilating the existing Catholic rites and obliterating their Catholic development.

F. The serious doubt which exists concerning Barlow's consecration totally removes all possibility of moral certainty which is required concerning his episcopal character; consequently the validity of the Anglican succession which is derived from him is subject to the same grave doubts. Moreover, if one remembers the *silent* and secondary part assigned to the assistant bishops in the Anglican rite, there can be no moral certainty that any defect in the principal consecrator could have been set right by Hodgkins or by the other assistant bishops consecrated after him.

THEOLOGICAL PART

[50] Anglican so-called orders should be regarded as totally invalid, because they were not conferred 'in the form of the Church', i.e. because the ordination rite composed under Edward VI in 1552 is totally insufficient, since Cranmer and his followers deliberately introduced changes which affected and destroyed the essence of the form.

Now it was according to this rite that Parker received his episcopal consecration; and from him, as pseudo-Archbishop of Canterbury, all these Anglican so-called orders derive their origin.

Two considerations reveal the insufficiency of the rite of

1552: (1) if the 'form' it contains is considered in itself objectively or *materially*, especially when it is compared with the various ordination rites which have been used with the Church's approval at different times and in different places; and (2) if it is considered *formally* with attention to the heretical beliefs which the authors of the rite held concerning Holy Orders – beliefs which are plainly manifested by the mutilation of the form of the Church.

I
THE OBJECTIVE OR MATERIAL INSUFFICIENCY OF THE RITUAL OF EDWARD VI

[51] The rite is in itself, or materially, insufficient, or, in other words, it differs substantially from the 'form of the Church'.

Attention to the following principles will help to make this plain:

1. A sacrament is a visible sign of invisible grace instituted by Christ our Lord.

2. All the sacraments were instituted by Christ, as is evident from the Council of Trent, Session 7 Canon 1: 'If anyone says that the sacraments of the New Law were not all instituted by our Lord Jesus Christ ... let him be anathema.'

3. Christ's institution of all these sacraments was direct and immediate.

4. Christ instituted the essentials of the sacraments, i.e. their matter and form, so that the Church has no authority to change their substance. This is again evident from the Council of Trent, Session 21, Chapter 2: 'Moreover (the holy Synod) declares that the Church has been endowed perpetually with the power to make any changes and arrangements in dispensing the sacraments which it judges will serve the needs of the recipients or promote devotion to the sacraments, as different times and places require, without however altering their substance.'

[52] 5. Christ certainly determined the individual 'form' of Baptism, and most probably that of the holy Eucharist. For the rest of the sacraments he determined the form at least

generically (*in specie*), leaving to the Apostles or the Church the *individual* determination.[28]

6. With regard to the sacrament of Order, Christ determined that it was not enough for *any* external signs and words to be used, but only those which express the effect and nature of the sacrament. For the Council of Trent (Session 23, Chapter 3) again makes it clear that ordination is performed by means of *words* and *external signs*. Moreover the essential words which unambiguously determine the meaning of the external signs, must be capable of signifying the sacrament of Order, differentiating it from any other sacraments, and expressing the distinction between Diaconate, Presbyterate and Episcopate.

If however the words are not capable of signifying the order conferred and differentiating it from the other orders, they are totally insufficient, and a form which consists of such words cannot be called 'the Form of the Church'.

The Rites of Ordination in the East and the West
used from the earliest times with the Church's approval
[53] On the basis of these principles careful examination of the ordination rites used from the earliest times in the West and the East with the approval of the Church will readily show that all these rites express the order conferred and differentiate it clearly from other orders. In both East and West, despite an evident diversity of *type* with regard to the arrangement and development of the sign and the words, and despite several discrepancies arising from inessential additions and omissions, we find the same external sign of the imposition of hands in constant use (cf the Council of Trent, Session 14, Chapter 3), and the same meaning expressed by the words which determine the external sign. Accordingly a remarkable

---

28. It makes no difference to the validity of the foregoing argument whether one holds that Christ assigned the matter and form of Order *generically* (*generica*) or determined it *individually* (*in individuo*), though we retain the statement adopted above in the text, which we think most probable. Moreover, as far as the strength of the argument is concerned, it is a matter of indifference if Christ's *immediate* institution of all the sacraments, which we hold to be certain, is questioned by anyone.

identity and substantial agreement is evident between the Eastern and the Western ordination rites approved by the Church throughout the ages. Consequently every discerning reader will agree with the learned scholar Muratori's conclusion that 'The variety and differences between the Eastern and Western Churches, and also among the Western Churches themselves, consists entirely in the variety of prayers, in the diversity of the words and in optional ceremonies. The Latins and the Greeks used different rites in administering the sacraments ... without affecting the substance of these sacraments' (De Origine S. Liturgiæ, c.11).

The Oriental Rites
[54] The oriental ordination rites can be found in Morin, *De Sacris Ordinationibus*; Denzinger, *Ritus Orientalium*; Goar, *Rituale Graecum*; Assemani, *Codex Liturgicus*, and *Bibliotheca Orientalis*, vol. 4, 'Dissertation on the Syrian Nestorians', p. dcccxviii, where he supplies the 'form' omitted by Morin; Estcourt, App. XXXIII.

The Western Rites
See the Gelasian Sacramentary (PL LXXIV); Gallican Liturgy (PL LXXII); the *Liber Sacramentorum* of St Gregory the Great (PL LXXVIII); the Pontifical of St Egbert of York (in Martène, *de Antiquis Ecclesiae Ritibus*, bk.1, p.2, n.340); Duchesne, *Origines du Culte Chrétien*, p. 346.

The Ancient Form in Book VIII
of the So-called Apostolic Constitutions
Book VIII, in which the form is found, is thought to be St Hippolytus' work 'the Teaching of the Apostles on Charisms', with later interpolations. There exist however two MSS of the Greek text, one in Oxford, the other in Vienna, which contain a purer text; in them we find a shorter 'form' of episcopal consecration, which is still sufficient, and even ample.[29] See

---

29. [The 'purer and shorter text' is now recognised to be a separate work, known as

Bunsen's comment (Hippolytus and his Age, vol.ii, pp. 412ff); he gives the purer and shorter text of the 'form' in Analecta Ante-Nicæna, London, 1854, vol.ii, p.378.

The Ritual composed under King Edward VI

[55] Let us turn now to the examination of the Ritual composed in 1552 by Cranmer and the other Reformers.

If these implacable enemies of Catholicism, who openly professed heretical opinions concerning the sacraments, including Holy Orders, had followed one of the *Pontificals* in use in England, the material sufficiency of such a rite would have been beyond question. But they rejected all the Pontificals in use among Catholics up to their time, and composed a totally new Ritual, which, as the reader can see, omitted the handing over of the chalice and paten with the accompanying words, and adopted words for the essential form of presbyteral and episcopal ordination which do not signify Holy Order, and fail to distinguish between Diaconate, Presbyterate and Episcopate. Although the Preface to the Ritual speaks of Deacons, Presbyters and Bishops as orders of ministry existing in Christ's Church since the time of the apostles, a profound silence is maintained about the nature and origin of these orders, so that the Preface is not incompatible with the errors of the Sacramentaries. We have shown above that this is what the authors of the Ritual manifestly intended. This is the sense too in which the Presentation, the Exhortation to the people, and the prayer following the Litany refer to Deacons, Presbyters and Bishops. Moreover according to the rubrics – to which modern Anglicans of the Ritualist party attach such great importance – at the ordination of a Presbyter (for the time being we say nothing about ordination to the Diaconate, not because we concede its validity, but because it is not relevant to the present discussion, and for the sake of brevity) after the prayer which in the Catholic rite follows the

the 'Epitome of the Apostolic Constitutions', or the 'Constitutions through Hippolytus'. Hippolytus' work which the authors call 'The Teaching of the Apostles on Charisms' is generally known today as the 'Apostolic Tradition'.]

imposition of hands, but which has been mutilated and evis-
cerated by these heretics and deprived of every indication of
the order of Presbyter, the Bishop and each of the Priests
present (according to the rubrics) lay hands on the head of
each person who *is receiving* (note the present tense) the
orders, while the recipients kneel humbly and the Bishop
says: 'Receive the Holy Ghost. Whose sins thou dost forgive,
they are forgiven; and whose sins thou dost retain, they are
retained. And be thou a faithful dispenser of the Word of God
and of his holy sacraments. In the name of the Father, etc.'

Finally he places a Bible in the hands of each of the candidates saying: 'Take thou authority to preach the word of God
and to minister the holy sacraments.'

[56] Now the first part of the words accompanying the
imposition of hands cannot constitute the essential form,
because they are not found in any of the ancient Western
or Eastern rites; their introduction into the Western
Pontificals is of very recent date, as is proved in Morin, *de
S. Ordine*, Part III, Ex. VII, c.11, n.2; Martène, II. 327;
Chardon, *Histoire des Sacraments*, Part II, ch.1; and in
many other works. For the time being we shall say nothing
about the *meaning* of these words according to the authors of
the Ritual. The following words, 'And be thou a faithful
dispenser, etc', were coined by these heretics; they neither
signify the priestly sacrament of Order, nor distinguish it
from Diaconate (for a Deacon also can preach the word of
God and dispense the sacraments) or from the Episcopate.
The same is true of the words accompanying the handing over
of the *Bible*. Therefore the 'form' which consists of the foregoing words is totally insufficient, and therefore is not 'the
form of the Church'.

Our statement that according to the Anglicans these words
serve as the form, and do not clearly differentiate between
Presbyterate and Episcopate, is confirmed by the following
fact: in 1662, wishing to show the difference between the two,
they inserted at this point the words: 'for the office and work
of a Priest'; thus they changed the form to: 'Receive the Holy
Ghost for the office and work of a Priest, etc.' They made a

corresponding change in the form for the consecration of a Bishop.

[57] The form of Episcopal consecration. In the form for the consecration of a Bishop we find the same defect. After the assistant Bishops have presented the godly and well-learned *man* to be consecrated as Bishop, prayers are recited in which there is no mention or suggestion of High Priesthood, except in the prayer after the Litanies in which the candidate is said to be called to the work and ministry of a Bishop. There follows the imposition of hands, where the rubric reads: 'Then the Archbishop and Bishops present shall lay their hands upon the head of the *elected* Bishop ..., the Archbishop saying: "Receive the Holy Ghost, and remember that thou stir up the grace of God which is given thee by this imposition of our hands; for God hath not given us the spirit of fear, but of power and love and soberness."'

The words 'Receive the Holy Ghost' are again of recent origin. The words which follow are taken from St Paul (2 Timothy 1.6–7), they had never been used anywhere previously, and make no distinction between Episcopate and Presbyterate. It is absurd to use them as a form to confer grace, because they imply, as they do in St Paul, that the grace of Order has already been conferred.

Therefore it is evident that the Ritual of Edward VI is an unprecedented, defective and distorted innovation, containing forms for Ordination substantially different from 'the form of the Church'. Accordingly the Holy See was right to reject it. For these reasons Orders conferred according to these forms must be judged to be not merely suspect and doubtful but absolutely null and invalid.

II
THE INSUFFICIENCY OF THE RITUAL OF EDWARD VI WHEN IT IS CONSIDERED FORMALLY

[58] Now that we have demonstrated the insufficiency of the forms for presbyteral and episcopal ordination contained in

the Ritual of Edward VI, when they are considered *materially* and compared with the forms used in the West and the East from earliest times, we must now proceed to examine the meaning which the authors of the time publicly attributed to the words of the forms. Such an examination shows beyond question that these forms are *formally* insufficient and inadequate. For if a heretical meaning concerning the sacraments, and concerning the nature and efficacy of holy orders in particular, can be deliberately read into words which are sufficient in themselves or *materially* and deprive them of all their force and validity, how much more so in the present case, when the *material* sufficiency of the words is not so much doubtful as altogether destroyed? For without any of the uncertainty of debate it can be shown that these words were given a meaning which is incompatible with the ability to designate a sacrifice.

[59] 1. First of all, Cranmer, the chief author of the Ritual, having embraced the errors of Zwinglianism, made every effort to remove from Holy Orders all references to sacramental character and grace; this is evident from his published writings. It is true he retained the titles of deacon, presbyter and bishop, but not in the Catholic sense; for he constantly denied that these orders are sacraments, unambiguously maintaining that they should be numbered among the various *states* of life which have none of the power or reality of a sacrament of the gospel. This doctrine can be found as clear as daylight in one of the XXXIX Articles which were composed about the same time. For Article XXV runs: 'There are two sacraments ordained of Christ our Lord in the Gospel, that is to say, Baptism, and the Supper of the Lord. Those five commonly called sacraments, that is to say, Confirmation, Penance, *Orders*, Matrimony and extreme Unction, are not to be counted for sacraments of the Gospel, being such as have grown partly from the corrupt following of the Apostles, partly are states of life allowed in the scriptures; but yet have not like nature of sacraments with Baptism and the Lord's Supper.' Again, Article X of Cranmer's XIII Articles runs thus: 'Concerning the ministers of the Church we teach that

no one ought to teach in public or minister the sacraments unless he is duly called by those in the Church who possess the right to call and admit according to the word of God and the laws and customs of each region.' Not one word is to be found in this article concerning the necessity of sacred ordination. Hence the mention of Deacons, Presbyters and Bishops in the Preface of the Ritual, and of each of the three orders in some of the prayers preceding the imposition of hands and during the presentation before the imposition, is not to be taken as a *formally* sufficient indication of intention, i.e. the intention of conferring orders in the Catholic sense or according to the will of Christ.

[60] 2. The heretical beliefs on this subject held by Bucer and Cranmer's other followers, who shared in the composition of the Ritual, are no less well known.[30]

3. They rejected the awe-inspiring and most holy sacrifice of the Mass, as we read in Article XXX: 'Wherefore the sacrifices of Masses, in the which it was commonly said that the priest did offer Christ for the quick and the dead, to have remission of pain or guilt, were blasphemous fables and dangerous deceits.'[31] The Council of Trent, on the contrary, teaches that sacrifice and priesthood are so joined together by divine ordinance that they exist together throughout the law. Since 'in the new covenant the Catholic Church has received by the Lord's institution the visible sacrifice of the holy Eucharist', the Council concludes that there is in the Church a new, visible and external priesthood (Session XXIII, Chap. 1). It clearly follows that the rejection of visible and external sacrifice entails equally the rejection of a visible and external priesthood. This makes it clear why the authors omitted from the ordination rite not only the handing over of instruments, but also every specific indication of priestly power.[32]

---

30. [The authors refer to their Historical Part, and to an Appendix collecting passages from the English Reformers.]

31. [The authors actually quote the Article in its 1563 form, in which it forms Article XXXI of the Thirty-Nine.]

32. [The authors refer to an Appendix setting out the Catholic and Anglican ordination rites in parallel columns.]

[61] 4. It would not be right to say that the words: 'Whose sins thou dost forgive, they are forgiven, etc', which occur in the form for presbyteral ordination, signify the specific power of a priest. For the authors and their followers rejected the power of the keys and the sacrament of penance with contempt, and understood by these words solely a sort of shadowy remission of sins by the preaching of the word of God.

5. Moreover, the heretical opinions according to which this defective and inadequate Ritual was composed were not concealed but made public, not cloaked in silence but proclaimed from the housetops; they were openly taught not only by the authors of the Ritual but also by those who used it at Parker's consecration. Consequently no comparison can be drawn between ordinations performed by these people and those performed according to the form of the Church by a Bishop whose heresy or lack of faith remained secret.

6. These observations are confirmed from the middle of the sixteenth century by Anglican doctrine and practice, which betrays itself in all sorts of ways throughout the Anglican system, as we have made clear in the Historical Part.

[62] 7. There has recently arisen in Anglican circles a new movement called '*Ritualist*' or '*Anglo-Catholic*'. The Ritualists, having borrowed a number of doctrines, ceremonies and other observances from the Catholic Church, have deceived themselves into thinking that they can as a consequence gradually get Anglicanism acknowledged as an integral part of the Catholic Church; accordingly they leave no stone unturned to obtain at least some degree of recognition from the Apostolic See. For this end some of their number make enormous and unwearying efforts and put together most subtle arguments to prove that their orders are genuine and valid; they employ every kind of wile to conceal the undoubted facts concerning the origin of the Anglican heresy, as if Holy Orders which were originally invalid could become valid with the passage of time. But these arguments deceive nobody. As we have proved, there is no reason for doubting that these orders are invalid, nor can there be shown to be any

well-founded doubt that they are totally and absolutely invalid because of the *material* and *formal* insufficiency of the Ritual of Edward VI, i.e. because they were not conferred 'in the form of the Church'.

8. It is precisely for this reason that the forms contained in the Edwardine Ritual cannot be given any Catholic sense, for, as the Historical Part made clear, this sense was deliberately and publicly excluded by those who composed the Ritual and those who used it. The conclusion is inescapable that Parker's Consecrator or Consecrators did not employ a form which was valid when considered either *materially* or (more importantly) *formally*, nor did they have the intention of doing what the Church does. For they openly and violently denied not only some of the *effects* of Holy Orders, but even the sacramental nature of Orders and their institution in any sense by Christ, teaching that Orders are *only an external* call and admission; finally, they positively intended to exclude Orders in the sense of the Church, and manifested their intention beyond doubt.

[63] 9. Consequently we hold the conclusion which the Apostolic See has ratified and pronounced on many occasions to be sound and certain: namely that *the Orders* (Episcopate, Presbyterate and Diaconate) *of the Anglican sect are to be regarded as certainly void and invalid on account of the defect of the form employed by these heretics and the defect of the intention of doing what the Church does.* This conclusion is based upon historical facts which have been conclusively proved and upon theological principles (not *opinions*) which have been irrefutably established. (See the 'Prologue'.)

[*There follow three Scholia. The first shows that the force of the foregoing argument does not depend on the fact that the rite contains no Handing Over of the Instruments. The third rebuts the argument that the sufficiency of the Anglican form 'Receive the Holy Ghost' follows from an alleged 1704 decree of the Holy Office approving of the same formula as used by the Ethiopians. The most important scholion is the second, which we give in full – Edd.*]

SCHOLION II
The rite is not determined by its adjuncts.

[64] As we showed in our theological argument against the sufficiency of the forms used in conferring Anglican Orders, they make no mention of the Order to be conferred, and no distinction between the various Orders is expressed in the forms themselves. Those who maintain the validity of these Orders counter this reasoning by arguing that the individual Orders are sufficiently determined by the fact that three distinct Orders are clearly indicated in the *Preface* of the *Ritual* or *Ordinal*, and that they are mentioned individually in some of the preceding prayers, in the Presentation and in the Rubrics. In addition, they argue, allowance must be made for the *intention* of the ordaining minister which is sufficiently manifested by these adjuncts. Finally they cite as an example the sacrament of matrimony, in which the words or signs are determined *by the adjuncts* so as to express consent to the marriage contract. The purpose of this second Scholion is to refute these arguments.

[65] 1. To begin with, we deny any parity between the sacraments of Order and Marriage; for the sacrament of Order *in its whole essence* is a matter of divine *positive* law (whether Christ instituted it immediately or mediately is of little relevance to this question), while the sacrament of Matrimony is a contract *already existing in the natural order* which Christ raised to the nature and dignity of a sacrament and endowed with certain characteristics. This is why the Church with regard to Matrimony has the right to determine the diriment impediments which directly affect the marriage contract. Again, this is why any signs, provided they are a clear enough expression of consent to the marriage contract, constitute a perfectly valid form, and why the Church has never insisted that the marriage contract is to be expressed *verbally*, as the Council of Trent did for Ordination. The Church accepts whatever external sign of consent is commonly held sufficient in society. Moreover (whatever a few writers may say), the Church has never claimed the right to determine impediments which invalidate the *conferring of*

Order as it is justified in doing for the sacrament of Matrimony.

[66] 2. As to the fundamental objection, i.e. that the forms in the Ritual or *Ordinal* of Edward VI are sufficiently determined *by the adjuncts*, we deny this totally. On the contrary, as we proved in the Historical Part, the adjuncts manifestly prove that the Rite was composed **expressly** in order totally to exclude Orders as understood by the Church and instituted by Christ. Therefore even if, *for the sake of argument*, it were true with regard to Order that a form which is indeterminate in itself can be made sufficient by the adjuncts, this would be of no help to the Anglicans' case, as they cannot escape the fact that, despite some trivial verbal resemblances (which could hardly be avoided), no reasonable doubt exists that those who composed and those who employed the Rite intended altogether to exclude Holy Orders in the Catholic sense.

[67] 3. Finally, just as the Anglicans specifically changed the forms for Episcopate and Presbyterate in 1662, as we have explained above, in the same way they added a certain specific determination to the Preface. Thus, there being no mention of ordination or consecration in the Preface to the 1552 Ritual or Ordinal, in 1662 they inserted the words: 'or hath had formerly Episcopal Consecration, or Ordination'. From this we are justified in concluding that in 1662 the Anglicans themselves did not consider that the 1552 Preface expressed a sufficient determination of the Rite.

Hence it indisputable that an appeal to the adjuncts in the case, so far from providing any basis for the argument put forward by some Anglicans, actually completely destroys it.

LETTER OF FR T. B. SCANNELL TO *THE TABLET*

PAUL IV. AND ANGLICAN ORDERS[1]

SIR,—The important document published in *St Luke's Magazine*, and reproduced by you last week, does not seem to me decisive against Anglican Orders. The Pope directs that all those promoted to Orders by any one other than a duly (*rite et recte*) ordained Bishop must be re-ordained; and, further, he declares that they are not duly ordained Bishops who have not been ordained *in forma Ecclesiæ*. The whole question turns on the meaning of this latter phrase. To make it equivalent to 'the old rite used in England' would be proving too much; for no one can deny the validity of other forms of ordination. What it would appear to mean is this: Just as the minister must have the internal intention *faciendi quod facit Ecclesia*, so the external rite must be one which the Church would recognize as sufficient. Whether in point of fact the new rite was, or was not, sufficient is not decided by the Pontiff. If he had distinguished between the old rite and the new rite, and had declared the former alone to be valid, the question would have been settled. But, with true Roman caution, he distinguishes between ordination *in forma Ecclesiæ* and ordination not *in forma Ecclesiæ*, and declares the former alone to be valid.

Your obedient servant,

T. B. SCANNELL

Sheerness, August 17 [1895]

---

1. [This was one of several letters which Scannell wrote as part of a running debate in *The Tablet* concerning Anglican orders.]

CONCERNING THE EPISCOPAL CONSECRATION AND THE SACRED ORDINATIONS AMONG THE ANGLICANS: WHETHER THEY ARE TO BE CONSIDERED AS VALID, AS DOUBTFULLY VALID, OR AS ABSOLUTELY INVALID.

Report and Votum of
Raffaele Pierotti, OP,

Master of the Sacred Apostolic Palace and Consultor of the Holy Office.

[1]. The question concerning the validity or invalidity of the episcopal consecrations and the sacred orders conferred by Anglicans and with the Anglican rite, seemed definitively settled in virtue of the various acts or decisions issued in their regard by the Holy See, either immediately by the Supreme Pontiffs, or through the Supreme Congregation of the Holy Office. Moreover, the unvaried and constant practice, observed up to our own day, of considering as simple lay persons those ordained with the Anglican rite, in the case of their conversion to Catholicism, and of ordaining absolutely and without condition, those Anglican ministers who, having embraced the Catholic faith, requested and were judged worthy of being promoted to the sacred Orders, seemed to demonstrate clearly, and I will say, superabundantly, the absolute invalidity of Anglican ordinations. However, the fact is that not only Protestant authors, especially those belonging to the sect of the so-called *Ritualists* or *Anglo-Catholics*, but even Catholic writers, have in our days raised

doubts, and have begun again to raise the question, holding that it is still undecided, and claiming that it can still be freely discussed, because, they say, previous decisions, even confirmed by constant practice, do not constitute a peremptory decision of the question. These Catholic writers are generally of the opinion that a more accurate study, supported by the new light that has come from the undeniable progress made in historical studies and from the publication of hitherto unedited or unknown documents, leads to the conclusion that if Anglican ordinations should not be considered absolutely valid, as some few maintain, they should be considered, with good reason, as at least doubtfully valid, and hence to be repeated conditionally. The question has been discussed by Catholic writers with more passion in recent times, and is discussed even now, with the result that they seem divided into two camps, on one side the upholders of invalidity, on the other side the few defenders of absolute validity, and the more numerous defenders of doubtful validity. It is useful however, to note that the latter are foreign to England, where all Catholic authors, including the recent ones, hold Anglican ordinations to be absolutely invalid. All, moreover, expect and many expressly request a definitive decision of the Holy See.

2. In this state of affairs, which has given rise to much perplexity and to heated arguments which have not always been edifying, since not kept within proper limits, the reigning Supreme Pontiff, in his fatherly solicitude and enlightened wisdom has judged it expedient to form a special Commission, made up of erudite and learned theologians, entrusting the presidency to the no less erudite and expert Cardinal Mazzella. The Commission thus formed and constituted since 24 March of the current year, under the enlightened direction of its Most Eminent President, diligently undertook the examination of the question, and considering it in all its parts and under every aspect, held no less than twelve sessions, thus accomplishing the task assigned to it. I will say right away that from the studies prepared and presented by the members of the Commission, and even more from the

very accurate minutes of the twelve sessions, drawn up by the Secretary and approved by the entire Commission, a providential fact has become evident: namely, that in the discussion of the question the two opposed opinions have been represented and sustained with learning and an abundance of argumentation, and the upholders of the absolute invalidity of Anglican ordinations and the defenders of validity, or at least doubtful validity, have been facing each other in exactly equal numbers. The Commission led by the Most Eminent Cardinal Camillo Mazzella was composed of the following persons: (1) Canon James Moyes; (2) Dom Aidan Gasquet, Benedictine; (3) Revd Fr David Fleming, Franciscan; (4) Revd Fr Giuseppe Calasanzio da Llevaneras, Capuchin and Consultor of the Holy Office. During the sessions these four constantly upheld the absolute invalidity of Anglican ordinations. (5) Monsignor Pietro Gasparri; (6) Revd Louis Duchesne. These two held for doubtful validity. (7) Revd Fr Emilio De Augustinis, SJ; (8) Revd Thomas Scannell. In the course of the discussion these two held for validity, but then at the end they too expressed their opinion in favour of doubtful validity. The Most Reverend Monsignor Merry del Val was Secretary.

3. Even before the Commission had finished its work, the Holy Father had decided to submit everything to the Supreme Congregation of the Holy Office, in order to have its authoritative opinion, before arriving at a definitive decision. Reflecting, however, that it would have been excessively burdensome for the Most Eminent General Inquisitors to undertake a detailed study, and to become familiar not only with what has been done and decided in regard to the question in the past, but also with everything that has been set forth recently, both in the written studies presented by the members of the Commission, and in the oral discussions, His Holiness was pleased to assign to the undersigned the task of examining attentively both the earlier and the present state of the question, and to prepare an accurate *votum* to be presented to the wise and enlightened discernment of the Most Eminent Fathers.

However conscious that the task assigned to me is far beyond my weak abilities and my very limited knowledge, I certainly cannot exempt myself from carrying out the order of the Holy Father, and I shall do my best to sum up the results as briefly and clearly as I can, expressing also my own feeble and humble opinion. In composing the present report and opinion, I think it opportune to follow the same order as the Commission, which first carefully examined not only the acts of the Holy Office but also the other documents concerning Anglican ordinations which are prior to the examination of the question that was undertaken by the Supreme Congregation in 1685, and was brought to a practical and decisive conclusion in 1704, in the Pontificate of Clement XI.

I. PAPAL DOCUMENTS AND HISTORICAL FACTS PRIOR TO 1685

4. Before entering on the matter in hand, it will be well to note that although Anglican Protestantism is said to have had its origin in the schism proclaimed by Henry VIII, beginning in 1534, it is nevertheless historically certain that at the time of that unfortunate monarch the public defection was limited to schism, when he attributed to himself that supremacy in the Catholic Church which belongs to the Roman Pontiff. However, it is also certain that Henry VIII was very soon personally imbued with the doctrines of Protestantism, and that the heresy spread in the kingdom with his connivance. Hence, the present question does not concern the ordinations of bishops or other sacred ministers which took place during the reign of Henry, who died on 28 January 1547, since those ordinations, although by schismatic and even heretical bishops, are undoubtedly valid, since they were done with the form and rite of the Catholic Church. Henry was succeeded by his son Edward VI who reigned, or, to put it more accurately, held the title of monarch, until 6 July 1553, the day of his death. Under this monarch who succeeded to the throne at the age of eight or nine years, through

the wickedness of his uncle the Earl of Hertford,[1] the heretical Protector of the king and the kingdom, England passed openly from schism to heresy. Also at this time the so-called new *Ordinal* was written, taking the place of the Catholic Pontifical in Sacred Ordinations; this was mainly the work of the apostate and heretic Thomas Cranmer, the intruder who was assigned the primatial see of Canterbury by Henry VIII. This new *Ordinal*, prepared by Cranmer and some of his associates, and called the Edwardine, was approved and made obligatory by public law in January 1550, and was published in March of the same year. It is moreover historically certain that under the reign of Edward VI, that is, from 1547 to 1553, there were ordinations celebrated in England according to the new *Ordinal*; it is also certain that at least from March, 1550 until 6 June 1553, they were all done according to the new rite. At the death of Edward, which took place, as I have said, on 6 July 1553, his legitimate sister Mary was proclaimed Queen; she reigned until her death, 15 November 1558. Queen Mary, being a Catholic, restored the Catholic religion in her realm, recalled the Catholic bishops from exile, and recognized and proclaimed the supreme authority of the Roman Pontiff.

5. From the beginning of the reign of Queen Mary, the Supreme Pontiff Julius III devoted his attention to England, to call her back to the bosom of the Catholic Church with the help of the pious Queen. With a Bull of 5 August 1553, he sent to England as his Legate the devoted, learned, and expert Cardinal Pole, bestowing on him the most ample and opportune faculties. This was the first papal document, issued at the beginning of the reign of Queen Mary, which occupied the attention of the Commission. Passing over all the rest, I shall at once refer to the passage of the document which concerns the question of the ordinations. The Supreme Pontiff gives to his Legate the faculty to rehabilitate or to habilitate for the exercise of the Sacred Ministry those who exercised it during the time of the schism or heresy, and to allow them to remain

1. [More usually known as the Duke of Somerset.]

in possession of the ecclesiastical benefices which they wrongly obtained, 'provided that prior to falling into this heresy, *they were rightly and legitimately (rite et legitime) promoted and ordained*; likewise, they could perform the ministry of the altar, and could retain as before any secular or regular benefices of whatever kind, provided that no other claim to them existed; moreover, *those who had not been promoted* [to sacred orders] could be promoted to all the sacred orders, including the presbyterate, by their Ordinaries, if they were found suitable and worthy, and receive ecclesiastical benefices etc.[2] For a correct understanding of the Pope's words which we have cited, it helps to recall what I have said in the preceding section, namely, that up to 1547, at least, the public defection of England was limited to schism. The heresy began in the reign of Edward; then the dogmatic error that denied the existence of the Sacrament of Order, first privately professed by Cranmer, was, so to speak, legalized with the publication of the new Ordinal, in March of 1550. In view of this, it seems to me quite obvious what the Pontiff meant by the words: '*provided that prior to falling into this heresy, they were rightly and legitimately promoted and ordained.*' According to the mind of the Pontiff, all those could be absolved by the Legate, and declared fit for the exercise of the sacred ministry, who had been ordained prior to the schism or were ordained during Henry's schism, and also those who had been ordained *rite et legitime* prior to the publication of the Ordinal, during the first years of Edward, i.e. up to 1550. But there must have been, and in fact there were, also those not ordained who not only illegitimately but altogether invalidly exercised the sacred ministry, because the Pontiff added that '*those who had not been promoted [to sacred orders] could be promoted to all the sacred orders, including the presbyterate, by their Ordinaries, if they were found suitable and worthy.*' Now who could those '*not promoted*' have been? Surely not the pure and simple laity,

---

2. [Pierotti gives this and all other quotations from official documents in the original Latin. Emphasis is always that of Pierotti's text, as published by Rambaldi.]

who never entered upon the exercise of ecclesiastical functions or ministry; there was no reason to mention them. Therefore, he could not have been referring to others than the false ministers who had either received the royal investiture of some greater or lesser ecclesiastical benefice, even before their ordination, or who had been ordained according to the Edwardine Ordinal, which was made obligatory in January 1550 and remained in force until July 1553. What I say here will become clearer from what follows.

6. The second papal document is a Brief of the same Pontiff Julius III addressed to his Legate Cardinal Pole, dated 8 March 1554. In regard to this document, one does well to note that in many publications it has been annexed to the Bull of which I have been speaking, whereas in reality it is quite distinct from the former document, which bears the earlier date of 5 August 1553, as has been verified in the Vatican Archives. This particular fact was not known to the Commission, since it was discovered only later, and it gave rise to various suppositions that rendered the Supreme Pontiff's meaning less intelligible. In fact in this second document, which had been annexed to the former one, the Pontiff mentions letters and faculties which had been previously granted to his Legate, and one could not know for certain which these faculties were, or where they were contained. But once the distinction between the two documents is established, it becomes clear that the faculties previously granted to the Legate by the Pope, were precisely those contained in the Bull of 5 August 1553.

Because some doubt had arisen in the minds of some who were 'perhaps excessively scrupulous' (these are the Pope's words) concerning the extent of the granted faculties, in regard to places and to persons, because the Legate, for reasons known to the Pontiff, had to reside not in England, but in Flanders, at least for a time, the Pontiff sent the Brief of which I speak for the purpose of removing such doubt. With this the Legate, *even residing outside the Kingdom itself* (i.e. of England), was authorised to make free use of the faculties granted him by the previous Bull, and those granted by the present Brief, in the entire Kingdom of England. And he was further authorised to make use of these faculties 'with regard to all Archbishops, Bishops, and Abbots, and other prelates of churches, whether of secular clergy or of whatever religious orders, as well as of monasteries and other houses of religious, and likewise with regard to other clergy of lesser rank; likewise with regard to other persons mentioned in the previous letters, however they are named, who have recourse to you during this time.'

7. This said, I at once transcribe the portion of the Papal Brief that concerns our question. The Pope authorises his Legate to make use of these faculties '*Also with regard to Orders which they never received*, OR RECEIVED BADLY (*male*), and the gift (*munus*) of consecration which was conferred on them by other Bishops or Archbishops, even heretics and schismatics, *or otherwise less rightly (minus rite) and without the customary form of the Church being maintained*, even though they have rashly exercised these orders and such office concerning the ministry of the altar. You are to make free use of these faculties, either by yourself or through others deputed for this by you for a period of time.' It seems to me to be clear, even I would say, evident, that in this passage of the Brief there are designated three classes of Sacred Ministers or men claiming to be ministers existing at that time in England. The first was made up of those *who had never received orders*, and those were the ones who had simply been invested with ecclesiastical benefices by royal power, prior to their ordination, as I have said above in n. 5. The second class was made up of those who had been *badly ordained*, since they had been ordained not only *less rightly*, i.e. by schismatic or heretical bishops, but even more, had been ordained *without the* CUSTOMARY *form of the Church being maintained*. The third class, finally, was made up of those ordained by schismatic or heretical Bishops, but *with the* CUSTOMARY *form of the Church being maintained*. The Papal Legate was authorised to provide for all of these with faculties that could be subdelegated. Now who were those alleged Sacred Ministers belonging to the second class who *had received*

orders badly, without the CUSTOMARY *form of the Church being maintained*? I do not know and cannot discover others than the ones who had been ordained with the new Edwardine form, that is, with the Ordinal. Even to put this deduction in doubt would seem to me to be nothing else than a subtle example of sophistry, for the purpose of denying or putting in doubt a truth that is evident of itself.

8. But if any doubt could still fall upon the interpretation which I have given of the Papal Document, this would be completely eliminated by the examination of two other documents, namely two letters sent by the Cardinal Legate: the first to Queen Mary and her husband Philip, dated 24 December 1554, and the second to the Bishop of Norwich dated 29 January 1555. In the first of these documents the Cardinal Legate declares that he has dispensed, and is ready to dispense in the future, from many irregularities that occurred in the time of the schism or the heresy, making use of the faculties granted him by the Pope in the Bull and Brief which we have examined. And with regard to our question, he expressed himself as follows: 'All those ecclesiastical persons, whether seculars or regulars of whatever orders, who have, by the alleged authority of the supremacy of the Anglican Church, received *invalidly and merely de facto* various grants, dispensations, concessions and indults, and *Orders* as well as ecclesiastical benefices or other spiritual goods, once they have sincerely returned to the unity of the Church, shall be mercifully *received in their Orders* and benefices either by ourselves or by those deputed for this by us, as indeed *many have already been received*, and we shall take these steps in due time in the Lord.' Thus the Legate declares that he has dispensed and is ready to dispense in favour of those persons who, for lack of jurisdiction and in virtue of the alleged supremacy of the Anglican Church *invalidly and merely de facto received dispensations and grants, both of Orders and of ecclesiastical benefices*, and that he receives such persons *in their Orders and benefices*. However, this concerns only the invalidity that results from the lack of jurisdiction, as he declares by adding the following:

'although *invalidly and merely de facto*; with regard to the *invalidity*, this arises ONLY *from the lack of the aforesaid jurisdiction.*' What then he would do, or his delegates would do, when there was not a valid ordination, and in some cases not even an invalid one, he explains in the second document, namely, the letter to the Bishop of Norwich, as we shall now see.

9. With regard to this second document, the letter written to the Bishop of Norwich on 29 January 1555, it will not be out of place to observe that although, among the documents published until now, we have only this letter addressed to this particular bishop, one can hardly believe that it was not addressed to other English Bishops as well, who, finding themselves in the same situation, had equal need to be authorised and subdelegated by the Papal Legate. In this letter Cardinal Pole, in his capacity as Legate, and making use of the faculties granted him by the Supreme Pontiff, of which he makes express mention, after having delegated to this Bishop various faculties, granted to him also the faculty of admitting *in their Orders* those who had been ordained by schismatic or heretical bishops, absolving them of the irregularity and other censures. Here are the Legate's words: 'Despite the irregularity and other aforesaid censures, they may be received in their orders which they have received even from heretical and schismatic Bishops, even LESS RIGHTLY, *provided that in their ordination the* FORM *and* INTENTION *of the Church was maintained.*' If one does not wish to say that the Cardinal Legate, in giving this sub-delegation and these practical dispositions, was speaking only theoretically and hypothetically (which would be most injurious to a man as learned and pious as was Cardinal Pole), one must recognize that in England at that time there were both Sacred Ministers and pseudo-ministers. The first were whose who had been ordained *less rightly*, but *with the form and intention of the Church being maintained*, or *in the customary form of the Church*, as was said in the Papal Brief. The latter, or the pseudo-ministers, were those who were not ordained (*they had never received orders*) or who had been

ordained not only *less rightly*, but *had received orders badly*, that is to say, *without the form and intention of the Church being maintained*, in other words, *not in the customary form of the Church*, precisely as I have said in my comment on the Papal Brief in no. 7. And because it is a question of a point which was much discussed by the Commission, as I shall say below, I ask again who those pseudo-ministers could have been who were ordained, but *without the form and intention of the Church being maintained*? I repeat that it seems to me not only clear, but evident, that they could not have been others than those ordained according to the Edwardine form. Those and not others are the ones who *received the orders badly*, and together with those who *never received orders*, form the catagory of the *not promoted*, and for all these the Legate disposes that *those who had not been promoted could be promoted to all the sacred orders, including the presbyterate, by their Ordinaries, if they were found suitable and worthy*. It is therefore clear, and in my view already evident, that the orders conferred according to the rite and form of the new Ordinal were declared absolutely invalid by the Supreme Pontiff Julius III. But if the matter is so clear, someone will say, how and with what reasons could four, that is to say, half the members of the Commission, uphold the validity of the Anglican ordinations, or at least maintain that the question is still entirely undecided? I shall try to respond to these questions after I have spoken of two other papal documents that concern our question.

10. Before speaking of the third papal document, that is, of the Bull *Praeclara nobis*,[3] issued in June 1555 by the Supreme Pontiff Paul IV, who succeeded Julius III in the Pontificate after the very brief reign of Marcellus II, who reigned only 22 days, I believe it opportune at least to mention some facts that preceded the publication of the Bull. Prescinding from other historical documents, it is known from a letter of Pope Paul IV, addressed to Queen Mary and her husband Philip, dated 30 June 1555, that at the beginning of that same year, that is,

---

3. [The title of Paul IV's Bull is usually given as *Praeclara charissimi*.]

in February, the King and Queen Mary of England, *persuaded to do this by Cardinal Pole*, had sent to the Supreme Pontiff a solemn embassy, with the purpose of obtaining the complete reconciliation of the Kingdom with the Holy See, of presenting the whole state of affairs to the Pontiff, and of obtaining the solemn and full confirmation of what had until then been done by the Legate. The soul, I shall say, and the head of this embassy was Bishop Thirlby, accompanied by Anthony Viscount Montague and Sir Edward Carne. Speaking of the first-named, the Pontiff declares in the aforesaid letter that in his presence, *the Bishop spoke with true eloquence and endowed with sound doctrine*. These ambassadors explained, both orally and in writing, what they desired to obtain for the full reconciliation of the Church of England, as one can see in a detailed document taken from the Vatican Archives (Arm. 64. T.28. f. 144 ff.) In this document, leaving aside the rest that is not relevant, one reads that among the other requests brought by the ambassadors and presented by the Parliament of England to the Legate, under n. 3 there were the following: 'That the provisions of benefices and dispensations and favours and other grants and indults of this kind, which concern ORDERS and benefices or other spiritual matters, might be confirmed.' There follows immediately: 'Granted. In this way: that those persons who sincerely returned to the unity of the restored church, should be received *in their orders* and benefices, by the Legate himself, or by those deputed by him, and that dispensation be granted them.' In another document taken from the same Archive, folio 199 of the aforesaid volume, one finds the following: 'Summary of those things whose confirmation is requested (i.e. by the Ambassadors) of the Holy See for the English.' Among other concessions granted by the Legate for which confirmation is sought, one finds: 'Dispensations granted to ecclesiastical persons, both secular and religious of various orders. THAT THEY MIGHT BE PROMOTED IN BOTH ORDERS *and* BENEFICES which had been obtained INVALIDLY. The Legate offered to give to others a similar dispensation.' Who those were who were dispensed so as to remain in possession of benefices and in the exercise of orders – *invalidly obtained* – and how the Legate provided for such as these, has been explained in the preceding number. One should note, however, that here also there were those who had been ordained altogether invalidly – *in orders obtained invalidly*.

11. I come now to speak of the Bull *Praeclara nobis* issued by Paul IV on 19 June 1555.[4] The Supreme Pontiff makes a detailed résumé of what had taken place, and of what the Cardinal Legate, endowed with Apostolic Authority, had done; he then confirms and, *as far as need might be*, he grants once more all the dispensations that the Legate had granted. With regard to the question with which we are occupied, he expressed himself as follows: 'To the very many ecclesiastical persons, priests and religious of various orders, who INVALIDLY and merely de facto had received various grants, dispensations, favours and indults, as well as ORDERS *and ecclesiastical benefices*, and other things concerning spiritual matters by the alleged authority of the supremacy of the Anglican church, and who sincerely had returned to the unity of the restored church, [the Legate] granted the dispensation that they could remain *in their orders* and benefices, and he offered to grant similar dispensation to others suffering from the same ills.' So the Pontiff also recognizes that there were some who had received not only benefices, but also orders *invalidly*, nor could one say, without falling into an absurdity, that the Legate had granted a dispensation to such as these, and that the dispensation was confirmed for them, so that they could remain in the exercise of Sacred Orders, *in their orders invalidly received*, without an entirely new and unconditional ordination.

12. Before going further, it will be well to note that Pope Paul IV did not proceed to confirm with his Supreme Authority what the Legate had done and intended to do, without first making an accurate and most diligent examination of the matter, as he himself tells us in the present Bull. In

---

4. [See note 3.]

fact, he says: 'All the foregoing *being explained and diligently discussed* with some of our brethren the Cardinals of the Holy Roman Church, and *a mature and minute deliberation being had* concerning them, [we approve] each of the dispensations, decrees, addition, healing, remission, easing, and *the intention of Reginald, Cardinal and Legate*, and also insofar as these things are relevant every single thing that has been done through the same Reginald Cardinal and Legate, and is contained in the same letters.' In view of this explicit declaration of the Supreme Pontiff, there falls of its own weight the hardly respectful supposition put forward by those who upheld the validity or doubtful validity of the Anglican Ordinations, namely, that Paul IV, shortly after becoming pope, did not have time to examine the question, and therefore either did not decide it, or decided it on the base of false suppositions. There falls also the other supposition, likewise disrespectful in regard to the Cardinal Legate, namely, that in giving his dispositions and especially in his letter to the Bishop of Norwich, of which I have spoken in n. 9, he could have acted on his own initiative and not altogether in accord with the mind of Pope Julius III, when he prescribed that those who *had not been promoted* to orders should be ordained, and when he declared that all those should be considered as not promoted who had been ordained *without the form and intention of the Church being maintained*, as I have said above. The Pontiff declares that everything done by the Legate had been subjected to a diligent examination: *explained [and] diligently discussed ... every single thing done through the same Cardinal Legate*.

13. The examination was so diligent, especially with regard to the ordinations, that before confirming what the Legate had done he added the following restriction: 'In such a way that if some were promoted *to ecclesiastical orders*, whether sacred or not sacred, *by someone other than a bishop rightly and correctly (rite et recte) ordained*, they are bound to receive the same orders again from their Ordinary, nor can they exercise those orders in the interim.' Having expressed and imposed this limitation, the pope *approves and confirms*

with Apostolic Authority what the Cardinal Legate had done. He then adds: 'And nevertheless, taking greater precaution, We again, with apostolic authority and by a grant of special favour, dispense all those whom Reginald, Cardinal and Legate, has dispensed in the manner described above but in such a way that those who were *ordained to the aforesaid orders* by someone other than a bishop or archbishop *who had been ordained* in the manner described above, must receive those orders again, and in the meanwhile are not to exercise the ministry. Moreover *We decree everything that the aforesaid Legate Reginald has decreed*, and we give the firmness of apostolic authority to everything which he has done by virtue of that authority.' After these words that are so clear and explicit, let me say that one could not, without rashness, put in doubt the validity of what was done by the Cardinal Legate, including, of course, the aforesaid letter to the Bishop of Norwich.

14. Some of the members of the Commission who upheld the validity or doubtful validity of the Anglican Ordinations, wandering into the region of hypotheses, have supposed that Pope Paul IV meant only to declare invalid the ordinations conferred by bishops who *had not been rightly ordained*, and in this he had intended to leave untouched the question concerning the other ordinations, including those conferred with the Edwardine Ordinal. In fact, some say that in this way he had declared those orders valid, because otherwise he would have mentioned them along with the others conferred by Bishops *not rightly ordained*. Those who argue in this way mutilate, so to speak, the weighty papal document; they stop with the aforesaid restriction, and they forget, or pretend to forget, what was said above in the same Bull, as I have faithfully reported in n. 11. When one compares the restriction, referred to in the preceding number, with the passage referred to in n. 11, one sees clearly that the Pope did not limit himself to speaking of ordinations received by bishops *not rightly ordained*, but he also speaks of all the other ordinations which were invalid on some other grounds. Here he was considering just one source from which the invalidity of ordi-

nations followed, or could follow. For the greater clarity of what I am asserting, against the false and hypothetical assertion of others, it is well to observe that – as is evident from the Bull of Julius III treated in n. 7, and from the letter of the Legate treated in n. 9, as well as from other documents to which we have referred – prior to the publication of the Bull of Paul IV one spoke of the invalidity of ordinations only by reason of defect of form: *the customary form of the Church not having been maintained –the form and intention of the Church* not having been maintained. There was no explicit consideration of the invalidity of ordinations arising from the lack of the episcopal character in the ordainer. It was for this, and for this alone, that Paul IV wished to provide with the aforesaid restriction. One can also say with good reason that up to the time of Paul IV, because of the immense confusion caused by the schism under Henry VIII, followed by the heresy under Edward, it was not clearly known that there were ordinations that were invalid for the lack of episcopal character in the ordainer, and that when Paul IV came to know this, he opportunely provided for it by introducing into his Bull the aforesaid restriction or clause, leaving intact what had been decided, and what he himself expressly wished to confirm, in regard to other ordinations that were invalid by reason of defect of form.

15. That afterwards, in the time of the restoration of Catholicism under Queen Mary, there really were some bishops or alleged bishops who were *not rightly ordained*, that is, ordained according to the new form and the new Edwardine Ordinal (which some have wished to call in doubt), is so evident a fact that to deny it or to call it doubtful is equivalent to denying a truth which is fully verified by history. The English theologians who were members first of a Commission established and presided over by His Eminence Cardinal Vaughan, and then of the Papal Commission, in their most praiseworthy work entitled *Ordines Anglicani*, published this year in London, give in Appendix VI, beginning on p. 172, a list naming no less than *seven* alleged bishops who were ordained with the Edwardine Ordinal. This list cannot

be put in doubt, since it is based on authentic documents and manuscripts containing the legal processes drawn up in the cases of those schismatic and heretical pseudo-bishops. In these processes no account whatsoever is taken of their alleged episcopal orders; on the other hand, in the processes drawn up in the cases of the bishops ordained according to the Catholic Pontifical, explicit account is taken of their episcopal character, from which rank they were degraded if unrepentant, or to which they were reinstated if repentant.

16. When the Bull of Paul IV had been brought to England by Bishop Thirlby and had been published by Cardinal Pole on 22 September 1555 (as is known from a letter of the same Cardinal, taken from the public Archives of Douai (Reg. Poli II f. 38d.)), there arose among some people the doubt as to who those Bishops were who should be considered *rightly ordained*. This brings us to the fourth papal document, i.e. the Brief issued by the same Supreme Pontiff Paul IV on 30 October 1555. In this Brief he was not satisfied merely to recall in its entirety the clause of the Bull to which I have referred in n. 13 (the only one about whose interpretation there was doubt), but he also made express mention of the dispositions he had made and confirmed in the first part of the same Bull, in reference to those *who had obtained* BOTH ORDERS *and ecclesiastical benefices INVALIDLY and merely de facto*. Going on to remove the doubt and to give the needed clarification, here is how he expressed himself: 'WE DECLARE that Bishops and Archbishops *can be said NOT to have been RIGHTLY AND CORRECTLY ORDAINED only if they were not ordained and consecrated in the form of the Church*. Consequently those who were promoted to orders by them did not receive the orders in question, and are obliged to receive the orders over again from their Ordinary, according to the contents and meaning of our aforesaid letters.' Then the Pontiff continues in his Brief: 'On the other hand, the persons on whom such orders were conferred by bishops and archbishops who had been *ordained and consecrated in the form of the Church*, even though those bishops and archbishops had been schismatics,

and had received the churches which they governed from the hand of Henry VIII or Edward VI, so-called kings of England, – such persons, I say, did receive the character of the orders conferred on them, and only lacked the execution of such orders.' This disposition of the Supreme Pontiff, although not wholly expressed in the same words, is nothing else than a repetition, with regard to the bishops and arch-bishops, of the disposition adopted by the Cardinal Legate and approved by Paul IV with regard to sacred ministers inferior to the episcopate. Just as the Legate recognized as valid the lesser ordinations conferred by schismatic or here-tical bishops, provided they were conferred *with the form and intention of the Church being maintained* as I said above in n. 9; so also Paul IV recognized that episcopal ordinations were valid, and bishops were to be held as validly ordained, even though they were schismatic and heretical, provided they were *ordained and consecrated in the form of the Church.* Having said this, I ask once more: who were and who could have been those bishops who were not absolutely unordained, but were ordained, but not *in the form of the Church, not rightly ordained?* And I repeat: to me it is clear to the point of evidence, that they cannot be others then those ordained according to the Edwardine form. Such men were present in England at the time, as I have proved in n. 15. Therefore it is clear and evident that all the ordinations conferred with the new Ordinal and according to the Edwardine form were declared absolutely invalid by the Supreme Pontiffs Julius III and Paul IV. Therefore the question regarding the Anglican Ordinations *is not an open one*, it cannot be said to be left to the free discussion of Catholic theologians, because the absolute invalidity of the same orders has been solemnly declared by the Supreme Authority of the Church, even from the year 1555.

17. Facts which are historically certain, and the constant practice and tradition, even prior to 1685, confirm the inter-pretation which I have given of the papal documents. One need refer to only a few facts. The English theologians, in their work cited in n. 15, Appendix 6, p. 172 ff., report that

the Bishop of Bath and Wells in England, Gilbert Bourne, in giving the commission to his Vicar General John Cottrell on 8 April 1554 to proceed against those ordained to sacred orders, or who claimed to be ordained, and were joined in marriage or in alleged marriage, among other things enjoined on the same Vicar General to proceed 'against those *married* LAYMEN, who, with the pretext and *under the cloak of the order of priesthood*, have rashly and illicitly involved themselves in matters that belong by right to the church.' There were, therefore, men who were invalidly ordained, they had intruded *under the cloak of the order of priesthood*, they were ordained with the Edwardine form. The fact that their alleged ordination was held to be absolutely invalid is clear from the texts of the sentences which are recorded in the manuscript of Harles n. 421, in about forty cases that are recorded there. Those charged were first of all asked *whether they were already ordained eight years ago*, that is, before the death of Henry VIII, during whose lifetime the Catholic Pontifical was still in use. Furthermore, from the list of names of the alleged bishops or others *in sacred orders* which is also recorded there, one finds that by the respective sentences that were handed down, no one was condemned to degradation from the episcopate or any other order that had been received according to the Edwardine Ordinal, but such action was taken only with regard to orders received according to the Catholic Pontifical. The former were, therefore, held and judged to be absolutely invalid. For further confirmation of this, it is useful to add that Bishop Bonner, the Principal Commissary of Cardinal Pole for the diocese of London, in the Preface of the work entitled '*Utilis et necessaria doctrina*', writes: '*Those so-called ministers*, who were appointed while the schism was still going on, *received through that newly fabricated ordination NO authority* to offer the body and blood of Our Saviour Jesus Christ in the Mass. (English theologians in their work entitled *Ordines Anglicani – Supplementum*, p. 13).[5]

---

5. [This little dossier also bears the title *Responsio ad votum Rev.mi de Augustinis sj.*]

18. These facts were certainly sufficient to prove that the interpretation given above of the papal documents was from the beginning confirmed by the facts. Even though, as the defenders of validity or doubtful validity complained, there was no express mention of the reordination of those who had received so-called ordination with the Edwardine form, this signified nothing, given the fact that those ordained with the Edwardine form were regarded as not ordained, or as laymen, and those who have not been ordained, but are laymen, are not reordained, but are unconditionally ordained. However, to remove any remaining doubt, there has come to light, at just the right moment, a document of the greatest importance, received by the English theologians on the 5th of this month, on the feast of the English Martyrs B. John Fisher, Thomas More and companions. This has been most opportunely published by them in a work entitled: *Documenta ad legationem Cardinalis Poli spectantia. Appendix II.* Here is what the document says: 'In a recent investigation of several episcopal archives, FOURTEEN cases have been found (of which EIGHT are in the Diocese of London alone) in which men who had been ordained *according to the Edwardine ritual* received THE SAME ORDERS AGAIN UNCONDITIONALLY *during the reign of Queen Mary.* The Anglican Bishop of Stepney of the city of London witnesses to this fact.[6] This undoubtedly shows that the directive given by the Holy See in the previous documents was put into execution and constantly followed in practice.' A sequel to this document is happily provided by a list, published by Estcourt and mentioned in the work we have cited at the end of the previous section, of Anglican Ministers, who, when converted to the faith, were again, and unconditionally, ordained in France, in the years 1575, 1577, 1578, 1579, 1580, 1581 and 1601. The Theologians add that with careful search, similar lists could be found in the English College in Rome. We shall see, when we speak of the Acts of the Holy Office,

---

6. [This was *actually* the information researched by W. F. Frere referred to in Lacey's diary entry for May 3rd – see p. 331.]

that this practice remained unvaried and constant. It is helpful to note that this document came to light only after the
work of the Commission was finished. Consequently I can
omit reporting or even mentioning some of the arguments
put forward in the course of the discussion by those who
upheld validity or doubtful validity, since they are completely
refuted by this same document.

19. The fact remains, however, that at the end of a long
discussion, lasting for *three* long sessions, the Most Eminent
President posed the question: 'Whether, on the sole grounds
of the words in the Brief of Julius III (the distinction between
the Bull and the Brief of Julius III was not known at that
time, as I observed at n. 6) the question could be decided or
not.' To this, four of the Consultors replied *Yes* and four *No*.
Then his Eminence posed a second question: 'Whether, in
view of the other facts in reference to the Brief of Julius III,
the validity or invalidity of the orders conferred according to
the new rite which had at that time been composed in
England, could be determined with certitude.' Those who
upheld validity or doubtful validity sought to evade this question rather than to give a categorical reply. The result was the
same after the examination of the Bull and Brief of Paul IV.
Here are the principal arguments on which those opposed to
absolute invalidity based their stand. (a) They said that the
two Pontiffs did not speak explicitly of ordinations conferred
with the Edwardine form; therefore one cannot say with
certainty that they declared them invalid. Reply: It is historically certain that, apart from the Catholic form and the
Edwardine form, no one has ever been able to find any
other form or forms that one could even suspect had been
used. Therefore those who had been ordained *invalidly*, those
ordained *not in the customary form of the Church*, '*without the
form and intention of the Church being maintained*', *those not
rightly ordained*, could not have been others than those
ordained with the *Edwardine form*. (b) They observed that
the expression *ordained invalidly* could be taken to mean
ordained illicitly. Although perhaps in very ancient times the
word *nulliter* had been used in place of *illicite*, at the time

when the papal documents were issued this was totally obsolete, nor can anyone bring forth a document, or even an author, who had used the word *nulliter* as the equivalent of the word *illicite*. (c) It was said that the words *in the form of the Church*, used to designate valid ordinations, could have meant not exclusively the Catholic form of the Pontifical, but rather *the essential form*, which is always the *form of the Church*. Reply: In the Brief of Julius III, as I have noted above in n. 9, the ordinations are declared invalid which were conferred *not in the CUSTOMARY form of the Church*. Therefore it was a question of a *new form*, which certainly could not be called *customary*. (d) They added that Paul IV, in declaring in his Brief which were the Bishops who were *rightly ordained*, limited himself to saying that they were those who had been *ordained in the form of the Church*, omitting the word *customary*, used by Julius III. Therefore he held as valid some other form besides that of the Catholic Pontifical. Reply: If, to say the impossible, this had been the meaning of the words used by Paul IV in replying to the question asked of him, he would have replied that the valid ordinations were valid, and the invalid ones invalid, thus giving an oracular reply, leaving everything to the judgment of the Legate who had asked the question. Since this is inadmissible, one must say that for the Pontiff those ordained *not in the form of the Church* were those ordained with the Edwardine form. (e) They said also that those *not promoted* could be those either never ordained, or those ordained without first receiving the lesser orders. Reply: I have already said in n. 7, that there could be some who were not ordained at all, but there were undoubtedly also some who were *ordained badly*, and these were the ones who were ordained according to the Edwardine form. The other interpretation is a mere hypothesis without any foundation. These and other similar arguments offered by the defenders of the validity or doubtful validity of Anglican orders have been drawn faithfully from the minutes of the sessions of the Commission, leaving aside various historical questions that were raised. They have no force at all to negate or to put in doubt the strength of the papal documents and the historical facts, from which the conclusion follows that all the ordinations conferred with the *Edwardine form* were from the beginning authoritatively declared and in practice held to be totally invalid, by reason of the defect of form and intention: *without the FORM and INTENTION OF THE CHURCH being maintained.*

II. ACTS AND DECISIONS OF THE HOLY OFFICE FROM 1684–85 TO THE PRESENT

20. To proceed with clarity, it will help to recall briefly what happened in England after the almost contemporary deaths of Queen Mary and of Cardinal Pole. After the death of Queen Mary on 15 November 1558 [actually 17 November], she was succeeded by her sister Elizabeth, the illegitimate daughter of Henry VIII and Anne Boleyn, who was proclaimed Queen on 15 November [actually 17 November] 1558. When Elizabeth died, on 4 April 1603, James King of Scotland succeeded her on the throne. When he died his son Charles I succeeded him; after Charles was beheaded in 1649, he had no successor until 1660, when Charles II became king. It is well known how deplorable were the conditions of the period from 1558 to 1660. Queen Elizabeth immediately restored the proscribed Edwardine Ordinal to use, and insisted that all the ordinations of bishops and other sacred ministers should be carried out according to the form contained in it. It was only in 1662, that is, after more than a century, when no one was left who had been ordained according to the Catholic form, that a change was introduced into the form of the ordination of bishops and priests. There had been a certain reaction in a somewhat Catholic direction during the time of Archbishop Laud. When therefore the question was brought to the Holy Office, this change had already been made; however, it had not been there when the papal documents of which I have been speaking were issued. But the Holy Office, in deciding the question, had no need to examine the form introduced in 1662; rather it had only to examine the Edwardine form, which had been in use for over a century.

When the invalidity of this form had been established, regardless of what form was then in use, the ordinations were certainly invalid for defect of succession, by reason of the invalidity of the form which had been in constant use for more than a century.

21. Before proceeding further, it occurs to me at this point to refer to one of the arguments brought up in the Commission by the defenders of the validity or doubtful validity of the Anglican ordinations, against the indisputable validity of the papal documents which were studied in the preceding section – arguments which I have deliberately omitted mentioning until now. They say: if the ordinations conferred with the Edwardine form had really been declared invalid by Popes Julius III and Paul IV, what need was there of a new examination by the Holy Office? Why did the Holy Office not simply refer to those decisions? Why did no one bring them up in the course of the long discussions that took place? According to them, this shows that the papal decisions were neither clear nor peremptory against the validity of the ordinations conferred with the Edwardine form. I admit that at first this argument struck me as having a solid foundation; however, after a more diligent study of the matter, I now see an obvious and easy solution to it.

First of all, one must not forget that from the time that the Brief of Paul IV was issued and remained in full observance, i.e. from 1555 until to 1558 when Queen Mary died, no less than one hundred and twenty-six years passed before the Holy Office began to study the question, in 1684–85.

Nor should one forget that during this long interval of 126 years, persecution raged ferociously and constantly against the Catholics, with the result, as Duchesne attests on page 5 of the position paper on Anglican ordinations which he presented to the Commission,[7] England remained without Catholic Bishops for the long period of 65 years, since it was only in 1623 that the first Vicar Apostolic was named.

---

7. [The reference seems to be to a paper Duchesne wrote during the sessions, not to the *Votum* published in the present volume.]

It is no surprise, then, that the papal documents of 1553–55 had fallen into oblivion, although the practice of holding the Anglican ordinations as invalid remained unchanged, as I have already said in nn. 17 and 18, and as I shall shortly confirm. It was presumed that this practice had its origin in dispositions coming from the Holy See, but that could not be proven then, as the documents came to light only later on. Nor should one wonder that in 1684–85 even the Holy Office was unaware of the existence of the papal documents, since it was only as a result of long and diligent search that they were rediscovered. The Bull and the Brief of Paul IV were found in the Vatican Archives only after the examination of 25 volumes of Acts relative to the Council of Trent among which they had been inserted. Searches had been carried out in the Archives of the Holy Office and of Propaganda, but nothing pertinent had been found there. Moreover one should observe that by 1684–85 a change of which I shall speak in due time had already been introduced into the Edwardine form since 1662. It was necessary, therefore, to carry on a most diligent examination, as was actually done, before one could come to know whether the Anglican ordinations were valid or invalid, and it would not even have been enough to know about the decision that was issued and adopted in 1555. In brief, one had to know the state of affairs not only as they were in 1555, but also as they were in 1684–85. It follows that from the silence of the Holy Office no argument can be drawn against the genuine interpretation and peremptory force of the papal documents which have been examined in the preceding section. Rather, as we shall now see, the decisions taken by the Holy Office are in full conformity with those documents, and seem as if taken with full knowledge of them.

22. On 24 July 1684, the Archbishop of Fano, Apostolic Nuncio in Paris, wrote that 'a young Calvinist heretic, having crossed from this Kingdom to England, was ordained to the diaconate according to the usage of that sect, and later on to the priesthood by the pseudo-bishop of London. When subsequently he returned to this country, and had embraced the

Catholic religion, he wished to marry, but was in doubt whether in that ordination he had received the character of the Sacred Order etc.' Here is the first case taken up by the Holy Office in regard to the validity of Anglican orders. And here it is well to note that the bishop who presented the doubt for resolution did not even mention the ordination of Parker, which he would certainly have done if the so-called *Tavern fable* had then been considered to be the one decisive argument that would prove the lack of apostolic succession in the English bishops, and hence the invalidity of their ordinations. He says rather that his doubt depended primarily on two matters of fact, which had to be known: the first was whether, after the apostasy, the ecclesiastical hierarchy had been maintained in England; the second was whether the Anglicans observed the form that is necessary for conferring sacred orders. 'The latter question,' he adds, 'should be easy to clarify, but the former seems to me to involve difficulty, since it requires accurate knowledge of what happened in that Kingdom, and of the successive ordinations of those pseudo-bishops, whence etc.'

We know from the dossier of the Holy Office that the learned and erudite Cardinal Casanata drew up an accurate report in which, for the solution of the doubt, he undertook to examine: '(1) How and by whom the bishops were consecrated in England, and whether they were consecrated by other bishops; (2) Whether those consecrated as bishops were successors to Catholic bishops, legitimately consecrated according to the rite of the Catholic Church; (3) What form and matter is presently used in England in the consecration of bishops; (4) Whether, if Chrismation is not practised, there is a lack of the matter necessary for the true conferral of the Sacrament of Orders.'

Casanata himself gave a definitive answer to the fourth question by showing that the lack of chrismation could not have caused the invalidity of the ordinations, and one must say that this issue was dropped, as it never came up again in the following studies. The other three questions were treated by the Cardinal with a great deal of historical erudition and theological doctrine, but in the end it must be said that he himself remained doubtful as to the final resolution of the case. When the doubt was put before the Congregation of Wednesday, 15 November 1684, 'the Eminent Fathers said that Cardinal Casanata should write to the Bishop of Chalcedon, the Internuncio in Belgium, for information concerning the doubt in question, according to the intention of the Eminent Fathers.' In the document it is not said what this intention was that was indicated by the Eminent Fathers to Cardinal Casanata; however, one can presume with good reason that they had indicated to the Cardinal what enquiries he should make and on which points he should focus his investigations.

23. From what is contained in the Holy Office dossier, it is clear that from that time Casanata began to make the most diligent and detailed enquiries, as is evident from the information which he received, and which forms part of the dossier. I do not intend to go into a detailed examination of the information and opinions which he received from the respectable persons whom he consulted, but I cannot fail to report the principal results of his investigation, to which the Cardinal himself gave special attention, since this is necessary in order to eliminate many of the doubts which the defenders of the validity or doubtful validity of the Anglican ordinations raised concerning the true and genuine sense of the resolution which was issued, as we shall see, by the Supreme Pontiff Clement XI.

In his second report, which begins at folio 686 of the dossier, Cardinal Casanata writes: 'Your Eminences ordered me to write to the Vicar Apostolic in Holland, and to the Internuncio in Flanders, to request that they endeavour to see if they could in some way obtain reliable information, whether the Bishops who are now in England (by one of whom the priest in question was ordained) can be said to be successors of the Apostles, in such wise that their ordinations can be said to descend, step by step, without any interruption, from one of those true and undoubted bishops who were in England while the true religion flourished there. And if this information cannot be had from the archives and registers of England, they should endeavour at least to find out, and to inform us, what opinion the English, both Catholics and heretics, have on this matter.'

24. Summing up the information he had received, he reports in brief the various opinions that were current in England, among both Catholics and Protestants. He says that the Catholics denied the apostolic succession, by reason of the spurious ordination of Parker, while the Protestants maintained that Parker had been validly ordained. He does not fail to note that the register in which the ordination of Parker is recorded was not produced by the Protestants until fifty years after it had taken place, that is, at the beginning of the seventeenth century. Nor should one believe that on the part of Catholics there had been no provocation, so to speak, that might have led to the production of the well-known document, since already in 1565 Thomas Harding had published in Louvain his refutation of the Apologia of the Anglican Church written by Jewell. Others who wrote against the Anglicans in 1565 were Holywood, also called Sacrobosco, Henry Fitzsimons, and Stapleton. I will not fail to observe that the celebrated document was not found in a regular register, which it would be difficult to alter; rather it was found in a pile of documents that had been put together and could easily be separated from one another. Having summed up other bits of information that were produced in favour of or against the validity of the ordinations, Casanata concludes this first part of his report and opinion, writing on folio 688 v., 'In this dispute between Catholics and heretics, although one should put more faith in the former than in the latter, nevertheless, *in a matter so grave and difficult, it is difficult to favour any one solution, since it would have such such great consequences.*'

From these most serious words of the learned Cardinal Casanata, one sees clearly that the so-called *fable of the Tavern, or of Parker*, was put out of the question, as they say, and in no way influenced the decisions that were taken and adopted in the matter.

25. Putting aside historical reports and conjectures that cannot provide a solid foundation for the solution to the question, Casanata went on to say, in the same section of his opinion to which we referred: 'The Vicar Apostolic of Holland proposes another reason for declaring invalid the ordination of the English priest on whose account this question has been raised: *and truly, in my judgment, it merits consideration. This is that since in England the formula used in the Roman Church in the ordination of bishops and priests had been changed, and since the new formula does not contain the form necessary for the Sacrament, it seems that all the ordinations of bishops and priests are invalid.* On this account, (the Cardinal continues) one must first of all observe that not only in the time of Edward and Elizabeth was a formula different from that of the Roman Pontifical composed, but also in the time of King Charles II, brother of the present King James, another one was made. I have thought it well to describe these, *since they are the PRINCIPAL OBJECT of the present discussion.*' He then goes on to examine both the Edwardine form, which remained in use for over a hundred years and the other one, which had been somewhat modified under Charles II in 1662. I shall not delay on this point for the moment, since I shall speak of it later on. For now it suffices to know that the discussion turned primarily on the validity or invalidity of the form, and the solution was based precisely on the invalidity of the form.

26. Lest anyone think that the treatment of the question was influenced by the opinion that was held at that time by various theologians, namely, that the handing over of the instruments, with the formula associated with it, was absolutely required for the validity of ordinations, the same Cardinal Casanata explicitly excludes this hypothesis, on which, in the course of the discussions in the Commission, the defenders of the validity or doubtful validity of Anglican ordinations based much of their case. Casanata focuses on the examination of the Anglican formulas in themselves, and he says explicitly: 'Since the words of the aforesaid formulas in no way signify the most essential POWER of the priest and

bishop, i.e. the power to offer the sacrifice and to consecrate the Body of Christ, they cannot effectively confer such a power or make one a true priest; moreover they do not include the handing over of the instruments of the sacrifice, as is done in the Latin Church.' It is to be noted that this lack of the handing over of the instruments is not presented as an essential defect that would make the form invalid; rather, he observes that besides this defect, what is absolutely lacking is the determination of the words in the form that was used, what is lacking is the designation of the *power* that one intends to confer. Furthermore, it was well known at the time that an ordination could be held as valid despite the lack of the handing over of the instruments. The same Cardinal adds: 'And although the Greek Church and other Eastern Churches do not have the handing over of the instruments, nonetheless, in the prayer which they call sacramental, *they always clearly confer the POWER to consecrate the Body of Christ.* I have taken pains to inform myself of this, and have had the formulas of the prayers of the *Armenians, Maronites, Syrians, Jacobites and Nestorians*, both Catholics and heretics, transcribed and appended to this document.' Therefore it was not the opinion concerning the handing over of the instruments that influenced the decision, since it was well known that even without this, an ordination could be valid, since it was held to be valid in the Churches of the various Eastern rites. Moreover, it is clear that the various Eastern formulas were known and were taken into consideration: a point which the defenders of the validity or doubtful validity of the Anglican ordinations believed was at least doubtful.

27. The careful report and opinion of Cardinal Casanata was presented by himself in the Congregation of the Most Eminent Fathers, on Wednesday, 4 July 1685, and the following Decree was issued: 'The report having been given by the Most Eminent Casanata concerning the information with regard to Anglican ordinations which he has obtained, and which is contained in these pages, the Most Eminent Fathers said that *this report is to be circulated*, and the Consultors are

to examine the doubt raised concerning the validity or invalidity of the ordination in question.' One should keep in mind that the question to be resolved, in order to reach a solution to the doubt, was precisely the doctrinal question regarding the validity of the *form*, as I have said at the end of n. 25. Let us now hear the decision of the Consultors. I have no need to say that the whole matter was studied and pondered by them for over a month; this is sufficiently said in the words: *let the aforesaid report be circulated by hand.*

'On Monday, 13 August 1685, the Consultors, having carefully considered the question, voted unanimously for the invalidity of the aforesaid ordination. As to whether, in the present case, it is expedient to issue a declaration to this effect, they left to the judgment of the Eminent Fathers.'

'On Tuesday, 21 August, the verdict was, by the Eminent Fathers, *Deferred.* '

Therefore the Congregation of Consultors, at that time, by unanimous vote, declared for the invalidity of the ordination, that is, for the invalidity of the *form*, and not only for the case that had been proposed, but in absolute fashion.

28. When the Eminent Fathers resolved the question which the Consultors had left to their discretion, with their verdict: *Deferred*, it would seem that they had left open to further discussion the basic question that had been decided by the Consultors. However, one cannot say with certitude whether or not there was doubt in their minds concerning the correctness of that decision. All one can say with certitude is that they pronounced the verdict '*Deferred*', for a motive that was totally extrinsic to the question. This was clearly indicated by Cardinal Casanata, who, after declaring for the invalidity of the ordination, added: 'Nevertheless, looking to the present state of England, and to the notable consequences that such a declaration could have, I would think that it would be well to go slowly with regard to the declaration.' As is known, England was in a great turmoil in 1684–85 by reason of the religious questions, and the Catholic King James II found himself in very grave difficulty at the time when the restora-

tion of the Catholic religion in his Kingdom was being contemplated.

29. In addition to what I have said thus far, and in order to explain what preceded and formed the basis of the solemn decision that was taken in 1704, I cannot fail to mention the fact that from a letter written on 15 April 1704 by Monsignor Francesco Genetti to Monsignor Casoni, at that time Assessor of the Holy Office, it is evident that even after 1685, the question continued to be studied. He says, in fact: 'At the time of Pope Innocent XI of holy memory, in 1686, by order of His Holiness, the question was proposed to various theologians: among others, to Don Giuseppe Charlas, to Archpriest Dorat, and to me.' He then says that after each one had separately studied and written on the quesiton, they consulted together in several meetings, in order the better to reply to the case. In fact one finds in the dossier several opinions which are not signed, but had certainly been requested. Genetti makes a point of noting the fact that one of these theologians 'besides various other reasons, proposed that an adequate decision had to be based, not on the very confused history of the various changes that had taken place in England in matters of religion, but rather on the defect of the intention and of the words that were used by the heretical Anglicans in conferring the priestly order, since they neither had nor could have had the intention of making true priests.' This was precisely as Cardinal Casanata had said and proposed back in 1685, as I have reported in n. 25.

Genetti goes on to say that, having been sent at that time, i.e. in 1686, to England: 'I found that the same question was hotly discussed among Catholics in London.[8] Monsignor

---

8. The fact that the question was being discussed among Catholics at that time should not be interpreted as a break in the constant tradition of holding Anglican ordinations to be invalid. The fact is easily explained if one reflects that precisely at that time or a little before, in consequence of the investigation made by Cardinal Casanata not only among Catholics but among heretics as well, it was quite natural that there should be discussion even among Catholics of the validity or invalidity of those ordinations, especially in view of the reaction the inquiry had aroused. In any case, the new inquiries and discussions that took place in London had no other result than to confirm the constant tradition.

Leyburn, at that time Bishop and Vicar Apostolic in London, asked my opinion about it, and I reported to him what had already happened. However, by order of Cardinal d'Alba, at that time designated Nuncio, and because the question had great consequences, and was coming up with some frequency, several meetings were held in which Mons. Leyburn presided and seven or eight of the most learned theologians among the clergy of England took part. Among these was Mr Gifford, subsequently made Bishop and Vicar Apostolic, Mr Bettan, at that time tutor to the King of England, and other doctors of the Sorbonne or of Douai, all men of consummate learning. I proposed to them the reasons explained above, and although, after some discussion, all came to agreement and were willing to decide in favour of my view, it was judged best to put off the decision for about fifteen days, so that they could the better study the matter and give grounds for their decision. I remember that at that time I made a great effort to arrive at certitude about the fact of the lack of episcopal succession, and for that reason I consulted Lord Belson, the most learned man among the Catholic laity and author of several books in defence of Religion. But seeing that this fact still remained doubtful, it was then decided, *by the unanimous vote of all*, and on the basis of the reasons given above, that English and Scottish bishops and priests who came to the Catholic faith should be received and treated as simple laymen. *And from that time on this was done without any difficulty*.' Leaving aside the historical question, Anglican ordinations were judged invalid by reason of the defect of form and intention; in other words, one kept to the same way that had been proposed and followed by Casanata.

30. It is now time to come to the solemn decision issued by the Supreme Pontiff Clement XI in the case of Gordon. The doubt concerning the validity or invalidity of the ordination and consecration of Gordon was proposed for the first time in the Congregation of Consultors on 10 March 1704. In that Congregation nothing was decided, but it was said: 'Let it be proposed in the next one.' On the 24th of the same month 'The Reverend Consultors voted that the aforesaid John

Clement Gordon should be ordained unconditionally.' On Wednesday, the 26th of the same month, the Eminences said: 'Let the enclosed writings be transmitted by the hands of the same Bishops.' What these *enclosed writings* were, will be made clear by the Decree, the full text of which I shall give. From this it is evident that the question was thoroughly discussed and studied all over again, for the space of 37 days, both by the Consultors and by the Eminent Inquisitors General. Here follows the authentic Decree, in its integrity.

31. 'On Thursday, 17 April 1704, in the customary Congregation of the Holy Roman and Universal Inquisition, held in the Palace of St Peter, in the presence of His Holiness Pope Clement XI.

'We have considered the petition of John Clement Gordon, an Anglican priest, converted to the Catholic faith, along with certain other writings or sworn testimonies which have been collected for a similar case, although previously nothing had been decided, or at least no decree with a vote of the Consultors had been issued in the matter. He has requested that despite his episcopal consecration conferred by bishops of the Anglican sect and with the rite commonly used by those pseudobishops, he should be granted the permission to be promoted to the Order of Priesthood, to be received with the Catholic rite, since his episcopal consecration was invalid, both by reason of the lack of legitimate succession in the bishops of England and Scotland who consecrated him, and for other reasons which rendered his consecration invalid.

His Holiness, having heard the opinions of the Most Eminent Cardinals *decreed*, that John Clement Gordon should be ordained afresh UNCONDITIONALLY to all the orders, and ESPECIALLY THE ORDER OF PRESBYTERATE, and since he has not been confirmed, he should first receive the Sacrament of Confirmation.'[9]

---

9. [De Augustinis ([3]) gives this quotation in a slightly different form.]

32. It is superfluous to observe, since the fact is obvious in itself, that strictly speaking this was not a Decree of the Holy Office, subsequently confirmed by the Supreme Pontiff; rather it was the Pontiff himself who issued it (*'His Holiness decreed'*) in the solemn Congregation held in the presence of His Holiness, with the consultors also present, as one sees in the acts of the Holy Office. On the other hand, it is well to stress the fact that the dossier that was examined again, i.e. 'the writings and testimonies that had been collected for a similar case', were not and could not have been other than the studies already made in 1684–85 with a view to the solution of the case of which I have spoken above. The motive which led the Pontiff to issue the solemn decree, therefore, was not the so-called *fable of the Tavern* concerning the ordination of Parker, as I have proved in n. 24 and further confirmed; nor was it the opinion of theologians who held ordination without the handing over of the instruments to be invalid; nor was it the lack of information about the form used by the Orientals, as I have proved in n. 26. Rather, his ordination was declared invalid solely, or at least primarily, by reason of the defect or invalidity of the form, as I have proved in n. 25. And if, in the presentation of the case, there is explicit mention of the lack *of legitimate episcopal succession*, one should not think that one was alluding to the fable concerning Parker; rather, that defect of succession must refer to the invalidity of the form: *'the succession being defective,'* as Cardinal Casanata said, *'by reason of the formulas, both that of Queen Elizabeth, and that of Charles II,'* as I have reported above at n. 25.

Therefore the decision issued by Clement XI was an explicit and formal declaration of the invalidity of Anglican ordinations, by reason of the defect of form, and this means that Anglican ordinations, after long and accurate investigations, were declared invalid for the very same reason for which Popes Julius III and Paul IV had declared them invalid a century and a half before, as I have shown in the first section.

33. Having arrived at this point, I can say in all truth that

along the way I have replied at least to the principal reasons, those that had at least the appearance of solidity, which in the course of the discussions were proposed by the defenders of the validity or doubtful validity of the Anglican ordinations. I have intentionally set aside various historical questions that were raised about particular facts in the course of discussions that lasted for six long sessions, so as not to be engulfed in labyrinths that will remain forever without exit. I have done this primarily because without all that one can still arrive at the true solution of the question. However, to complete this part of my treatment of the case, and to make it even clearer that the Decree of Clement XI, although issued for the solution of a particular case, was in reality an absolute and general decision of the invalidity of Anglican Ordinations, I shall refer now to another decree issued by the Holy Office in 1724.

34. On 7 October 1724, the Vicar Apostolic of England wrote to the Assessor of the Holy Office, saying that an anonymous book had appeared (the work of Canon Regular Courayer) in which the claim was made that the ordinations of the heretical Anglican Church were valid – note well that it says 'ordinations' and not one or another ordination – and that those who return from this to the Catholic Church ought not to be reordained. Desiring to respond to that book, and to put in clearer light the proposition which he said was *held universally by all English Catholics*, namely that those ordinations were invalid, the aforesaid Prelate asked for instructions and clarifications about the matter. The question having been submitted to the Holy Office by the Bishop's agent, 'the Consultors on Monday, 27 November 1724 expressed their opinion that writings and *decisions* concerning the matters in question should be communicated to the Priest Laurence Mayes, Agent of the Bishop of Thespis.' Further on one reads: 'On Wednesday, 29 November the Most Eminent Fathers approved the opinion of the Consultors,' and one finds inserted in the documentation precisely the Decree that had been issued in the Gordon case. Hence one has the authentic

interpretation of the Papal Decree, from which it is clear that the same Decree had truly universal scope. In conclusion, I find myself totally in accord with Cardinal Franzelin of blessed memory, who, after an accurate study of all the documents of the Holy Office up to 1875, concluded the first part of his opinion on the matter by saying: 'Prescinding therefore from the question of fact, whether Matthew Parker had ever been ordained by a bishop, and whether this was done with the Anglican rite of Edward VI, *IT IS CERTAIN from the Edwardine form in itself, and from its origin and history, that the orders of that sect ARE ENTIRELY NULL AND VOID.*'

35. There is no doubt at all about the practice which has constantly been observed, of treating those ordained with the Anglican rite as simple laymen, or of reordaining them unconditionally, once they had returned to Catholicism. That this was the constant practice up to 1704 is evident from the document of the Holy Office. To show that this practice was maintained even up to the present, omitting many other testimonies, I shall refer only to that of the Cardinal Archbishop of Westminster, who, proposing a doubt to the Holy Office regarding Anglican ordinations, wrote on 25 August 1874: 'By a CONSTANT consensus of Catholics in England, the orders conferred by the Anglican sect have always been held to be invalid. However, there has always been some controversy about the cause to which that invalidity is to be attributed. For *in earlier times* (note well his words) Catholics condemned those orders for two reasons: first, because of the lack of the requisite *intention* on the part of the ordainers, and secondly, because of the lack of the requisite *form.*' Thus, not only had the practice been maintained, but also the formal reason for it: *for the lack of intention, for the lack of form*, precisely as Cardinal Casanata had said about two centuries before. Therefore the practice had not originated after 1704, as the defenders of the validity or doubtful validity of Anglican ordinations had thought, or rather had surmised, but it existed in full force in 1685, as is clear from the documents of the Holy Office. It existed from

the time of Queen Mary, as is evident from what I reported in n. 17, and especially in n. 18. This practice has undergone no change up to the present, so that the Decree of Clement XI remains even now in full force, and all the doubts raised in the Commission by the defenders of Anglican Ordinations provide no basis for questioning the continuation of the existing practice.

36. I will not fail to note that the defenders of validity or doubtful validity, besides the fact that they do not agree among themselves, have not been able to produce a single case in which Anglican ordinations have been recognized as valid, or have been repeated conditionally as doubtfully valid. One of them had asserted that three bishops had been rehabilitated, even though consecrated with the Edwardine form; but that assertion has been found to be evidently false, since authentic documents have shown that they had been ordained in the time of the schism, according to the Catholic rite of the Pontifical.

There remains only the case of a certain John Scory, who had been ordained priest according to the Pontifical, and bishop according to the Edwardine form. It is said that this man was rehabilitated by the Catholic Bishop Edmund Bonner in 1554. However, it is clear from authentic documents that that alleged rehabilitation would have taken place in the month of July 1554, whereas Bonner, who was much behind in regard to theology, was authorised by Cardinal Pole to rehabilitate clergy, but never bishops, only in January 1555. There is no evidence that Cardinal Pole confirmed that alleged rehabilitation, for which even he was not authorised by Julius III, since Scory was married, or rather was living in concubinage. Besides, it is clear from the writings of Bonner that he held as invalid the ordinations conferred with the *newly fabricated ordinations*, nor is it proven that he really rehabilitated Scory other than as a simple priest.

One must therefore conclude with complete assurance that not one Anglican ordination was in practice held as valid or even as doubtfully valid.

37. I would prefer to pass directly to the last part of the work of the Commission, with regard to the validity or invalidity of the Anglican ordinations by reason of the *form* and the *intention*; but since the Commission itself, besides the discussion it had already had concerning the ordination of Parker, spent the whole of the seventh session and part of the eighth in a historical discussion of the episcopal consecration of Barlow, the first consecrator of Parker, I think it opportune to add a few words concerning this matter. From the document, whether fabricated or genuine, of the consecration of Parker, one learns that his consecrator was this William Barlow, already an apostate from the year 1536 in the time of Henry VIII, by whom he was named Bishop of St Asaph and St David's. He was assisted by three co-consecrating Bishops, only one of whom, John Hodgkins, had been ordained with the Catholic rite. After a long discussion it was not possible to produce an authentic and decisive document that would prove that Barlow had really been consecrated bishop; hence, at the end of the long discussion, the question of his episcopal consecration remained still doubtful. On the other hand, it is historically certain that Parker was made bishop with the Edwardine form. It is also certain that according to the Anglican ritual the words of the spurious form are pronounced only by the consecrator. Here is the rubric of the ritual: 'The Archbishop and Bishops present shall lay their hands upon the head of the elected Bishop, *the Archbishop saying: Receive the Holy Ghost, etc.*' Therefore one would have to prove that a special change had been made when Barlow was consecrated. Now, even if the Lambeth register, which reports his consecration, could be held to be substantially trustworthy, it cannot provide certainty, especially with regard to the details of the ceremony that was performed at that time. For these reasons, and for others that were discussed in the Commission, the consecration of Barlow remains doubtful. The defenders of validity or doubtful validity were not able to eliminate this doubt; hence, even on this account the alleged consecration of Parker would still remain doubtful.

III. CONCERNING THE FORM AND INTENTION
OF THE MINISTER IN
THE ANGLICAN ORDINATIONS

38. I shall begin by saying that, as I have mentioned above, the Edwardine form certainly remained in use for over a century without any change, that is, from the reign of Elizabeth in 1558 until 1662, which fact was certainly sufficient to interrupt the succession in the Anglican hierarchy. Given the invalidity of the Edwardine form, it follows that after the change was introduced into the ritual, even supposing that this change would have rendered the form of ordinations valid, they must still be held as invalid by reason of the defect of the minister, who was certainly ordained with the Edwardine form. For good reasons, then, the discussions and studies of the members of the Commission focussed primarily on the validity or invalidity of the Edwardine form, and in order that the discussion might proceed more expeditiously special attention was given to the Edwardine form of episcopal consecration.

According to the Anglican ritual, the form was the following: 'Receive the Holy Ghost, and remember that thou stir up the grace of God which is given thee by this imposition of our hands. For God hath not given us the spirit of fear, but of power, and love, and soberness.'

39. In order to simplify the question as far as possible, it will be well to observe that the discussion focused almost exclusively on the first three words of the alleged form: Receive the Holy Ghost; because obviously the following words do not indicate, and even less express, the conferral of a power of any kind. They are rather an admonition by which the candidate is exhorted to stir up in himself a gift already given – remember that thou stir up – and one certainly cannot stir up what is not yet there. Limiting myself, then, to the words Receive the Holy Ghost, I say that even joined, as they are, to the following words remember that thou stir up, etc., they constitute a form that is absolutely invalid for episcopal ordination, considering the form materially, or

REPORT AND VOTUM – PIEROTTI

objectively in itself, prescinding for now from the intention of the minister, about which, in accord with the order followed by the Commission, I must speak later on. In order that one may more clearly recognize the invalidity of this form, I shall quote the questions which the Most Eminent President wisely put to the members of the Commission, requesting each one to give concisely the reply that he judged to be true.

40. The first question is as follows: 'Whether for the validity of episcopal ordination it is necessary that the form express the order or power that is conferred.'

That the answer to this question must be absolutely in the affirmative is proven by many reasons, among which I shall mention briefly the two principal ones: (a) as St Thomas teaches (III, q.60, a.7), speaking in general of the form of the sacraments: 'The principle of determination is had on the part of the form, which is in some fashion the end and aim of the matter. Since therefore in sacraments there must be determined sensible things, which in sacraments are like the matter, *much more* it is required that there be a determined form.' Now in the Anglican episcopal consecration there is, to be sure, determined matter, which, as all agree, is the laying on of hands; but this is an ambiguous sign in itself, since there is also the laying of hands in priestly ordination. This sign, therefore, as in all the other sacraments, needs to be determined by the form. *The word is added to the matter and a sacrament takes place.* If therefore in the form of episcopal consecration there is no expression of the power or the order which one intends to confer, the form remains undetermined and is consequently invalid. (b) What always and in all liturgies has been held to be necessary and essential for the validity of episcopal consecration certainly belongs to the essence or is constitutive of the form; but the fact is that always and everywhere in all the liturgies accepted by the Catholic Church one finds in the form, despite all other variants, the designation of the order or power that is conferred; therefore we must hold that such designation is absolutely necessary. The major premise of the argument has no need of proof. The minor is proven by the following facts.

(1) In the ancient Roman liturgy one finds: *To the ministry of the high priesthood.* (2) In an old Gallican Codex: *to the ministry of the high priesthood.* (3) In the Greek liturgy: *to episcopal dignity.* (4) In the liturgy of the Syrian Maronites: *to the sublime order of bishops.* (5) In the Nestorian liturgy: *to the great work of the episcopate.* (6) In the liturgy of the Jacobites of Alexandria: *to a bishop.* (7) In the liturgy of the Armenians: *to the episcopate.* (8) In the liturgy of the Jacobites of Syria: *to the sublime order of bishops.* (9) In the liturgy of the Apostolic Constitutions: *to the episcopate.* (10) In the text of the rite of ordination found in the so-called canons of St Hippolytus: *grant to him the episcopate.* Since the minor of the argument remains abundantly proven, we must therefore hold that such designation is absolutely necessary, and any form that lacks it is invalid.

41. To the question put to them, the members of the Commission who maintained the invalidity of the Anglican ordinations unanimously replied *Yes* without restriction of any kind. Of the two who argued for validity, one replied *Yes*, adding: 'inasmuch as the form determining the matter constitutes with it the sacramental sign, which signifies the grace and power of the order, according to Christ's institution.' The other replied *No!!* adding: 'It is enough that from the whole rite one can judge what order or what power is being conferred.' Of the two defenders of doubtful validity one replied: *More probably! Yes.* The other replied *No!!* I shall not take the time to report the motives that led two of the Consultors to reply *No* to the question put to them, nor the motives that led the third one to reply *More probably*, since the matter seems to me so evident, both for the reasons that I have proposed in the preceding number, and for other reasons that could easily be brought forth. I shall only observe that the very disagreement among the replies given by the defenders of validity or doubtful validity shows by itself that the truth is to be found on the part of those who maintain the invalidity of a form in which the order or power that is being conferred is not designated.

42. The second was as follows: 'Whether this, i.e. the des-

ignation of the order or power, is expressed in the Anglican Ordinal, and if so, in which words.' From the very words of the Anglican alleged form which were faithfully reported and transcribed at the end of n. 38, to me it is evident that the required designation is not to be found in the Anglican Ordinal, and therefore it is also evident that to the question proposed the answer ought to be *No*. As I have already said in n. 39, where I have also given my reason, the only words in the alleged form to which one could attribute the semblance of a form are *Receive the Holy Ghost*. Now it is evident that these words offer a meaning that is absolutely undetermined. In fact, what do they express? Nothing else than a simple invocation of the Holy Spirit. And even if someone wished at all costs to claim that they signify the conferral of an order, what would that order be? The Diaconate? the Priesthood? or the Episcopate? It seems clear to me, therefore, that the alleged form is in itself undetermined, whereas, as we have already seen, it is absolutely necessary for the validity of a sacrament that the form be in itself determined, since this, to use the words of St Thomas quoted above, is the *determining principle*, and not what is to be determined.

43. To this question also the reply of those maintaining invalidity was completely uniform, that is, *No*. Of the two who defended validity, one answered *Yes*, claiming that the designation of the episcopal order or power is found right in the words of the form; but this cannot be admitted, as has already been proven. The other replied *Yes*, and he claimed to find the determination in the difference between the rite prescribed in the Ordinal for the ordination of a bishop, and that prescribed for the ordination of deacons and priests. But neither can this be sustained because the form, as I have said, must be what determines, and not what is to be determined. Of the two who defended doubtful validity, one replied *Yes*, but he claimed to find such a determination *in parts of the Anglican consecration that are certainly accidental*, that is, especially in the rubrics. But this seems to me not only false, but even absurd, and not much different from the condemned proposition of Le Courayer (Prop. 23).

The other, avoiding a categorical response said: 'In the formula *Receive the Holy Ghost*, nothing of the kind is expressed, at least explicitly. In the prayer of consecration the episcopal dignity and power is *somehow* expressed in the words: *Grant, we beseech Thee, to this Thy servant such grace, etc.*' To this it suffices to reply that according to him the form is undetermined and therefore is invalid.

44. Although the defenders of the validity or doubtful validity of the Anglican ordinations were not in agreement in deciding which were the words of the sacramental form for the consecration of a bishop, and where they were to be found in the Edwardine Ordinal, nevertheless I must report that they put much emphasis and stress on the words of the prayer which is found in the Ordinal after the litanies. These words are: 'Almighty God ... who by thy Holy Spirit hast appointed divers Orders of Ministers in Thy Church; Mercifully behold this thy servant now called to the Work and Ministry of a *Bishop*, etc.' I do not deny that the quoted words could at least provide reason for some doubt, if they were found in the right place, and joined either physically or morally to the imposition of hands, especially since, according to the common opinion, the form of episcopal consecration even in the Latin rite is not *imperative*, but *imprecatory*. And here I must say that the defenders of validity or doubtful validity grasped at all possible subtleties and all minutiae in their effort to prove that the cited imprecatory form is found at least morally united to the matter, i.e. to the imposition of hands which comes much later, and they argued their case at great length, producing the various opinions of the theological school and the authority of various approved theologians. All this, however, in no way helped their cause. First of all, it is not at all certain that this prayer was recited by the consecrator, since this is not prescribed in the Anglican ritual, and reliable persons testify that in fact this prayer is sometimes recited by the consecrator, and at other times by someone else. But what is more important is the fact that, according to the Ordinal, at the time when this prayer is recited the rite of ordination properly so called has not yet

begun. In fact, in the very ritual, the one chosen is still called *the one to be consecrated*, and the *consecrator* is required to pose a long series of questions to the *one to be consecrated*, to which he could even reply in the negative, and on that account be dismissed. Therefore it is only after the chanting of the *Veni Creator* that properly speaking the so-called rite of consecration begins. Therefore not only is the imposition of hands, the matter, found separated from the form, but this alleged imprecatory form is found outside the rite of consecration; hence it is separated from the matter not only physically but also morally.

45. This is so true that the Protestants themselves, with the exception, as far as I know, of a few recent ritualist writers, pay no attention to that alleged form, separated as it is from the matter and outside the rite of consecration; instead, they insist on the words *Receive the Holy Ghost*. In fact, when in 1874, as Cardinal Manning reports in a letter to the Holy Office of 25 August of that year, it was falsely supposed that what Antoin asserts in his Moral Theology was true, namely, that the Holy Office had declared priestly ordination according to the Coptic rite to be valid, with the imposition of hands and only the form *Receive the Holy Ghost*, the ritualists made great capital of this, as a decision favourable to the validity of their ordinations, and even some Catholics were disconcerted by it. And since the matter has come up, it is well to report at once that when the question raised by Archbishop Manning had been examined, and a learned and carefully prepared opinion had been given by Franzelin, at that time Consultor and subsequently Cardinal, it became clear that the alleged decision had never been pronounced. It was decided that Cardinal Patrizi, at that time Secretary of the Holy Office, should write to the Archbishop of Westminster in the following terms: 'From the Coptic rite itself, as found in their own Pontificals, it is evident that the words: *Receive the Holy Ghost* do not *constitute the entire form*; nor is the decision that was issued in 1704[10] to be understood to mean anything

---

10. Note well that here it was not a question of the decision taken with regard to

else than that priestly ordination among the Copts, with the imposition of hands and the recital of the form that is prescribed in their ancient rite, is to be held as valid. On the other hand, the Holy Office *never, either implicitly or explicitly declared* that the imposition of hands accompanied only by the words *Receive the Holy Ghost* would be sufficient.

46. Despite this explicit decision and declaration, Fr De Augustinis, defender in the Commission of the absolute validity of the Anglican ordinations, endeavoured, with much erudition and an abundance of quotations from eminent Catholic theologians, to prove that the words *Receive the Holy Ghost* constitute the valid form of episcopal ordination, even though in his writings he had taught the contrary. The eminent theologian, however, would have had to prove that those words constitute, as Franzelin put it, *the entire form*. Furthermore, he would have had to prove that according to the theologians whom he cited, those words not only belong to the form, but constitute it by themselves, so that, torn from some Catholic Pontifical and transferred to the Ordinal, from then on they constituted the complete and valid form of episcopal ordination. This he has not proved, nor could he ever prove it. Moreover, if one takes the opinion of the theologians to mean what De Augustinis takes it to mean, namely, that those words by themselves constitute the entire form, his argument would prove too much, and therefore would prove nothing. I say that it would prove too much, because it would follow that in the Catholic Church in England there had been no episcopal ordinations, since in the ancient Pontifical those words are not to be found, but only the imprecatory form. It would further prove that the whole Western Church lacked episcopal ordinations, since those words were introduced into the Pontifical only about the eleventh century, as Marino among others testifies.[11]

Gordon, but of another alleged decision of the same year and the same month of April; hence all the more improbable, as Franzelin observes with good reason.

11. [We presume that Marino stands for Morino, i.e. he refers to J. Morin, *Commentarius de sacris Ecclesiae ordinationibus*, Antwerp 1695, p. III, ex. II, cap. II, p. 18 – G. Rambaldi.]

With regard to the following words of the alleged form, namely *remember that thou stir up the grace*, etc., which were also much stressed by De Augustinis, I have already observed that in no way do they or can they signify exclusively episcopal ordination. Even if he wished to maintain that they allude exclusively to episcopal ordination because Timothy to whom they are directed was a bishop (which is not commonly admitted by exegetes), I will say only that with these words St Paul did not ordain or consecrate Timothy as a bishop, but he considered him already ordained and consecrated.

The Anglicans themselves in 1662 recognized the uselessness and invalidity of the aforesaid alleged *form*, seeing that after more than a hundred years they thought it necessary to change it into another: '*Receive the Holy Ghost* for the Office and Work of a Bishop in the Church of God, now committed unto thee by the imposition of our hands; In the name of the Father, and of the Son, and of the Holy Ghost. Amen. And remember . . .' as in the older form. However, this also is to be considered invalid, at least for defect of *intention*, concerning which I must speak presently. In any case the reply to the second question remains certain, namely, that in the alleged consecration of a bishop according to the Ordinal, the form does not express in any way the order or the power that one intends to confer.

47. Before entering upon the question of the defect of *intention* in the minister of Anglican ordinations, I must mention two other questions which were opportunely proposed by the Most Eminent President of the Commission, also concerning the *form* in itself. The third question is the following: 'Whether these words (that is, the words with which in the Ordinal the episcopal order or power is expressed) are explicit and clear, or rather somewhat ambiguous, so that their meaning needs to be further determined. If the answer is negative to the first part and affirmative to the second part, then Question 4 is: Whether and from what source these words might have a certain and definite meaning.'

The reply of those arguing for invalidity was explicit and

uniform, and in replying to these two questions they referred to the answer already given to the first and second questions. The reply of the defenders of validity or doubtful validity was discordant as usual. Some of them also referred to the reply already given, as did Gasparri, who held for doubtful validity. Duschesne replied 'No' to the first part of the third question, and 'Yes' to the second part. Then, to the fourth question he replied that the determination is drawn *from the rite as whole*. Of the two who defended validity, De Augustinis in replying to the third question, said: 'Yes to the first part, No to the second part.' Replying to the fourth question, he said: 'The reply has been given in my answer to the preceding question.' The second defender of validity, Scannell, although at the end he concluded for doubtful validity, replied to the third question with a simple 'Yes.' An inappropriate answer, even though he also referred to his previous reply. To the fourth question he replied simply: *Provided for by my previous answers*. I have already summarized the reasons given by the defenders of validity or doubtful validity, and have shown that they lack substance. Therefore, what those who argue for invalidity have asserted remains certain: namely, that the order or power which is conferred in episcopal ordination, in the form of consecration according to the Anglican rite is not expressed explicitly with words that have a determined meaning. Nor can it be said that they receive such a determination from some other part of the ritual. Therefore I agree with them that the *form* of the Ordinal, looked at objectively in itself, *is invalid*, since it lacks the essential quality, namely the determination of the order or power which is conferred in episcopal ordination.

48. Turning now to speak of the intention of the minister, it is well to note that here it is not a question of the faith or the intention of a minister who uses a Catholic sacramental form that is unchanged, or is changed only in some accidental way through ignorance or some slip of the tongue. Rather, the question is specific, and refers to the intention of a minister who uses a form that has been changed, and changed precisely for the purpose of introducing one's heresy into it,

or of promoting one's heresy by it, even though the change
itself were a minor one. To the question thus proposed we
find the answer in the reply given by Pope Zacharias to St
Boniface, Bishop of Mainz. St Boniface posed a question to
the Pope concerning the validity or invalidity of a baptism
conferred with a form whose words remained ambiguous, and
could have either a true or a false meaning. The Pope replied:
'The baptism is to be held as valid, if the one baptizing used
those words, not to introduce error or heresy, but merely
from ignorance of the Latin tongue, mangling the language'
(Mansi XII, 325). St Thomas answers the question with his
usual precision, first in III, q. 60, a. 7 ad 3, where he says:
'One who pronounces the sacramental words in a distorted
way, *if he does this intentionally*, does not seem to intend to do
what the Church does, and hence it does not seem that he
confers the sacrament.' In the place to which he refers, a. 8,
where he directly treats the question, he teaches: 'I reply that
one should say that with regard to ALL *those changes that
can happen in the forms of sacraments*, there are two things to
be considered: first *on the part of the one saying the words*,
whose intention is required for the sacrament. Thus, *if by this
addition or omission he intends to introduce another rite which
is not accepted by the Church, it does not seem that the sacrament is conferred, because it does not seem that he intends to do
what the Church does*.' Hence, in the light of the aforesaid
decision of Pope Zacharias and the teaching of the Angelic
Doctor, when we are dealing with a change of any kind that
has been introduced into the form of sacraments: '*with regard
to all those changes that can happen in the forms of sacraments*,' in order to judge correctly about the validity or invalidity of the sacrament, we ought to look not only to the
material change of the form, but also to whether the change
has been introduced deliberately, with the intention of introducing another rite not accepted by the Church, or, as the
Pontiff put it, with the intention of introducing error or heresy.
If such a perverse intention is not only present in the mind,
but is manifested externally, either by the one who introduced
the change, or by the one who uses the altered form, and even

more if by both, then the sacrament must be judged invalid, not only because of the defect of the form, but also because of the defect of the intention of the minister.

49. Most opportunely, therefore, the Most Eminent President proposed the fifth question, which reads as follows: 'Can words which taken in themselves can have the force and meaning of a Catholic form, or are compatible with it, if they are knowingly twisted into the contrary meaning, with a change of rite being made with the same intent, still be considered to retain the Catholic meaning in this new rite?'

In accord with the doctrine briefly explained in the preceding number, it seems clear to me that one must reply to this question with an unconditional 'No'. In fact, such was the unanimous reply of the four who argued that the Anglican ordinations were absolutely invalid, relying more or less on the reason that with regard to the form of sacraments, one must pay attention not only to the material words, but also, and indeed primarily, to the meaning that is given to the words by the one who pronounces them. When such words, in the common language of the one who pronounces them, have a meaning that is destructive of the essence of the sacrament, they cannot be used to confer a valid sacrament. With this reason, thus briefly summed up, I am in full agreement.

The defenders of validity or doubtful validity, having to reply to the aforesaid question, saw themselves in dire straits. Therefore Gasparri replied: 'If in the words of the rite there is positively conveyed an error that is contrary to the substance of episcopal consecration, No. If by the words of the rite there is not conveyed an error that is contrary to the substance of episcopal consecration, Yes.' Whether this reply will hold up, we shall more opportunely see later on. De Augustinis replied 'Yes,' adding: 'if the words of the form truly, of themselves, signify the grace and power, according to Christ's institution, for that sacrament whose form it is.' I shall speak of this also later on. Scannell seconded the reply given by Gasparri, distinguishing between an error expressed positively and negatively. Duchesne said more or less the same things with a different turn of phrase.

50. We come now to the sixth question proposed by His Eminence, and from the reply to this question we shall be led to the definitive solution of the problem we are discussing. Here is the question: 'Is it evident that the Catholic doctrine on the Sacrament of Orders and on what pertains to this sacrament was repudiated by the authors and promoters of the Anglican Ordinal, and that changes in accord with their new doctrine were introduced into the rite?'

With regard to the first part of the question, it is not my intention to present in detail the numberless proofs that could be adduced, to show beyond a shadow of a doubt that the authors and compilers of the Ordinal rejected and denied the Catholic doctrine on the Sacrament of Orders, and what is dogmatically pertinent to Orders. If anyone desires a full and detailed exposition of this, supported by reliable historical documents, he can read Appendix II, inserted by the English theologians in their learned work entitled *Ordines Anglicani*, from page 71 to p. 86. After examining this learned and erudite Appendix, I am convinced that it proves beyond a shadow of doubt that the compilers of the Ordinal denied the existence of the Sacrament of Orders, the real presence of Jesus Christ in the Eucharist, the Sacrifice of the Mass, and the power to absolve and remit sins, in the true and Catholic sense. To prove that the compilers of the Ordinal defended and publicly propagated the aforesaid heresies, the English theologians patiently investigated the perverse doctrines, in matters of faith, of all those who took part in the compilation of the Ordinal, either as principal authors, as collaborators or as adherents. However, since it is also proven beyond any doubt, as is shown in Appendix I contained in the same work, that the heretical and schismatic Archbishop Cranmer was, as I have said before, not only the principal author of the Ordinal, but its true compiler, it will suffice to indicate briefly what the perverse doctrine of this heresiarch was. To prove that Cranmer was the true compiler of the Ordinal, it suffices to cite the Anglican Strype, historian of the Reform, and held in high repute by all the Anglicans, who wrote toward the middle of the seventeenth century. Speaking of the compiler of the new liturgy, he says, among other things, 'Just as they introduced nothing into this liturgy without his (scil. Cranmer's) approval, so neither did they reject or wish to exclude anything that he judged should be included in it.'

51. What the perverse doctrines of this compiler of the Ordinal were regarding the Sacrament of Orders, he himself clearly manifested when Henry VIII asked him: 'Whether in the New Testament be required any consecration of a bishop and priest, or only appointing to the office be sufficient.' His reply was: 'In the New Testament, he that is appointed to be a bishop or a priest, *needeth no consecration by the scripture*, for election or appointing thereto is sufficient' (Stillingfleet MSS, Lambeth. 1108, fol. 69).[12] And in his detestable work entitled *De Oblatione*, Bk. V, ch. 11, he says clearly that '*there is no difference between the priest and the layman*', and that the priest is nothing but a '*common minister of the Church*'.[13] Speaking of the Sacrifice of the Mass, in chap. 14 of the work cited, he blasphemes saying: 'And as for the saying or singing of the mass by the priest, as it was in time past used, it *is neither a sacrifice propitiatory*, nor yet a sacrifice of laud and praise, nor in any wise allowed before God, but *abominable and detestable.*'[14] Then, regarding the real presence of Jesus in the Sacrament, in the cited work, Bk. III, ch. 11 he teaches: 'The eating of Christ's flesh and drinking of his blood … is a *figurative* speech *spiritually* to be understand … And this our belief in him is *to eat his flesh and drink his blood, although they be not present with us.*'[15] I have no need of producing other proofs, since from the denial of the Sacrament of Orders there follows the necessity of denying all the dogmas intimately connected with the same. Moreover, that the error of Cranmer which is basic to our question was not a private one, but publicly professed,

12. [Cranmer's *Works*, Parker Society, 24.117.]
13. [Parker Society, 12.350.]
14. [Parker Society, 12.352.]
15. [Parker Society, 12.115–116.]

besides other proofs that could be adduced, is perfectly clear
from the 25th of the 39 so-called doctrinal Articles, which
were compiled and publicly adopted at the same time the
Ordinal was introduced. This article reads as follows:
'There are *two* Sacraments ordained of Christ our Lord in
the Gospel, that is to say, Baptism and the Supper of the
Lord. Those five commonly called Sacraments, that is to
say, Confirmation, Penance, Orders, Matrimony, and
extreme Unction, are not to be counted for Sacraments of
the Gospel, being such as have grown partly of the corrupt
following of the Apostles, partly are states of life allowed in
the Scriptures; but yet have not like nature of Sacraments
with Baptism, and the Lord's Supper.' It is therefore evident
that the principal author of the Ordinal rejected the Catholic
doctrine on Sacred Orders, and on what pertains to Orders.
The same doctrine was publicly professed by his collaborators
Ridley, Hooper, Holbeach et al.

52. Whoever would wish to see, clearly and in detail, that
modifications and innovations were introduced into the
Ordinal that are completely in accord with the heresies professed by its principal Author, could read Appendix IV compiled by the English theologians, in pages 113 to 160 of their
work, where, with great accuracy, the rite of ordination
according to the Catholic Pontifical used in England is compared with the rite according to the Ordinal. One sees at once
that everything which referred to the Sacrament of Orders has
been carefully removed from the Ordinal, every mention of
Priesthood, Priest, Altar, Sacrifice has been consistently
avoided, and specifically in episcopal consecration everything
has been removed that referred to *Priesthood*, to the *fullness
of Priesthood*, to *the Power of the Keys*. Moreover, besides the
other changes the Bishop-elect is invited to make a positive
promise to hold and teach only what is contained in Holy
Scripture, without paying any attention to Tradition, as
something that is not necessary for eternal salvation. Now
we have already seen that according to Cranmer and the
explicit profession of the 25th doctrinal article, Holy Orders
would not be a Sacrament according to Holy Scripture; hence

in this promise, one explicitly rejects the existence of Orders as a sacrament of the new law.

53. From all that has been said up to now, and from what has been written in a scholarly way and maintained in the Commission by those who argued for the invalidity of the Anglican ordinations, it seems to me clear that to the sixth question proposed by the Eminent President, one ought to reply *Yes on all accounts*, as indeed the proponents of the absolute invalidity of the ordinations have unanimously done. It is perfectly clear that the innovations made in the ritual, and specifically in the form of ordinations, including episcopal consecration, were made by the compiler of the Ordinal not by chance or by mistake, or from ignorance, but with the deliberate intention of introducing heresy into it, of establishing a new rite, and consequently the ordinations and episcopal consecrations performed according to this new rite are invalid by defect of intention, as has been proven in n. 48. And here it is well to observe that as far back as 1685, Cardinal Casanata had concluded to the invalidity of Anglican Ordinations by reason of the defect *of form, and of intention* on the part of the minister, and for the same reason they are still considered invalid by the Catholics of England, as we have seen in n. 25.

54. I must now add a few words about the replies given to this question by the defenders of validity or doubtful validity. Gasparri replied that in the new ritual heresies are not expressed *positively* but only *negatively*, and therefore the heretical doctrine of the compilers is not clearly expressed in it. To this I reply that there are sins both of commission and of omission, and that in order to call a rite heretical, it is not necessary that heresy be positively professed in it, when the Catholic dogma has been removed from it, nor does it follow that the dogma has to be denied. For example, to render the form of Baptism invalid, it is not necessary that there be in it an explicit denial of the existence or divinity of the Holy Spirit; it would be enough to omit the mention of this third divine Person, precisely in the way that the compilers of the Ordinal have acted in omitting the mention of the

order or the power that is being conferred. By this they have said clearly enough that they do not believe in the existence of the Sacrament of Orders. Furthermore, I have already observed in n. 52 that the principal compiler of the Ordinal, and Anglicans generally, reject divine Tradition, accepting only Sacred Scripture, according to which, they say, Order is not a sacrament. The Bishop-elect, therefore, being required in his profession of faith to reject divine tradition, and to profess *positively* the heretical doctrine imposed by law (*the law of this realm*), by doing so, *positively* rejects the Sacrament of Orders.

55. De Augustinis, mind you, said that the compilers of the Ordinal intended only to restore the rite of ordination to the practice of Apostolic times, to its original institution, hence one cannot say that in the new rite they have rejected the Sacrament of Orders. While that might have been their intention, they have not expressed this in the rite; in fact, they have expressed the opposite, recognizing that there are deacons, priests and bishops, as in Sacred Scripture, and furthermore it is not proven that all the compilers of the Ordinal were heretics.

I reply: one can easily admit that the compilers of the Ordinal have claimed that they only intended to restore the Church to the purity of apostolic times; this has almost always been the sheep's clothing with which the heretics have tried to disguise themselves. But that this is what they have actually done in compiling the Ordinal must be absolutely denied, as has been shown. In fact, among all the various Pontificals which are accepted by the Catholic Church and were kept intact even by schismatics and heretics, those compilers could not find one that satisfied their heretical tastes, and for that reason they took it upon themselves to make those radical changes.

Nor can their work receive a benign interpretation merely on the grounds that in the Ordinal and their common usage they retain the names of deacons, priests and bishops. They did not intend to return to paganism, but claimed to establish a new Church, a true Church, called 'national', removed from legitimate subjection to the Roman Pontiff and subject to their own Sovereign. They had need, therefore, of an external appearance to support their claim that they intended to establish a Christian church, and for that reason they retained the names designating the sacred hierarchy. Indeed they could not suppress the names that are found in the very Sacred Scriptures on which they mainly wished to base themselves. However, they were careful officially to give to these names a meaning totally contrary to the reality of divine institution and of Catholic dogmatic doctrine. Since they denied the Sacrament of Orders, the Sacrifice of the Mass, and the Power of the Keys, their alleged bishops, priests and deacons were nothing more for them than simple *administrators and superintendants* (*presbus, episkopos*), appointed to perform one or another office, as they themselves said, men without any sacred character whatsoever. Moreover, they could not suppress in their hierarchy the names found in the very Sacred Scriptures on which they mainly wished to base their new doctrine. There is no need, therefore, to evaluate the varied replies given to the sixth question by the defenders of validity or doubtful validity, since they are based primarily on the aforesaid reasons which have an appearance of truth, but are completely false.

56. The seventh question proposed by His Eminence was the following: 'What judgment, therefore, should be made about the form and intention in this new rite?'

I think that in the whole of the present chapter, I have sufficiently demonstrated that this new rite absolutely lacks the valid form and the requisite intention. This is the unanimous reply given by those who argued for the invalidity of the ordinations, and this is the reply that I intend to give to the question. With regard to the reply given by those who defended validity or doubtful validity, I must observe that while De Augustinis, in the course of the discussions, had almost always spoken in favour of the validity of the ordinations, he seems, in his reply to this last question, to have modified the opinion he had previously held, associating himself with those who argued for doubtful validity. In fact he replied as follows: 'I judge the form to be *probably* or *more probably* valid, and the intention to be *sufficient* for validity.' Here, then, it is no longer a question of absolute validity, but of doubtful validity. It seems one can draw the same conclusion from the final replies of Scannell.

Reflecting on the whole long discussion, lasting through twelve long sessions, and on the documents presented by those who argued against the absolute invalidity of the ordinations, I must confess that the defenders of doubtful validity were strongly represented in the Commission formed by the Holy Father, and had powerful, and, if I may say so, obstinate representatives, especially in Gasparri and De Augustinis, men certainly worthy of defending a better cause, which they would no doubt have brought to the desired victory, provided that their case had been based not on mere hypotheses, but on the truth and reality of the facts.

CONCLUSION

57. From what has been said so far, it seems to me that it has been clearly enough demonstrated that the Anglican Ordinations were declared invalid: (a) by Pope Julius III in the Bull *Dilecte Fili* of 5 August 1553, and with the Brief of 8 March 1554. (b) They were declared invalid by Pope Paul IV with the Bull *Praeclara charissimi* of 19 June 1555 and with the Brief of 30 October of the same year, as is clear from what I have said in Chapter I. (c) They were declared invalid, first by the Consultors of the Holy Office in 1685, and then solemnly in the Thursday session by Pope Clement XI in 1704, as I have shown in Chapter II. (d) They are to be judged invalid for defect of form and of intention, as was shown in Chapter III. (e) The constant practice of Catholics has always held them to be invalid, as is clear from what I have said on this point in Chapters I and II. (f) The solemn declarations of nullity, confirmed by constant practice, are not and cannot be said to be motivated by a lack of knowledge of the various liturgies, or by other incomplete knowledge of documents

that have subsequently come to light; rather, they are based on the defect of the requisite form and the requisite intention.

I maintain therefore that Anglican ordinations have been declared absolutely invalid by the Supreme Authority of the Church, and are to be held as such by all Catholics, for the lack of the requisite form and the requisite intention.

IV. WITH REGARD TO THE NECESSITY, OPPORTUNENESS AND MODALITY OF A NEW AND SOLEMN DECLARATION

58. From all that I have said thus far, it might seem that a new declaration of the nullity of Anglican ordinations should be considered superfluous, since the matter has been so many times declared and has been constantly held in practice. In my humble opinion, such a new, solemn, formal and explicit declaration has at the present moment become more necessary than ever. In fact, it is not only the dissidents, especially the Ritualists and Anglo-Catholics, who for some time have been maintaining the validity or at least the doubtful validity of Anglican ordinations, but, as I have said at the beginning, the question has been raised, and is being vigorously raised, by Catholic theologians and writers, who claim that at least the definitive and unappealable decision of the Supreme Authority of the Church, the Supreme Pontiff, has not yet been pronounced.

The very fact of the difference of opinion among the members of the Commission, which has persisted throughout the whole course of the discussions, makes it evident that despite the declarations and decisions of three Popes and of the Supreme Congregation of the Holy Office, perplexities and differences of opinion remain among some Catholics. Perhaps someone will say: in order to put an end to the disputes and eliminate the confusion, it would be enough to publish the declarations and decisions already made, which might easily be unknown, at least in their full complexity, to Catholic theologians and writers. But the facts show that this would not suffice. The Commission, made up of learned and erudite men, was shown everything, it knew everything, it pondered and discussed everything at great length; nonetheless the difference of opinion and the perplexity remained. In my opinion, therefore, a new papal decision is not only useful but necessary. Silence on the part of the Supreme Pontiff, or merely recalling the earlier declarations and decisions, after having entrusted the study and discussion of the question to a special Commission, would contribute to an increase of perplexity and differences of opinion, and would give new life to the dispute.

59. As regards the opportuneness, some have thought that a new authoritative declaration could perhaps impede, or at least slow down, the very welcome movement of return to Catholicism that has been taking place for some time in England, and has even grown stronger after the publication of the well-known Apostolic Letter of the reigning Supreme Pontiff. To eliminate such unfounded doubts and fears, it is enough to know that the whole English Catholic Episcopate, in a collective letter addressed to the Holy Father, has expressed the opinion that a new and peremptory decision would not only not be inopportune, but would provide a new and most powerful impulse, leading to the return of numberless dissidents to the bosom of the Catholic Church.

Now who are the people who, in these recent times, have been 'moving heaven and earth' in their efforts to obtain from the Holy See a declaration of at least the doubtful validity of the Anglican ordinations? They are, in the first place, the so-called Ritualists, who form one group of that part of the English Church called the 'High Church', which is distinguished in beliefs and attitudes from the two other parts of the same Church, namely, the 'Broad Church', with its elastic doctrines, and the evangelical 'Low Church'. All these use the same Ordinal of Edward VI for the consecration and installation of their ministers, nor can they use another as long as they remain in the Anglican Church.[16] Among all these, even

---

16. They are not to be confused with the 250 or more dissident sects which have legally abandoned the Established Church, and which number twelve million adherents.

including the Ritualists, every one has his own opinion on every point of doctrine. On their personal initiative, many belonging to the 'High' Church have again adopted a great many Catholic ceremonies, practices and doctrines, except for the Petrine Primacy in the sense of '*jurisdiction*', and they want to be certain that they have sacraments that are valid and are recognized by the rest of Christianity.

In the second place are all those belonging to the various parts of the Anglican Church who, whether or not they believe in the true Priesthood, in the Sacrifice of the Mass and in the Eucharist (in the sense of 'transubstantiation'), seek to propagate their theory of a Catholic Church that is divided into various national branches which are more or less united in '*essential*' beliefs and in sharing the same sacraments (Cf. Letter of Gladstone, *Times*, 1 June 1896).

They earnestly wish to be called '*Catholics*'; they are '*English Catholics*', we are '*Roman Catholics*'. To provide a firm basis for this theory of theirs, which is practically so attractive, and to hold in the broad bosom of the Church of England all those who feel ever more strongly the necessity of being in union with the See of Peter, it is essential that their sacraments be recognized in some way by the rest of Christianity (Cf. Letter of the English Episcopate to the Holy Father).

Here is the real reason for the efforts that have been made recently. To those whose conscience is troubled by doubt, one replies as the Archbishop of York did in his celebrated discourse of the past October at the Norwich Congress: 'To the eye of our Blessed Lord, however obscure to our imperfect vision, the countless multitudes of those who have been baptized into His Name and grafted into Him are bound together in a union, not less real because it is spiritual; they are one body in Christ.... Whatever may be our differing conceptions as to the nature of the future life or the conditions under which it shall be obtained, throughout the length and breadth of Christendom there is one hope.... There may be varied conceptions of His Incarnate life or His atoning death: but everywhere and at all times He is the Lord – the

Lord of the Church ... which is his Body ... And there is one baptism ... There may be different estimates as to its efficacy or its administration; but among all the divisions of Christendom there is one baptism' (cf. *Guardian*, 9 October 1895). It is by people such as these, if I may speak frankly, that all those Catholic writers have been deluded and misled, who for some time now have undertaken to defend the validity or doubtful validity of Anglican ordinations. This is proven by the fact that it is from their writings that Catholics have drawn almost all the arguments which they have advanced to prove this thesis.

60. Now it is quite natural that these Neo-Catholics constitute one of the principal obstacles to the return of England to Catholicism. To adopt biblical language, they are still outside the sheepfold; they are still ravenous wolves; but at the same time they wish to disguise themselves as Catholics, they have put on sheep's clothing, and in this way they more easily approach and delude simple folk, getting them to believe that to obtain their eternal salvation, to be Catholics, it is enough to belong to them, it is enough to have the sacraments without going to Rome, without having to be subject to the Vicar of Jesus Christ. Thus they impede the salutary movement toward the Catholic Church and the return to Catholicism. A new and solemn decision declaring Anglican ordinations to be absolutely invalid would not only manifest the constancy and unchanging conduct of the Holy See; it would serve also to tear off the sheep's clothing, so to speak, with which these new reformers have wished to disguise themselves. For these and other reasons which could easily be produced, I maintain that a new and solemn declaration is not only necessary but also most opportune.

61. To further confirm what I have said about the necessity and opportuneness of a new and explicit declaration, I think it well to add that already in 1868, among the preparatory documents of the Vatican Council, one finds an admirable *votum* of the Reverend Professor Fejie, in which, after having given solid proof of the absolute invalidity of Anglican ordinations, he studies the question and offers a suggestion about

the way to deal with the Anglicans before and during the Council. He concludes: 'Since Anglican *ordinations are null and void, the Anglican bishops, as such, should be completely ignored.* Taking into account the great number of Anglican people and ministers (not bishops) who are returning to the Catholic faith, and the great hope of this that shines more brightly every day, I think that at the close of the Council there would be a place for a special approach to the Anglicans as a whole, calling them *all, without further specification,* back to Catholic unity.' What the Consultor suggested in this part of his *votum* was done by the reigning Supreme Pontiff in his memorable Apostolic Letter *Ad Anglos.* And even earlier, Pius IX of happy memory, before the Vatican Council began, invited the schismatic Orientals to unity, and he also invited the *Protestant factions.* The invitation to the schismatics was addressed to the bishops, but in the invitation to the Protestants, including the Anglicans, no mention was made either of bishops or of Sacred Orders. The same Consultor added: 'In that document it seems that there are two things that should not be omitted. First of all, it seems that one should not omit *express mention of the invalidity of Anglican ordinations, since this would seem to favour the work of conversion*; on the other hand, if this were omitted, it could seem that the Apostolic See was still in doubt about this, and thus perhaps one of the primary motives for conversion would be taken away.'

In the second place, the Consultor suggested that the sect of the Ritualists, already condemned by the Holy Office on 16 September 1864, should be censured again.

62. Finally, with regard to the way it should be done, it is my opinion that the new declaration should not only be explicit and peremptory, but should also be given all those qualities that would cause it to be recognized as an act issued by the Supreme Authority of the Church, from which there is no appeal. I also think it expedient that the declaration should be aimed at the very essence of those alleged ordinations, declaring them null *by reason of the defect of the requisite form and the requisite intention.* That would make it

evident that in a matter like the present, which is doctrinal and dogmatic, the Holy See maintains not only unity of doctrine, but also unity of language. To further manifest this unchanging unity, one could recall the previous acts of the Holy See, especially those of Popes Julius III, Paul IV and Clement XI. One could also mention the preparatory studies on which the solemn declaration of Clement XI was based, likewise noting the fact that all those decisions were based not on false or dubious hypotheses, but on the proven lack of the requisite form and the requisite intention.

Thus I express my humble opinion, and submit it wholly and entirely to the wise and enlightened discernment of the Eminent Fathers Inquisitors General, and to the definitive judgment of the Holy Father, of whom I humbly beg the Apostolic Blessing.

Rome, the Vatican,   Fr RAFFAELE PIEROTTI, OP
28 May 1896   Master of the Sacred Palace
                                and Consultor of the Holy Office.

APOSTOLICAE CURAE

Apostolic Letter of Pope Leo XIII

[1] The apostolic solicitude and charity with which, helped by His grace, We strive in the fulfilment of Our office to imitate 'the great pastor of the sheep, our Lord Jesus Christ',* have been devoted in no small measure to the noble people of England. Our affection for them was shown particularly in the special Letter addressed by Us last year 'to the English who seek the kingdom of Christ in the unity of faith',† wherein We recalled the memory of that nation's ancient union with Holy Mother Church and appealed for earnest prayers to God that it might soon become happily reconciled to her. And again when, not long ago, We thought fit to treat more fully of the unity of the Church in an Encyclical Letter‡ We had England prominently in mind, hoping that Our words might bring not only encouragement to Catholics but also salutary guidance to those who are separated from Us. In that Letter We spoke emphatically and freely, urged thereto by no mere human considerations; and the fact that it received so warm a welcome from the English people shows a courtesy in that nation and a widespread concern among them for the salvation of souls to which We gladly pay tribute.

[2] In the same spirit and with the same end in view We have resolved now to turn Our attention to an equally

---

*Heb. 13:20.

†Apostolic Letter *Amantissimæ* of the year 1895; *Acta Leonis XIII*, XV, pp. 138–155.

‡*Satis cognitum*, *Acta*, XVI, pp. 157–208.

important matter which is connected with the aforesaid subject and with Our own hopes.

[3] It has been the common theological opinion – and one confirmed on several occasions by the pronouncements of the Church and by her consistent practice – that the true sacrament of Order as Christ instituted it, and therewith the hierarchical succession, lapsed in England because, shortly after her secession from the centre of Christian unity, an entirely new rite for the conferring of sacred orders was publicly introduced in the reign of King Edward VI. In recent times, however, and especially during the past few years, a controversy has arisen whether sacred ordinations performed according to the Edwardine rite possess the nature and efficacy of a sacrament, the opinion in favour of their validity being held, with greater or less assurance, not only by a number of Anglican writers but also by a few Catholics, for the most part not English. The former have been moved by an awareness of the excellence of the Christian priesthood and a desire that their ministers should not be without its twofold power concerning the body of Christ, while the latter have been prompted by the wish to remove an obstacle in the way of the Anglicans' return to unity. Both have appeared to share the conviction that it would be opportune, now that time has matured the study of this subject and some documentary evidence has been newly rescued from oblivion, to have the question re-examined under Our authority.

[4] Having regard to these proposals and desires, and paying heed above all to the bidding of apostolic charity, We resolved for Our part that nothing ought to be left untried which might seem to contribute in any way to averting harm to souls or promoting their well-being. We therefore decided to accede to the request for a re-examination of the question, in order that a complete and thorough investigation might remove even the least shadow of doubt for the future.

[5] We accordingly commissioned a number of persons of eminent learning and erudition, known to differ in their views on this question, each to draw up in writing a reasoned report of his opinion; they were then summoned to Our presence and

directed to communicate their reports to one another and to make such further investigations and studies as the subject seemed to demand. We further arranged that they should be afforded every facility to re-examine all the known relevant documents in the Vatican archives, and to bring any new documents to light; also that they should have at their disposal all the acts relating to the subject which were in the keeping of the Supreme Council, as well as the hitherto published works of learned writers in favour of either view. Thus equipped, We required them to hold special sessions, twelve of which took place under the presidency of a Cardinal appointed by Ourself, every member being allowed full freedom of discussion. We finally directed the findings of these sessions, together with the other documents, to be placed before Our Venerable Brethren the Cardinals of the same Council; these were to study the matter, then discuss it in Our presence, and each pronounce his opinion.

[6] Such was the procedure determined upon. But a due prerequisite for a thorough-going investigation was first to make a most careful inquiry to discover how the matter stood already in regard to the enactments and established custom of the Apostolic See. It was of great importance to consider the origin and the force of that custom.

[7] In the first place, therefore, consideration was given to the chief documents by which Our Predecessors, at the request of Queen Mary, made special provision for the reconciliation of the English Church. For this task Julius III appointed Cardinal Reginald Pole, an Englishman of outstanding merits, to be his Legate *a latere*; he sent him as 'his angel of peace and love', giving him extraordinary instructions or faculties and laying down directions for his guidance,* all of which were subsequently ratified and explained by Paul IV.

[8] Now in order to grasp the exact force of these documents it is a necessary presupposition to understand that they

---

*These were conveyed in August 1553 by the Bulls *Si ullo unquam tempore* and *Post nuntium Nobis*, and by other letters.

were not abstract treatises, but were intended to deal with concrete and specific conditions. The faculties granted by these Popes to the Apostolic Legate had reference precisely to England and to the state of religion existing in that country. Consequently the instructions given by them to the same Legate in answer to his request could not have had the scope of laying down what was essential for the validity of sacred ordinations in general; they had to be specifically directed to making provision for holy orders in England itself, as required by the conditions and circumstances described. That this is so is abundantly clear from the nature and tenor of the documents themselves; moreover it would plainly have been quite incongruous to send such a lesson to the Legate, a man whose learning had been conspicuous at the Council of Trent itself, as if he needed to be told what was essentially required for conferring the sacrament of Order.

[9] If these considerations are borne in mind it is not difficult to see why, in the letter of Julius III to the Apostolic Legate dated 8 march 1554, distinct mention is made first of those who, 'having been regularly and lawfully promoted', were to be retained in their orders, and, secondly, of those who, 'not having been promoted to sacred orders', might 'if found worthy and suitable, be promoted' thereto. Two classes of persons really existing are plainly and definitely described: on the one hand those who had truly received sacred ordination, that is to say, who had received it either before Henry's secession or, if after it and at the hands of ministers who were in error or schism, had nevertheless been ordained according to the customary Catholic rite; and on the other hand those who had been initiated according to the Edwardine Ordinal, and who were able to 'be promoted' precisely because they had received an ordination which was invalid.

[10] And that this was in fact the Pope's meaning is very clearly confirmed by a letter of the Legate himself, dated 29 January 1555, in which he delegates his faculties to the Bishop of Norwich. It is also of great importance to consider what Julius III himself says in his letter on making free use of the Papal faculties even for the benefit of those upon whom an

[episcopal] consecration had been conferred 'irregularly (*minus rite*) and without the observance of the customary form of the Church'; an expression which undoubtedly indicated those who had been consecrated according to the Edwardine rite, since apart from this form and the Catholic form there was none other existing in England at the time.

[11] Further evidence is provided by the delegation which the sovereigns Philip and Mary, on the advice of Cardinal Pole, sent to the Pope in Rome in the month of February 1555. The royal envoys, three 'illustrious and most virtuous men', among them Thomas Thirlby, Bishop of Ely, were charged to inform the Pope more fully concerning the state of religion in England, and in particular to ask for his ratification and confirmation of all that the Legate had done and caused to be done in the matter of reconciling that kingdom with the Church; for which purpose all the necessary written evidence, together with the relevant portions of the new Ordinal, was submitted to the Pope. Paul IV received the delegation with great ceremony and, the aforesaid documents having been 'carefully discussed' by certain Cardinals, 'after mature deliberation' he issued his Bull *Praeclara carissimi* on the 20th of June in the same year. Herein, after full approval and confirmation of Pole's action, the following instruction is given concerning ordinations: 'Those who have been promoted to ecclesiastical orders ... by any other than a bishop regularly and rightly ordained shall be bound to receive the same orders anew.'

[12] Who these bishops were that had not been 'regularly and rightly ordained' had already been made sufficiently clear by earlier documents and by the faculties which the Legate had used in the matter: they were those who had been promoted to the episcopate, as others had been promoted to other orders, 'without the observance of the customary form of the Church', or, as the Legate himself had written to the Bishop of Norwich, without the observance of 'the Church's form and intention'. And these were certainly none other than those who had been promoted according to the form of the new rite, to the examination of which the

appointed Cardinals had devoted careful attention. Another pertinent passage in the same letter is to be noted, in which the Pope mentions among the persons needing the benefit of dispensation those who 'had obtained both orders and ecclesiastical benefices *nulliter* and *de facto*'. To have obtained orders *nulliter* means to have obtained them by an act which is null and void, that is, invalidly, as both the etymology of the word and its ordinary use denote; indeed, this usage is confirmed here because the same term that is used in regard to orders is used likewise in regard to 'ecclesiastical benefices', which by certain provisions of the sacred canons were manifestly null because they had been conferred with a voiding defect.

[13] Finally, a doubt having arisen as to who in fact might be said and held to be bishops 'regularly and rightly ordained' according to the mind of the Pope, the latter shortly afterwards, on the 30th of October, issued a further letter in the form of a Brief, in which he said:

'Wishing to dispel this doubt and, by explaining more clearly what was Our mind and intention in Our aforesaid letter, to make opportune provision for the peace of conscience of those who had been promoted to orders during the schism, We declare that the bishops and archbishops who cannot be said to be "regularly and rightly ordained" are only those who were not ordained and consecrated in the form of the Church.'

[14] This declaration must have related precisely to the existing circumstances in England, that is, to the Edwardine Ordinal; otherwise the Pope would certainly have done nothing by his further letter 'to dispel doubt' or 'to make provision for peace of conscience'. Moreover, it was in this sense that the Legate understood the documents and instructions of the Apostolic See, and it was according to this sense that he duly and diligently observed them. The same is true also of Queen Mary and the others who co-operated with her in the work of restoring the Catholic religion and practice to its former condition.

[15] The authorities which We have quoted of Julius III and Paul IV clearly show the origin of the rule, which has now been constantly observed for more than three centuries, of treating ordinations according to the Edwardine rite as null and void, a rule which is abundantly testified by many instances, even in this City, in which such ordinations have been repeated unconditionally according to the Catholic rite.

[16] The observance of this customary rule is significant for the question before us. For if any doubt lingers as to the sense in which the aforesaid Papal documents are really to be understood, one may apply here the axiom: 'Custom is the best interpreter of law'. As it has always been the unvarying and accepted teaching of the Church that it is unlawful to repeat the sacrament of Order, it was accordingly quite impossible that the Apostolic See should tacitly allow or tolerate such a custom. And yet in this matter she has not only tolerated it but has approved and sanctioned it whenever a particular case of this sort has come up for judgement.

[17] We quote two such cases, out of the many which from time to time have been submitted to the Supreme Council: that of a certain French Calvinist in the year 1684, and that of John Clement Gordon in the year 1704 both of them ordained according to the Edwardine ritual.

[18] In the first case, verdicts (or '*vota*') were delivered in writing by many of the consultors after a careful examination, the remainder unanimously concurring with them in giving a verdict 'for the invalidity of the ordination'; it was only for considerations of expediency that the Cardinals decided upon the reply, 'Judgement postponed'.

[19] In the second case the proceedings of the former were presented again and reconsidered; in addition further *vota* were obtained from consultors, leading doctors of the Sorbonne and of Douai were asked their opinion, and no measure which far-sighted prudence could suggest was neglected to ensure a thoroughly accurate knowledge of the question.

[20] It is to be observed also that, although both Gordon himself, whose case was in question, and some of the con-

sultors had included among the grounds of nullity the account of Parker's ordination as then alleged, this argument was in fact entirely set aside in arriving at a decision, as documents of incontestable authenticity show. No other reason was given weight than 'defect of form and intention'. And in order that the judgement on this form might be as complete and certain as possible, care had been taken to have a copy of the Anglican Ordinal available, and a comparison was made between this and the forms of ordination taken from various Eastern and Western rites. Thereupon Clement XI, with the unanimous vote of the Cardinals concerned, issued the following decree on Thursday, 17 April 1704:

'John Clement Gordon is to be ordained *completely and unconditionally* to all the orders, including sacred orders and especially the priesthood, and, inasmuch as he has not been confirmed, he is first to receive the sacrament of Confirmation.'

[21] This decision, it is important to consider, was in no way influenced by the omission of 'the tradition of the instruments'; for then the direction would have been given, as usual in such cases, to repeat the ordination *conditionally*. It is still more important to notice that this same decision of the Pope applies in general to all Anglican ordinations; for although it refers to a particular case, yet the ground upon which it was based was not particular. This ground was the 'defect of form', a defect from which all Anglican ordinations suffer equally; and therefore whenever similar cases have subsequently come up for judgement this decree of Clement XI has been quoted every time.

[22] It thus becomes quite obvious that the controversy which has been recently revived had already long ago been settled by the judgement of the Apostolic See; and the fact that one or two Catholic writers should have ventured to treat it as an open question is perhaps due to lack of sufficient knowledge of the aforesaid documents.

[23] But because, as We observed at the beginning, it is Our most earnest desire to be of service to men of good will, by

using the greatest possible consideration and charity towards them, We directed that the Anglican Ordinal, which is the crux of the whole question, should once more be very carefully examined.

[24] In the rite for the performance and administration of any sacrament a distinction is justly made between its 'ceremonial' and its 'essential' part, the latter being usually called its 'matter and form'. Moreover it is well known that the sacraments of the New Law, being sensible signs which cause invisible grace, must both signify the grace which they cause and cause the grace which they signify. Now this signification, though it must be found in the essential rite as a whole, that is, in both matter and form together, belongs chiefly to the form; for the matter is by itself the indeterminate part, which becomes determinate through the form. This is especially apparent in the sacrament of Order, the matter of which, so far as it needs to be considered here, is the imposition of hands. This by itself does not signify anything definite, being used equally for the conferring of certain orders and for administering Confirmation.

[25] Now the words which until recent times have been generally held by Anglicans to be the proper form of presbyteral ordination – 'Receive the Holy Ghost' – certainly do not signify definitely the order of the priesthood (*sacerdotium*) or its grace and power, which is pre-eminently the power 'to consecrete and offer the true body and blood of the Lord'* in that sacrifice which is no 'mere commemoration of the sacrifice performed on the Cross'.†

[26] It is true that this form was subsequently amplified by the addition of the words 'for the office and work of a priest'; but this rather proves that the Anglicans themselves had recognized that the first form had been defective and unsuitable. Even supposing, however, that this addition might have lent the form a legitimate signification, it was made too late when a century had already elapsed since the adoption

---

*Council of Trent, Sess. XXIII, *de sacr. Ord.*, can. 1.

†Ibid., Sess. XXII, *de sacrif. Missae*, can. 3.

of the Edwardine Ordinal and when, consequently, with the hierarchy now extinct, the power of ordaining no longer existed.

[27] Some have latterly sought a help for their case in other prayers of the same Ordinal, but in vain. To say nothing of other reasons which show such prayers, occurring in the Anglican rite, to be inadequate for the purpose suggested, let this one argument serve for all: namely that these prayers have been deliberately stripped of everything which in the Catholic rite clearly sets forth the dignity and functions of the priesthood. It is impossible, therefore, for a form to be suitable or sufficient for a sacrament if it suppresses that which it ought distinctively to signify.

[28] The case is the same with episcopal consecration. Not only was the formula 'Receive the Holy Ghost' too late amplified by the words 'for the office and work of a bishop', but even these additional words, as We shall shortly declare, must be judged otherwise than in a Catholic rite. Nor is it of any use to appeal to the prayer of the preface 'Almighty God . . .', since from this in like manner the words which denote 'the high priesthood' have been eliminated.

[29] It is not relevant here to inquire whether the episcopate is the complement of the priesthood or an order distinct from it; or whether the episcopate conferred *per saltum*, that is, upon one who is not a priest, is valid or not. It is quite certain in any event that the episcopate by Christ's institution belongs most truly to the sacrament of Order and is the priesthood in the highest degree; it is what the holy Fathers and our own liturgical usage call 'the high priesthood, the summit of the sacred ministry', Therefore, since the sacrament of Order and the true priesthood of Christ has been totally expunged from the Anglican rite, and since accordingly the priesthood is in no wise conferred in the episcopal consecration of the same rite, it is equally impossible for the episcopate itself to be truly and properly conferred thereby; the more so because a chief function of the episcopate is that of ordaining ministers for the Holy Eucharist and for the sacrifice.

[30] But for a just and adequate appraisal of the Anglican Ordinal it is above all important, besides considering what has been said about some of its parts, rightly to appreciate the circumstances in which it originated and was publicly instituted. It would take too long to set out a detailed account, nor is it necessary; the history of the period tells us clearly enough what were the sentiments of the authors of the Ordinal towards the Catholic Church, who were the heterodox associates whose help they invoked, to what end they directed their designs. They knew only too well the intimate bond which unites faith and worship, *lex credendi* and *lex supplicandi*; and so, under the pretext of restoring the order of the liturgy to its primitive form, they corrupted it in many respects to bring it into accord with the errors of the Innovators. As a result, not only is there in the whole Ordinal no clear mention of sacrifice, of consecration, of priesthood (*sacerdotium*), of the power to consecrate and offer sacrifice, but, as We have already indicated, every trace of these and similar things remaining in such prayers of the Catholic rite as were not completely rejected, was purposely removed and obliterated.

[31] The native character and spirit of the Ordinal, as one may call it, is thus objectively evident. Moreover, incapable as it was of conferring valid orders by reason of its original defectiveness, and remaining as it did in that condition, there was no prospect that with the passage of time it would become capable of conferring them. It was in vain that from the time of Charles I some men attempted to admit some notion of sacrifice and priesthood, and that, later on, certain additions were made to the Ordinal; and equally vain is the contention of a relatively small party among the Anglicans, formed in more recent times, that the said Ordinal can be made to bear a sound and orthodox sense. These attempts, We say, were and are fruitless; for the reason, moreover, that even though some words in the Anglican Ordinal as it now stands may present the possibility of ambiguity, they cannot bear the same sense as they have in a Catholic rite. For, as we have seen, when once a new rite has

been introduced denying or corrupting the sacrament of Order and repudiating any notion whatsoever of consecration and sacrifice, then the formula, '*Receive the Holy Ghost*' (that is, the Spirit who is infused into the soul with the grace of the sacrament), is deprived of its force; nor have the words, '*for the office and work of a priest*' or '*bishop*', etc., any longer their validity, being now mere names voided of the reality which Christ instituted.

[32] The majority of Anglicans themselves, more accurate in their interpretation of the Ordinal, perceive the force of this argument and use it openly against those who are vainly attempting, by a new interpretation of the rite, to attach to the orders conferred thereby a value and efficacy which they do not possess. The same argument by itself is fatal also to the suggestion that the prayer 'Almighty God, giver of all good things', occurring towards the beginning of the ritual action, can do service as a legitimate form of Order; although, conceivably, it might be held to suffice in a Catholic rite which the Church had approved.

[33] With this intrinsic *defect of form*, then, there was joined a *defect of intention* – of that intention which is likewise necessary for the existence of a sacrament.

Concerning the mind or intention, inasmuch as it is in itself something interior, the Church does not pass judgement: but in so far as it is externally manifested, she is bound to judge of it.

Now if, in order to effect and confer a sacrament, a person has seriously and correctly used the due matter and form, he is for that very reason presumed to have intended to do what the Church does. This principle is the basis of the doctrine that a sacrament is truly a sacrament even if it is conferred through the ministry of a heretic, or of one who is not himself baptized, provided the Catholic rite is used.

But if, on the contrary, the rite is changed with the manifest purpose of introducing another rite which is not accepted by the Church, and of repudiating that which the Church does and which is something that by Christ's institution belongs to the nature of the sacrament, then it is evident, not merely that the intention necessary for a sacrament is lacking, but rather that an intention is present which is adverse to and incompatible with the sacrament.

[34] All these considerations We weighed long and carefully in Our own mind and in consultation with Our Venerable Brethren the Judges of the Supreme Council, whom We also summoned to a special meeting in Our presence on Thursday 16 July last, the feast of our Lady of Mount Carmel. They unanimously agreed that the case proposed had already been adjudicated with full cognizance by the Apostolic See, and that the renewed investigation had only served to bring into clearer light the justice and wisdom with which the Holy See had settled the whole question. We nevertheless thought it best to postpone a decision, taking time to reflect whether it was fitting and expedient to make a further declaration on the same subject by Our own authority, and also to pray humbly for a greater measure of divine guidance.

[35] And now, taking into consideration the fact that this matter, although it had already been duly settled, has by certain persons for one reason or another been called again in question, and that not a few may in consequence be led into the dangerous error of thinking themselves to find the sacrament of Order and its fruits where in fact they do not exist, We have resolved in the Lord to pronounce Our judgement.

[36] **Therefore adhering entirely to the decrees of the Pontiffs Our Predecessors on this subject, and fully ratifying and renewing them by Our authority, on Our own initiative and with certain knowledge, We pronounce and declare that ordinations performed according to the Anglican rite have been and are completely null and void.**[1]

[37] It remains for Us, still in the name and spirit of 'the great Pastor' in which We approached the task of setting forth the most certain truth of this grave matter, now to address a word of exhortation to those who with sincerity

---

1. [Also translated: 'absolutely null and utterly void'.]

of will desire and seek the blessings of Orders and Hierarchy.

[38] Hitherto perhaps, while striving after the perfection of Christian virtue, while devoutly searching the Scriptures, while redoubling their fervent prayers, they have yet listened in doubt and perplexity to the promptings of Christ who has long been speaking within their hearts. Now they see clearly whither He is graciously calling and bidding them come. Let them return to His one fold, and they will obtain both the blessings they seek and further aids to salvation; the dispensing of which He has committed to the Church, as the perpetual guardian and promoter of His redemption among the nations. Then will they 'draw waters with joy out of the fountains of the Saviour', that is, out of His wondrous sacraments; whereby the souls of the faithful are truly forgiven their sins and restored to the friendship of God, nourished and strengthened with the bread of heaven, and provided in abundance with the most powerful aids to the attainment of eternal life. To those who truly thirst after these blessings may 'the God of peace, the God of all consolation', grant them in overflowing measure, according to the greatness of His bounty.

[39] Our appeal and Our hopes are directed in a special way to those who hold the office of ministers of religion in their respective communities. Their position gives them pre-eminence in learning and authority, and they assuredly have at heart the glory of God and the salvation of souls. Let them, then, be among the first to heed God's call and obey it with alacrity, thus giving a shining example to others. Great indeed will be the joy of Mother Church as she welcomes them, surrounding them with every mark of affection and solicitude, because of the difficulties which they have generously and courageously surmounted in order to return to her bosom. And how shall words describe the praise which such courage will earn for them in the assemblies of the faithful throughout the Catholic world, the hope and confidence it will give them before Christ's judgement seat, the rewards that it will win for them in the kingdom of heaven! For Our part We shall

continue by every means allowed to us to encourage their reconciliation with the Church, in which both individuals and whole communities, as We ardently hope, may find a model for their imitation. Meanwhile We beg and implore them all, through the bowels of the mercy of our God, to strive faithfully to follow in the open path of His truth and grace.

[40] We decree that the present Letter and the whole of its contents cannot at any time be attacked or impugned on the ground of subreption, obreption, or defect in Our intention, or any defect whatsoever; but that it shall be now and for ever in the future valid and in force, and that it is to be inviolably observed both judicially and extrajudicially by all persons of whatsoever degree or preeminence; and We declare null and void any attempt to the contrary which may be made wittingly or unwittingly concerning the same by any person, by any authority, or under any pretext whatsoever, all things to the contrary notwithstanding.

[41] It is moreover Our intention that copies of this Letter, even printed copies, provided they are signed by a Notary and sealed by a person constituted in ecclesiastical dignity, shall be accorded the same faith as would be given to the expression of Our will by the showing of these presents.

Given at St Peter's, Rome, on the thirteenth day of September in the year of the Incarnation of our Lord 1896, the nineteenth of Our Pontificate.

LEO PP. XIII

ANSWER TO THE APOSTOLIC LETTER OF POPE LEO XIII ON ENGLISH ORDINATIONS

To the whole body of Bishops of the Catholic Church, from the Archbishops of England, Greeting.

I. It is the fortune of our office that often, when we would fain write about the common salvation, an occasion arises for debating some controverted question which cannot be postponed to another time. This certainly was recently the case when in the month of September last there suddenly arrived in this country from Rome a letter, already printed and published, which aimed at overthrowing our whole position as a Church. It was upon this letter that our minds were engaged with the attention it demanded when our beloved brother Edward, at that time Archbishop of Canterbury, Primate of all England and Metropolitan, was in God's providence taken from us by sudden death. In his last written words he bequeathed to us the treatment of the question which he was doubtless himself about to treat with the greatest learning and theological grace. It has therefore seemed good to us, the Archbishops and Primates of England, that this answer should be written in order that the truth on this matter might be made known both to our venerable brother Pope Leo XIIIth, in whose name the letter from Rome was issued, and also to all other bishops of the Christian Church settled throughout the world.

II. The duty indeed is a serious one; one which cannot be discharged without a certain deep and strong emotion. But since we firmly believe that we have been truly ordained by the Chief Shepherd to bear a part of His tremendous office in the Catholic Church, we are not at all disturbed by the opinion expressed in that letter. So we approach the task which is of necessity laid upon us 'in the spirit of meekness;' and we deem it of greater importance to make plain for all time our doctrine about holy orders and other matters pertaining to them, than to win a victory in controversy over a sister Church of Christ. Still it is necessary that our answer be cast in a controversial form lest it be said by any one that we have shrunk from the force of the arguments put forward on the other side.

III. There was an old controversy, but not a bitter one, with respect to the form and matter of holy orders, which has arisen from the nature of the case, inasmuch as it is impossible to find any tradition on the subject coming from our Lord or His Apostles, except the well-known example of prayer with laying on of hands. But little is to be found bearing on this matter in the decrees of Provincial Councils, and nothing certain or decisive in those of Œcumenical and General Assemblies.

Nor indeed does the Council of Trent, in which our Fathers took no part, touch the subject directly. Its passing remark about the laying on of hands (*Session* XIV. *On Extreme Unction, chap.* III.), and its more decided utterance on the force of the words 'Receive the Holy Ghost,' which it seems to consider the form of Order (*Session* XXIII. *On the Sacrament of Order, canon* IV.), are satisfactory enough to us, and certainly are in no way repugnant to our feelings.

There has been a more recent and a more bitter controversy on the validity of Anglican ordinations, into which theologians on the Roman side have thrown themselves with eagerness, and in doing so have, for the most part, imputed to us various crimes and defects. There are others, and those not the least wise among them, who, with a nobler feeling, have undertaken our defence. But no decision of the Roman pontiffs, fully supported by arguments, has ever before

appeared, nor has it been possible for us, while we knew that
the practice of re-ordaining our Priests clearly prevailed
(though this practice has not been without exception), to
learn on what grounds of defect they were re-ordained. We
knew of the unworthy struggles about Formosus, and the
long vacillations about heretical, schismatic and simoniacal
ordinations. We had access to the letter of Innocent IIIrd on
the necessity of supplying unction and the Decree of Eugenius
IVth for the Armenians; we had the historical documents of
the XVIth century, though of these many are unknown even
to the present day; we had various decisions of later Popes,
Clement XIth and Benedict XIVth, but those of Clement were
couched in general terms and therefore uncertain. We had
also the Roman Pontifical as reformed from time to time,
but, as it now exists, so confusedly arranged as to puzzle
rather than enlighten the minds of inquirers. For if any one
considers the rite *Of the ordination of a Presbyter*, he sees that
the proper laying on of hands stands apart from the utterance
of the form. He also cannot tell whether the man, who in the
rubrics is called 'ordained,' has really been ordained, or
whether the power, which is given at the end of the office
by the words—'Receive the Holy Ghost; whose sins thou
shalt have remitted they are remitted unto them, and whose
sins thou shalt have retained they are retained'—with the
laying on of pontifical hands, is a necessary part of the priesthood (as the Council of Trent seems to teach[1]) or not necessary. In like manner if any one reads through the rite *Of the
consecration of an elect as Bishop*, he will nowhere find that he
is called 'Bishop' in the prayers and benedictions referring to
the man to be consecrated, or that 'Episcopate' is spoken of in
them in regard to him.[2] As far as the prayers are concerned
the term 'Episcopate' occurs for the first time in the Mass
during the consecration.

From these documents therefore, so obviously discordant

---

1. *Sess.* xxiii. *On the Sacrament of Order, Canon* 1, where a certain power of consecrating and offering is claimed for the priesthood together with one of remitting
and retaining sins. Cp. *ib. Chap.* 1. See below Chaps. xv. and xix.

2. 'Episcopal chair' is mentioned in the blessing after unction.

and indefinite, no one, however wise, could extract with certainty what was considered by the Roman Pontiffs to be truly essential and necessary to holy orders.

IV. Thus our most venerable brother in his letter dated the 13th of September, which begins with the words *Apostolicae curae,* has approached this question after a manner hitherto unexampled, although the arguments urged by him are sufficiently old. Nor do we desire to deny that in entering upon this controversy he has consulted the interests of the Church and of truth in throwing over the very vain opinion about the necessity of the delivery of the 'instruments,' which was nevertheless widely accepted by scholastic theologians from the time of S. Thomas Aquinas up to that of Benedict XIVth, and even up to the present day. At the same time he has done well in neglecting other errors and fallacies, which for our part also we shall neglect in this reply, and in regard to which we hope that theologians on the Roman side will follow his example and neglect them for the future.

V. His whole judgment therefore hinges on two points, namely, on the practice of the Court of Rome and the form of the Anglican rite, to which is attached a third question, not easy to separate from the second, on the intention of our Church. We will answer at once about the former, though it is, in our opinion, of less importance.

VI. As regards the practice of the Roman Court and Legate in the XVIth century, although the Pope writes at some length, we believe that he is really as uncertain as ourselves. We see that he has nothing to add to the documents which are already well known, and that he quotes and argues from an imperfect copy of the letter of Paul IVth *Praeclari carissimi.* Where, for example, are the faculties granted to Pole after 5th August 1553 and before 8th March 1554, which Julius confirms in his letter of the latter date, to be 'freely used' in respect to orders received with any irregularity or failure in the accustomed form, but does not detail and define? Without these faculties the 'rules of action' to be observed by Pole are imperfectly known. For the distinction made in the letters of both those dates between men 'promoted' and 'not promoted,' to which the Pope refers, does not seem to touch the position of the Edwardian clergy, but the case of those who held benefices without any pretence of ordination, as was then often done. Who in fact knows thoroughly either what was done in this matter or on what grounds it was done? We know part; of part we are ignorant. It can be proved however on our side that the work of that reconciliation under Queen Mary (6th July 1553 to 17th Nov. 1558) was in very great measure finished, under royal and episcopal authority, before the arrival of Pole.

In the conduct of which business there is evidence of much inconsistency and unevenness. Yet while many Edwardian Priests are found to have been deprived for various reasons, and particularly on account of entering into wedlock, none are so found, as far as we know, on account of defect of Order. Some were voluntarily re-ordained. Some received anointing as a supplement to their previous ordination, a ceremony to which some of our Bishops at that time attached great importance.[3] Some, and perhaps the majority, remained in their benefices without re-ordination, nay were promoted in some cases to new cures. Pole did not return to England after his exile until November 1554, and brought the reconciliation to a conclusion in the fifteen months that followed. The principle of his work appears to have been to recognize the state of things which he found in existence on his arrival, and to direct all his powers towards the restoration of papal supremacy as easily as possible. In this period one man and perhaps a second (for more have not yet been discovered) received new orders under Pole, in the years 1554 and 1557; but it is uncertain in what year each of them began the

---

3. See James Pilkington, *Exposition on the Prophet Aggeus*, ii. 10–14, published in 1560 (*Works*, Parker Society, p. 163):– 'In the late days of Popery, our holy Bishops called before them all such as were made ministers without such greasing, and blessed them with the Pope's blessing, anointed them, and then all was perfect: they might sacrifice for quick and dead, but not marry in no case, etc.' Cp. Innocent IIId, *cp.* vii. 3 (1204).

process of being re-ordained. At any rate very few were re-ordained after Pole's arrival. Others perhaps received some kind of supplement or other to their orders, a record of which is not to be found in our Registers.

But if a large number had been re-ordained under Pole, as papal legate, it would not have been at all surprising, inasmuch as in his twelve legatine constitutions, he added, as an appendix to the second, the Decree of Eugenius IVth for the Armenians, saying that he did so 'inasmuch as very great errors have been committed here (in England) with respect to the doctrine concerning the head of the Church and the Sacraments.'[4] And this he did, not as our Archbishop, but as papal legate. For these constitutions were promulgated at the beginning of the year 1556. But Pole was only ordained Presbyter on the 20th March of the same year; and said Mass for the first time on the following day, being the day on which our lawful Archbishop, Cranmer, was burnt alive; and on the 22nd he was consecrated Archbishop.

We quote here the Decree of Eugenius IVth, as re-issued by Pole, because it shows how slippery and weak the judgment of the Church of Rome has been in this matter. Further when Pope Leo extols the learning of Pole on this point and writes that it would have been quite irrelevant for the Popes to instruct the legate 'as to the conditions necessary for the bestowal of the sacrament of orders,' he seems wholly to forget Eugenius' Decree, which he has silently thrown over in another part of his letter. (Cp. §5 and §21.) 'The sixth sacrament is that of Order: the matter of which is the thing by the delivery of which the order is conferred: as for instance the order of the presbyterate is conferred by the porrection of the chalice with wine and the paten with bread: the diaconate by giving of the book of the Gospels: the sub-diaconate by the

---

4. See Labbe and Cossart, *Councils*, vol. xiv. p. 1740, Paris, 1672, and vol. xiii. p. 538 on the year 1439. Compare also *Councils of Great Britain*, Wilkins, vol. iv. p. 121, col. 2, which differs slightly and omits the words of the Decree of Eugenius. It is obvious that Eugenius generally borrows the language of Aquinas' *Exposition of the articles of the Creed and of the Sacraments of the Church* (*Works*, vol. viii. pp. 45–9, Venice, 1776).

delivery of the empty chalice with the empty paten on it: and in like manner as regards other orders by the assignment of the things pertaining to their ministries. The form of priest-hood is as follows: *Receive the power of offering sacrifice in the Church for the living and the dead. In the name of the Father, and of the Son, and of the Holy Ghost.* And so as regards the forms of the other orders as is contained at length in the Roman Pontifical. The ordinary minister of this Sacrament is the Bishop: the effect, an increase of grace, so that a man may be a fit minister.' Here the laying on of hands, and the invocaion of the Holy Spirit upon the candidates for orders, are not referred to even by a single word. Yet Eugenius, as is clear by his explanation of other Sacraments, is not speaking of things to be supplied by the Armenians, as writers on the Roman side are sometimes fond of saying, but is teaching the Church, as if he were its master, in careful adherence to Aquinas, about what is absolutely necessary to the adminis-tration of the Sacraments. So also he writes in the earlier part of his Decree: 'All these Sacraments have three requisites for their performance, things as their "matter," words as their "form," and the person of the minister who celebrates the Sacrament with the intention of doing what the Church does: *and if any of these be absent, the Sacrament is not performed*' (*Conc.* xiv. p. 1738).

Now in our Church from March 1550 to 1st November 1552, though the delivery of the instruments still remained in some degree (*i.e.* of the chalice with bread in the case of Presbyters, and of the pastoral staff in that of Bishops, and of the Bible in both) yet the forms attached to them had already been changed very nearly into those which now are in use. In the year 1552 the delivery of the chalice and the staff was dropped and that of the Bible alone remained. King Edward died on the 6th July 1553.

According to this Decree, then, all these Presbyters ought to have been re-ordained. But Pole's opinion scarcely agreed with his practice. Nor does Paul IVth himself, in his Brief *Regimini universalis*, make any demands as to the form in which Presbyters are ordained, though careful about 'properly and rightly ordained' Bishops. (See last page of Appendix.)[5]

VII. The second, but scarcely stronger, foundation of the papal opinion about the practice of his Court appears to be the judgment of Clement XIth in the case of John Gordon, formerly Bishop of Galloway, delivered on Thursday 17th April 1704 in the general Congregation of the Inquisition, or, as it is usually called, the holy Office.

We here make a short answer on this case, inasmuch as it cannot be treated clearly on account of the darkness in which the holy Office is enveloped, a darkness insufficiently dispersed by Pope Leo's letter. The fuller treatment of this has been relegated to the Appendix. There are, however, four reasons in particular for considering this case as a weak and unstable foundation for his judgment. In the first place, inasmuch as Gordon himself petitioned to be ordained according to the Roman rite, the case was not heard on the other side. Secondly, his petition had as its basis the old 'Tavern fable,' and was vitiated by falsehoods concerning our rite. Thirdly, the new documents of 'incontestable authenticity' cited by the Pope are still involved in obscurity, and he argues about them as if he were himself uncertain as to their tenor and meaning.[6] Fourthly, the decree of the Congregation of the holy Office, if it is to be considered to agree with Pope Leo's judgments can scarcely be reconciled with the reply of the consultors of the holy Office on Abyssinian ordinations, said to have been given about a week before, and often published as authoritative by Roman theologians up to 1893. Therefore all those documents ought to be made public if the matter is to be put on a fair footing for judgment.

Finally, it must be noted, that Gordon never went beyond

---

5. [Not included in this edition.]

6. Compare the letter 'Apostolicae curae,' § 21. 'It is important to bear in mind that this judgment was in no wise determined by the omission of the tradition of instruments, for in such a case, according to the established custom, the direction would have been to repeat the Ordination conditionally,' etc. Which mode of argument differs widely from the quotation of a clearly expressed document. See the Appendix.

minor orders in the Roman Church. That is to say, he only did enough to receive a pension for his support from certain benefices.[7]

VIII. The Pope has certainly done well not to rest satisfied with such weak conclusions, and to determine to re-open the question and to treat it afresh; although this would seem to have been done in appearance rather than in reality. For inasmuch as the case was submitted by him to the holy Office, it is clear that it, being bound by its traditions, could hardly have expressed dissent from the judgment, however ill founded, which was passed in the case of Gordon.

Further when he touches upon the matter itself and follows the steps of the Council of Trent, our opinion does not greatly differ from the main basis of his judgment. He rightly calls laying on of hands the 'matter' of ordination. His judgment on the 'form' is not so clearly expressed; but we suppose him to intend to say that the form is prayer or benediction appropriate to the ministry to be conferred, which is also our opinion. Nor do we part company with the Pope when he suggests that it is right to investigate the intention of a Church in conferring holy orders 'in so far as it is manifested externally'. For whereas it is scarcely possible for any man to arrive at a knowledge of the inner mind of a Priest, so that it cannot be right to make the validity of a Sacrament depend upon it, the will of the Church can both be ascertained more easily, and ought also to be both true and sufficient. Which intention our Church shews generally by requiring a promise from one who is to be ordained that he will rightly minister the Doctrine, Sacraments and Discipline of Christ, and teaches that he who is unfaithful to this promise, may be justly punished. And in our Liturgy we regularly pray for 'all Bishops and Curates, that they may both by their life and doctrine set forth (God's) true and lively word, and rightly and duly administer (His) holy Sacraments'.

But the intention of the Church must be ascertained 'in so

7. See Le Quien, *Nullity of Anglican Ordinations*, Paris, 1–25, ii. pp. 312 and 315.

far as it is manifested externally,' that is to say from its public formularies and definite pronouncements which directly touch the main point of the question, not from its omissions and reforms, made as opportunity occurs, in accordance with the liberty which belongs to every Province and Nation—unless it may be that something is omitted which has been ordered in the Word of God, or the known and certain statutes of the universal Church. For if a man assumes the custom of the middle ages and of more recent centuries as the standard, consider, brethren, how clearly he is acting against the liberty of the Gospel and the true character of Christendom. And if we follow this method of judging the validity of Sacraments, we must throw doubt upon all of them, except Baptism alone, which seems according to the judgment of the universal Church to have its matter and form ordained by the Lord.

IX. We acknowledge therefore with the Pope that laying on of hands is the matter of ordination; we acknowledge that the form is prayer or blessing appropriate to the ministry to be conferred; we acknowledge that the intention of the Church, as far as it is externally manifested, is to be ascertained, so that we may discover if it agrees with the mind of the Lord and His Apostles and with the Statutes of the Universal Church. We do not however attach so much weight to the doctrine so often descanted upon by the Schoolmen since the time of William of Auxerre (A.D. 1215), that each of the Sacraments of the Church ought to have a single form and matter exactly defined. Nor do we suppose that this is a matter of faith with the Romans. For it introduces a very great danger of error, supposing any Pope or Doctor, who may have great influence over the men of his own time, should persuade people to acknowledge as necessary this or that form or matter which has not been defined either in the word of God or by the Catholic Fathers or Councils.

For, as we have said, Baptism stands alone as a Sacrament in being quite certain both in its form and its matter. And this is suitable to the nature of the case. For—inasmuch as the

Baptism of Christ is the entrance into the Church for all men, and can be ministered by all Christians, if there be a pressing need—the conditions of a valid Baptism ought to be known to all. As regards the Eucharist (if you set aside, as of less importance, questions about unleavened bread, and salt, about water, and the rest), it has a sufficiently certain matter: but up to the present day a debate is still going on as to its full and essential form. But the matter of Confirmation is not so entirely certain; and we at any rate do not at all think that Christians who have different opinions on the subject should be condemned by one another. The form of Confirmation again is uncertain and quite general, prayer, that is to say, or benediction, more or less suitable, such as is used in each of our Churches. And so with respect to others.

X. But this topic of Confirmation requires to be treated rather more at large: for it throws much light on the question proposed by the Pope. He writes truly that laying on of hands is a 'matter' 'which is equally used for Confirmation.' The matter therefore of Confirmation seems, in his judgment, to be laying on of hands, as we too hold in accordance with Apostolic tradition. But the Roman Church for many centuries has, by a corrupt custom, substituted a stretching out of hands over a crowd of children, or simply 'towards those who are to be confirmed,' in the place of laying on of hands to be conferred on each individual.[8]

The Orientals (with Eugenius IVth) teach that the matter is chrism, and use no laying on of hands in this rite. If therefore the doctrine about a fixed matter and form in the Sacraments were to be admitted, the Romans have ministered Confirmation imperfectly for many centuries past, and the Greeks have none. And not a few amongst the former practically confess

---

8. In the so-called 'Gelasian' Sacramentary (perhaps of the VIIth century) we still read the rubric *In sealing them he lays his hands on them with the following words*: then follows the prayer for the sevenfold gift of the Spirit. And in the 'ordines' called those of S. Amand, which are perhaps of the VIIIth century, in ch. iv. the pontiff touches *their heads with his hand*. But in the 'Gregorian' we read, *raising his hand over the heads of all he says*, etc. In the ordinary editions of the Pontifical we read again: *Then stretching out his hands towards those who are to be confirmed he says*, etc.

the corruption introduced by their Fathers, having joined laying on of hands to the anointing, as we have learnt, in many places, while a rubric on this point has been added in some Pontificals. And it is fair to ask whether Orientals who are converts to the Roman communion require a second Confirmation? or do the Romans admit that they, who have changed its matter, have had as good a right to do so as themselves who have corrupted it?

Whatever the Pope may answer, it is clear enough that we cannot everywhere insist very strictly on that doctrine about a fixed form and matter; inasmuch as all Sacraments of the Church, except Baptism, would in that way be rendered uncertain.

XI. We inquire therefore what authority the Pope has for discovering a definite form in the bestowal of holy orders? We have seen no evidence produced by him except two passages from the determinations of the Council of Trent (*Session* XXIII. *On the Sacrament of Order, canon* I., and *Session* XXII. *On the sacrifice of the Mass, canon* III.) which were promulgated after our Ordinal was composed, from which he infers that the principal grace and power of the Christian priesthood is the consecration and oblation of the Body and Blood of the Lord. The authority of that Council has certainly never been admitted in our country, and we find that by it many truths were mixed with falsehoods, much that is uncertain with what is certain. But we answer as regards the passages quoted by the Pope, that we make provision with the greatest reverence for the consecration of the holy Eucharist and commit it only to properly ordained Priests and to no other ministers of the Church. Further we truly teach the doctrine of Eucharistic sacrifice and do not believe it to be a 'nude commemoration of the Sacrifice of the Cross,' an opinion which seems to be attributed to us by the quotation made from that Council. But we think it sufficient in the Liturgy which we use in celebrating the holy Eucharist,—while lifting up our hearts to the Lord, and when now consecrating the gifts already offered that they may become to us the Body and Blood of our Lord Jesus Christ,—to signify the sacrifice which is offered at that point of the service in such terms as these. We continue a perpetual memory of the precious death of Christ, who is our Advocate with the Father and the propitiation for our sins, according to His precept, until His coming again. For first we offer the sacrifice of praise and thanksgiving; then next we plead and represent before the Father the sacrifice of the cross, and by it we confidently entreat remission of sins and all other benefits of the Lord's Passion for all the whole Church; and lastly we offer the sacrifice of ourselves to the Creator of all things which we have already signified by the oblations of His creatures. This whole action, in which the people has necessarily to take its part with the Priest, we are accustomed to call the Eucharistic sacrifice.

Further, since the Pope reminds us somewhat severely of 'the necessary connection between faith and worship, between *the law of believing and the law of praying*,' it seems fair to call closer attention, both on your part and ours, to the Roman Liturgy. And when we look carefully into the 'Canon of the Mass,' what do we see clearly exhibited there as to the idea of sacrifice? It agrees sufficiently with our Eucharistic formularies, but scarcely or not at all with the determination of the Council of Trent. Or rather it should be said that two methods of explaining the sacrifice are put forth at the same time by that Council, one which agrees with liturgical science and Christian wisdom, the other which is under the influence of dangerous popular theology on the subject of Eucharistic propitiation. Now in the Canon of the Mass the sacrifice which is offered is described in four ways. Firstly it is a 'sacrifice of praise,'[9] which idea runs through the whole action and so to say supports it and makes it all of a piece. Secondly it is the offering made by God's servants and His

9. 'Sacrifice of praise,' that is a Eucharistic sacrifice, like the peace-offerings and thank-offerings of the Old Testament, the ritual peculiarity of which was that the man who offered was a partaker with God. 'Sacrifice of praise' is the expression of the old Latin version: see the Lyons Pentateuch; 'Offering of thanksgiving' is from that of S. Jerome (*Lev.* vii. 12, 13). Hence in our Liturgy both are united: 'this our sacrifice of praise and thanksgiving.'

whole family, about which offering request is made that it 'may become to us the Body and Blood' of His Son our Lord. Thirdly it is an offering to His Majesty of His 'own gifts and boons' (that is, as Innocent IIIrd[10] rightly explains it, of the fruits of the fields and trees, although the words of the Lord have already been said over them by the Priest), which are called the holy Bread of eternal life and the Chalice of everlasting salvation. Fourthly and lastly (in the prayer *Supra quae propitio*[11]) the sacrifice already offered in three ways, and according to Roman opinion now fully consecrated, is compared with the sacrifices of the patriarchs Abel and Abraham, and with that offered by Melchisedech. This last, being called 'holy sacrifice, unblemished victim,' shews that the comparison is not only in respect to the offerer, but also to the things offered. Then the Church prays that they may be carried up by the hands of the holy Angel to the altar of God on high. Lastly, after the second series of names of Saints, there occurs the piece of a prayer (*Per quem haec omnia*) which appears rather suitable to a benediction of fruits of the earth, than to the Eucharistic sacrifice.

It is clear therefore from what has been already said that the *law of believing*, set forth by the Council of Trent, has gone some distance beyond the boundaries of the *law of praying*. The matter is indeed one full of mystery and fitted to draw onwards the minds of men by strong feelings of love and piety to high and deep thoughts. But, inasmuch as it ought to be treated with the highest reverence and to be considered a bond of Christian charity rather than an occasion for subtle disputations, too precise definitions of the

---

10. *On the Sacred Mystery of the Altar*, v. chap. 2.

11. This prayer has given a good deal of trouble to the commentators. We may compare for example Innocent IIIrd *On the sacred mystery of the altar*, v. 3; Bellarmine *On the Sacrament of the Eucharist* (*on the Mass*), vi. 24; and Romsée, *Literal meaning of the Rites of the Mass*, art. xxx. Its older form appears in [Pseudo-Ambrose] *On the Sacraments*, iv. 6, § 27, where its parts are found in inverse order; and where we also read 'by the hands of Thy angels.' It seems to have been already added to the Roman Canon in the time of Leo Ist, if the statement about the words 'holy sacrifice, unblemished victim' added by him, which is found in his *Life*, is a true one. Cp. his *Sermon*, iv. 3, where he speaks of Melchisedech as 'immolating the sacrifice of that sacrament, which our Redeemer consecrated as His body and blood.'

manner of the sacrifice, or of the relation which unites the sacrifice of the eternal Priest and the sacrifice of the Church, which in some way certainly are one, ought in our opinion to be avoided rather than pressed into prominence.

XII. What therefore is the reason for impugning our form and intention in ordaining Presbyters and Bishops?

The Pope writes, if we omit things of less importance, 'that the order of priesthood or its grace and power, which is especially the power *of consecrating and offering the true Body and Blood of the Lord* in that sacrifice which is *no nude commemoration of the sacrifice* offered on the cross,' must be expressed in the ordering of a Presbyter. What he desires in the form of consecration of a Bishop is not so clear; but it seems that, in his opinion, in some way or other, 'high priesthood' ought to be attributed to him.

Both however of these opinions are strange, inasmuch as in the most ancient Roman formulary used, as it seems, at the beginning of the third century after Christ (seeing that exactly the same form is employed both for a Bishop and a Presbyter, except the name), nothing whatever is said about 'high priesthood' or 'priesthood' nor about the sacrifice of the Body and Blood of Christ. 'The prayers and oblations which he will offer (to God) by day and by night' are alone mentioned, and the power of remitting sins is touched on.[12]

Again in the old Roman Sacramentary, which may perhaps be assigned to the VIth century, only three prayers are employed for the ordination of Presbyters. Two are short collects, namely *Oremus dilectissimi*, and *Exaudi nos*, and a third longer, like a Eucharistic preface, which is the real Benediction, and was in former times attached to the laying on of hands, which begins *Domine sancte pater omnipotens aeterne Deus, honorum omnium*, etc. These prayers from the VIth to the IXth century and perhaps later, made up the whole rite for ordaining a Presbyter in the Church of

---

12. See the *Canons of Hippolytus* in the edition of Hans Achelis in the 6th volume of the series of *Texte und Untersuchungen*, edited by Gebhardt and Harnack, Leipzig, 1891, pp. 39–62.

Rome, with no other ceremonies whatever. These prayers, scarcely altered, are retained in the Roman Pontifical, and form as it were the nucleus of the service *For the ordering of a Presbyter*, although the laying on of hands which used to be attached to the longer form has passed to the commencement of the office, and is given again at the end of the Mass. But in the Benediction 'priesthood' is not attributed to Presbyters, and in none of that series of prayers is anything said of the power of sacrificing or of the remission of sins. 'Priestly grace' too, which is prayed for in the second collect in most of the Pontificals, is simply 'spiritual grace' in some other uses both English and foreign.[13] Yet this form is undoubtedly valid.

Similar things may be said about the form for the consecration of a Bishop. The Collects and the Benediction remain in the modern Pontifical, only slightly changed. They begin *Exaudi Domine supplicum preces* (now *Adesto*), *Propitiare Domine*, and *Deus honorum omnium*. The second of these mentions 'the horn of priestly grace,' the third, 'the high priesthood,' but nothing else which can be alleged as confirming the Pope's position. All the rest of the matter in the Pontifical is derived from the usage of later times and especially from Gallican rites.[14]

And this also may be said as to the power of remitting sins, which is mentioned by the Council of Trent (see ch. III. n. 1) together with 'a certain power of consecrating and offering,' and with equal emphasis. It appears nowhere up to the XIth century in the ordination of a Presbyter; nowhere in the old Roman form for the consecration of a Bishop. It appears only

---

13. See *e. g.* Edm. Martenne (or Martene), *Anc. Rites of the Church*, t. ii. pp. 429, 493. Rouen, 1700.

14. The old Roman Sacramentary may be collected from three books especially, as far as the prayers are concerned, viz., the 'Leonine,' 'Gelasian,' and 'Gregorian,' as they are called. But the first alone is Roman without any admixture. The Gelasian was introduced into Gaul about the beginning of the VIIIth century, and the Gregorian under Charles the Great, being sent thither by Pope Hadrian about A.D. 780. Both of them contain Gallican rites and prayers mixed with Roman. Three 'Ordines' should also be consulted for the knowledge of the rites, namely the 8th and 9th of Mabillon, and those called by the name of 'S. Amand,' which were first printed by the learned L. Duchesne in the Appendix of his book *Antiquities of Christian Worship*, Paris, 1889. All of which shew the same simplicity.

in the long Gallican interpolation in the blessing of a Bishop *Sint speciosi munere tuo pedes eius* up to *ut fructum de profectu omnium consequatur*.

But the Pope who appeals to the Council of Trent must submit to be judged by it. Either then these Roman formulas were valueless because of their defect in the matter of sacrifice and remitting sins, or else the authority of that Council is of no value in settling this question about the necessary form of Order.

We may here quote another ancient form[15] of consecrating a Bishop which was used both in England and elsewhere during the XIth century and displays the same simplicity. It begins, *Pater sancte omnipotens Deus qui per Dominum*, and prays for those about to be consecrated, 'that they may be enabled to celebrate the mysteries of the Sacraments which have been ordained of old. May they be consecrated by Thee to the high-priesthood to which they are called;' but it says not a word about sacrifice nor about the power to remit sins.

XIII. On the subject of the title of Bishops our simple and immediate reply is that the name of high Priest is in no way necessary to describe this office in the form of consecration. The African Church openly forbad even her Primates to use this title;[16] the words 'pontifical glory,' which sometimes appear in Sacramentaries, denote a secular or Jewish

---

15. This form occurs in the Missal of Leofric of Exeter (p. 217 of the edition by F. E. Warren, Oxford, 1883), in a Pontifical of Jumièges (Martenne *On the Ancient Rites of the Church*, t. ii. p. 367, Rouen, 1700), and in the Sarum Pontifical (see Maskell, *Ritual Monuments of the Eng. Ch.*, 2nd ed. Oxford, vol. ii. p. 282). The words about celebrating the mysteries and the *Admonition to Priests* (ib. p. 246) seem to have served our fathers as a precedent in the ordination of a Presbyter. This form, which has a certain affinity to those in the *Canons of Hippolytus* and the *Apostolic Constitutions*, has an air of great antiquity, and except for the expression 'high priesthood,' appears equally applicable to the ordering of a Presbyter. It is believed by some to be of Roman origin and to have been adapted by Augustine of Canterbury to our use.

16. See Third Council of Carthage, can. 26 A.D. 397: 'The Bishop of a chief see may not be called chief of the Priests, or high Priest, or anything else of the kind, but simply Bishop of a chief see.' S. Augustine of Hippo is believed to have been present at this Council. The passage cited for this title by Baronius, etc. is certainly not from Augustine.

distinction rather than a rank in the Church. We are content with the name of Bishop to describe the office of those who, when they were left, after the removal of the Apostles, to be chief pastors in the Church, exercised the right of ordaining and confirming, and ruled, together with a body of presbyters, over a single 'parochia' or diocese, as it is now called. And to this order the Pope, in the beginning of his letter, following the sound custom of antiquity, reckons himself to belong. Bishops are undoubtedly Priests, just as Presbyters are Priests, and in early ages they enjoyed this title more largely than Presbyters did; nay, it was not till the IVth or Vth century that Presbyters, in the Latin Church at any rate, came to be called Priests in their own right. But it does not therefore follow that Bishops nowadays ought to be called high Priests in the form of Consecration. The question of the priesthood of Bishops was perhaps different in early times, certainly up to the IXth and possibly to the XIth century, when a simple Deacon was often made Bishop *per saltum*, i.e. without passing through the presbyterate.[17] In those days of course it was fitting, if not indeed necessary, to apply to the Bishop the term Priest, as, *e.g.*, is done in the Prayer still used in the Pontifical, which speaks of 'the horn of priestly grace.' But inasmuch as this custom of consecration

---

17. On this point cp. Mabillon, *Commentary prefixed to the Ordo Romanus*, chaps. xvi. and xviii. (Migne, *Pat. Lat.* vol. 78, pp. 912–3 and 919–20) and Martenne, *Ancient Rites of the Church*, lib. 1, c. viii. art. 3, sec. 9, t. ii. p. 278 foll., and the 8th 'Ordo' of Mabillon (=Martenne i.), which is found in MSS. of the IXth century, where it is clear that there was no distinction in the form if the man to be consecrated was only a Deacon. The XIIIth canon of the Council of Sardica was but poorly observed in the West, as appears incidentally from the translation by Dionysius Exiguus, who renders the words of the canon ἐὰν μὴ καὶ ἀναγνώστου καὶ διακόνου καὶ πρεσβυτέρου ὑπηρεσίαν ἐκτελέσῃ as follows: "unless he have discharged the duty of Reader and the office of Deacon or Presbyter." As instances are quoted John the Deacon, the disciple of S. Gall (Walafrid Strabo in the *Life of S. Gall*, c. 23–25, A.D. 625), Constantine the anti-pope (A.D. 767), and the Popes Paul I. (A.D. 757), Valentine (A.D. 827), and Nicolas I. (A.D. 858). This custom was one amongst the charges brought against the Latin Church by Photius of Constantinople. Nicolas did not deny the fact, but retorted on the Greeks their custom of promoting a layman to be a Patriarch. (Ep. lxx. in Labbe and Cossart, *Councils*, viii. p. 471 B). The ordination of a Deacon to the Episcopate *per saltum* is further implied in the Ritual of the Nestorian Syrians in Morinus, *On Ordinations*, pt. ii. p. 388, Antwerp, 1695 = Denzinger, *Rites of the Orientals*, vol. ii. p. 238 (1864).

per saltum has long since died out (though perhaps never expressly forbidden by statute) and every Bishop has already, during the period of his presbyterate, been a Priest, it is no longer necessary to confer the priesthood afresh, nor, if we give our candid opinion, is it a particularly good and regular proceeding. Nor ought the Romans to require it, inasmuch as the Council of Trent calls preaching of the Gospel 'the chief duty of Bishops' (*Session* V. *on Reform.* ch. II. and *Sess.* XXIV. *on Ref.* ch. IV.). It is not therefore necessary that either high priesthood or any other fresh priesthood should be attributed to Bishops.

But although in our Ordinal we say nothing about high Priests and Pontiffs, we do not avoid using the terms in other public documents. Examples may be taken from the Latin edition of the *Book of Common Prayer*, A.D. 1560, Archbishop Grindall, A.D. 1580, and from Archbishop Whitgift's Commission to his Suffragan the Bishop of Dover, A.D. 1583.[18]

XIV. Two of the arguments advanced against our form, which specially commend themselves to the Pope, shall receive a somewhat larger answer.

The first of these is, that about a century after the Ordinal was published, in 1662, we added to the words 'Receive the Holy Ghost' other words intended to define the office and work of a *Bishop* or *Priest* (ch. chap. XV. notes 1 and 3). The Pope suggests that these words of our Lord without the subsequent addition are in themselves insufficient, imperfect, and inappropriate. But in the Roman Pontifical, when a Bishop is consecrated by the laying on of the hands of the consecrating Bishop and assisting Bishops, the only form is 'Receive the Holy Ghost.' In our later Pontificals, on the other hand, the Holy Spirit was invoked by the Hymn 'Come, Holy Ghost,' with the exception of the Exeter book, in which the Roman form is added. Then came the prayer

---

18. See the collect for the clergy and people after the Litany, and *Councils of Great Britain*, iv. pp. 293 and 304. In the latter passage Grindall is styled by his brethren 'Noble Christian Prelate and High Priest of God in the Church of England.'

about the 'horn of priestly grace.' As we have already said, the words Bishop or Episcopate do not appear in any prayer of the Pontifical until *after* the Consecration; so that if, according to the Pope's suggestion, our fathers of the year 1550 and after, went wrong in the form of omitting the name of Bishop, they must have gone wrong in company with the modern Roman Church. At that time too there immediately followed in our Ordinal those words of S. Paul which were believed to refer to the consecration of S. Timothy to be Bishop of Ephesus, and were clearly used in this sense:— 'And remember that thou stir up the grace of God which is in thee by imposition of hands; for God hath not given us the spirit of fear, but of power, and love, and of soberness' (2 Tim. 1.6, 7).

You may remember, brethren, that these are the only words quoted by the Council of Trent to prove that Order confers grace (*Session* XXIII. *On the Sacrament of Order* c. III.). This form then, whether contained in one sentence as in the Roman Church, or in two as in ours, is amply sufficient to create a Bishop, if the true intention be openly declared, which is done in the other prayers and suffrages (which clearly refer to the office, work and ministry of a Bishop), in the examination, and other like ways. We say that the words 'Receive the Holy Ghost' are sufficient, not that they are essential. For they do not occur in the more ancient Pontificals whether Roman or English, nor in any Eastern book of any date. But we gladly agree with the Council of Trent that the words are not vainly uttered by Bishops[19] either in consecrating a Bishop or in ordering a Presbyter, since they are words spoken by our Lord to His Disciples from whom all our offices and powers are derived, and are fit and appropriate for so sacred an occasion. They are not equally appropriate in the case of the diaconate, and are accordingly not used by us in admitting to that office.

XV. The form of ordering a Presbyter employed among us in

---

19. See *Council of Trent, Sess.* xxiii. *On the sacrament of Order, can.* iv.

1550 and afterwards was equally appropriate. For after the end of the 'Eucharistic' prayer, which recalls our minds to the institution of our Lord, there followed the laying on of hands by the Bishop with the assistant Priests, to which is joined the 'imperative' form taken from the Pontifical, but at the same time fuller and more solemn (cp. ch. XIX.). For after the words 'Receive the Holy Ghost' there immediately followed, as in the modern Roman Pontifical (though the Pope strangely omits to mention it), 'Whose sins thou dost forgive, they are forgiven; and whose sins thou dost retain, they are retained,' and then the words from the Gospel (S. Luke xii. 42) and S. Paul (1 Cor. iv. 1), which were very rightly added by our fathers, 'and be thou a faithful Dispenser of the word of God and of His holy Sacraments: in the Name of the Father, and of the Son, and of the Holy Ghost.' This form is suitable to no other ministry of the Church but that of a Priest, who has what is called the power of the keys and who alone with full right dispenses the word and mysteries of God to the people, whether he remains a Presbyter or be advanced to higher duties as Bishop. Then there followed, as there still follows, the ceremony of conferring the power to preach and to minister the Sacraments in the sphere where a man has been appointed to that ministry, together with the delivery of the holy Bible, which is, in our opinion, the chief instrument of the sacred ministry and includes in itself all its other powers, according to the particular order to which the man is ordained. And in view of Gordon's case it may not perhaps be idle to explain that these forms are not only verbally but really different.

The former, 'Receive the Holy Ghost,' with what follows, together with laying on of hands, confers the general faculties and powers of priesthood, and as is generally said, imprints the character. The second, together with the delivery of the Bible, gives a man the right to offer public service to God and to exercise authority over the Christian people who are to be entrusted to his charge in his own parish or cure. The two commissions taken together include everything essential to the Christian priesthood, and, in our opinion, exhibit it more clearly than is done in the Sacramentaries and

Pontificals. Nor indeed do we avoid the term *Sacerdos* and its correlatives either in the Latin edition of the '*Book of Common Prayer or of the Ministry of the Sacraments as administered in the Church*,' published in 1560 in the reign of Elizabeth, nor in other public documents written in Latin.[20]

That this was not done without intention appears from the fact that in our translations of the Bible published in the XVIth century the word ἱερεὺς is rendered by Priest (the word which is always used in the Anglican Ordinal, and very often in the Communion Office and elsewhere), while πρεσβύτερος is translated Elder.

When therefore in 1662 the addition 'for the office and work of a Bishop *or* Priest' was made, it would not seem to have been done in view of the Roman controversy, but in order to enlighten the minds of the Presbyterians, who were trying to find a ground for their opinions in our Prayer Book. Historians are well aware that at this period, when the king had been killed, his son driven into exile, and the Church Government upset, the Church of England's debate with the Presbyterians and other innovators was much more severe than it was with the Romans. These words then were not added to give liturgical completeness to the form. For the changes mentioned drew us further away from the Pontificals instead of bringing us nearer. The object of the addition therefore was to declare the difference in the orders. And at this period other similar additions were made by way of protest against the innovators, as for example the suffrages in the Litany against rebellion and schism, the prayer for the High Court of Parliament and for the establishment of religion and peace at home, and the Ember Week Collects.

That these facts should escape the Pope's notice is perhaps

---

20. In the *Articles of Religion* 1562, in the *Canons* of 1571 and elsewhere: See *Councils of Gt. Brit.* vol. iv. pp. 236, 263, 429. Similarly in the Greek translation of our Prayer Book (Cambridge 1665) Ἱερωσύνη and ἱερεὺς occur in the Ordinal, the Order for the Holy Communion, and elsewhere. In certain Latin versions Presbyter seems to be used in preference.

not strange; they only prove the difficulty in interpreting our Prayer Book that has arisen from the separation of our nationalities and churches.[21]

But the XVIth century form was not merely in itself sufficient but more than sufficient. For the collect *Almighty God, giver of all good things*, which beseeches God on behalf of those called 'to the office of the priesthood,' that they may faithfully serve Him in that office, was at that time part of the form, and used to be said by the Bishop immediately before the examination.[22] Now however, since the new words clearly express the same sense, it has been moved elsewhere and takes the place of the collect for the day.

That the Pope should also have been unaware of this change is no matter of wonder: but the fact is worthy of your attention. For we note that he shows some hestitation in this part of his letter, when he suggests that the form of 1662 ought perhaps to be considered sufficient if it had only been a century older (§ 26). He also seems to adopt the opinion of those theologians who believe that the form does not consist of one prayer or benediction, whether 'precative,' as they call it, or 'imperative,' but in the whole series of formulas which are bound together by a moral union. For he goes on to argue about the help which has been 'quite recently' (as he believes) sought for our case from the other prayers of the same Ordinal; although this appeal on our part is by no means recent, but was made in the XVIIth century when first the argument on the Roman side about the additional

---

21. See G. Burnet, *Hist. of Ref.* vol. ii. p. 144 (1680), and *Vindication of Ord. of Ch. of Eng.* p. 71 (1677); H. Prideaux, *Eccl. Tracts*, pp. 15, 36, 69–72, etc. (1687), ed. 2, 1715; cp. his letter in Cardwell, *Conferences*, pp. 387–8 n., ed. 3, Oxf. 1849.

22. It is worth while quoting this collect here, as used in 1550 and 1552, since such stress is laid at Rome upon the words 'to the office and work of a Presbyter or Priest.'

'Almighty God, giver of all good things, which by thy Holy Spirit hast appointed divers Orders of Ministers in thy Church; mercifully behold these thy servants now called to the Office of Priesthood; and replenish them so with the truth of thy doctrine, and innocency of life, that, both by word and good example, they may faithfully serve thee in this Office, to the glory of thy Name and profit of the Congregation; through the merits,' etc. This collect expresses shortly the idea of the 'blessing,' *Deus honorum omnium*. It is even thought by some that 'bonorum' (='of all good things') is a variant of 'honorum.'

words was brought to our notice.[23] Nor do we suppose that the Pope disagrees with Cardinal John de Lugo in his teaching that the whole ordination service is a single action, and that it makes no difference if the matter and form are separated from one another (as is the case in the Pontifical), if what intervenes make up a moral whole.[24]

XVI. The argument, however, which the Pope appears to consider of chief importance and stability is not that which concerns the addition of any words to our form, but that which lays to our charge the removal of certain acts and prayers from the rest of the rite. His letter says (§ 27): 'For, to put aside other reasons which show these (prayers) to be insufficient for the purpose in the Anglican rite, let this argument suffice for all:[25] from them has been deliberately removed whatever sets forth the dignity and offices[26] of the priesthood in the Catholic rite. That form consequently cannot be considered apt or sufficient for the Sacrament which omits[27] what it ought essentially to signify.' And a little later he adds words which are in one way untrue and in another very likely to mislead the reader, and are unfair to our Fathers and ourselves:—'In the whole Ordinal not only is there no clear mention of the sacrifice, of consecration, of the Sacerdotium,[28] and of the powers of consecrating and offering sacrifice, but every trace of these things ... was deliberately removed and struck out' (§ 30). In another passage he speaks (with great ignorance of the facts, we regret to say) of 'that small[29] section of the Anglican body, formed in recent

23. See Burnet, *Vindication*, pp. 8, 71, who writes that the additional words are not essential to Ordination, but are merely explanations 'of what was clear enough by the other parts of these offices before'; and Prideaux, *Eccl. Tracts*, p. 117, who quotes the prayer *Almighty God* in full and argues from it. Bramhall had written similarly in 1658, *Works*, A. C. L. iii, pp. 162–9, Oxf. 1844.

24. *On the Sacraments in General*, disp. ii, sec. v. § 99, t. iii. pp. 293–4, Paris, 1892.

25. *Latin* instar omnium.

26. *Latin* officia. The English version inaccurately has 'office.'

27. *Latin* reticet.

28. This word is left untranslated.

29. *Latin* non ita magna.

times, whose contention is that the said Ordinal can be understood and interpreted in a sound and orthodox sense.'

Next he declares that we deny or corrupt the Sacrament of
Order, that we reject (viz. in the Ordinal) all idea of consecra-
tion and sacrifice, until at last the offices of Presbyter and
Bishop are left 'mere names without the reality which
Christ instituted.'

The answer to these harsh and inconsiderate words has
already been partly made when we gave the warning that he
who interprets the acts of our Church by mere conjecture and
takes it upon himself to issue a new decree as to what is
necessary in the form of Order, condemning our lawful
bishops in their government of the Church in the XVIth
century by a standard which they never knew, is entering
on a slippery and dangerous path. The liberty of national
Churches to reform their own rites may not thus be removed
at the pleasure of Rome. For, as we shall show in part later,
there is certainly no one 'catholic rite,' but even the forms
approved by the Roman Church vary much from one
another.

The Pope says nothing, however, of the well-known intention of our Church set forth in the preface to the Ordinal, and
nothing of the principle which our Fathers always set before
themselves and which explains their acts without any adverse
interpretation.

XVII. Now the intention of our Church, not merely of a
newly formed party in it, is quite clearly set forth in the
title and preface of the Ordinal. The title in 1552 ran 'The
fourme and maner of makynge and consecratynge Bishoppes,
Priestes and Deacons.' The preface immediately following
begins thus:—'It is euident unto all men, diligently readinge
holye Scripture and auncient aucthours, that from the
Apostles tyme there hathe bene these ordres of Ministers in
Christ's Church: Bishoppes, Priestes, and Deacons: which
Offices were euermore had in suche reuerent estimacion,
that no man by his own private aucthoritie might presume
to execute any of them, except he were first called, tried,

examined, and knowen to have such qualities as were requisite for the same; And also, by publique prayer, with imposi-
cion of hands, approued, and admitted thereunto. And
therefore, to the entent that these orders shoulde bee continued, and reuerentlye used and estemed, in this Church of
England; it is requysite that no man (not beyng at thys pre-
sente Bisshope, Priest nor Deacon) shall execute anye of
them, excepte he be called, tryed, examined and admitted,
accordynge to the form hereafter folowinge.' Further on it
is stated incidentally that 'euery man which is to be consecrated a Bishop shalbe fully thyrtie yeres of age.' And in the
rite itself the 'consecration' of the Bishop is repeatedly mentioned. The succession and continuance of these offices from
the Lord through the Apostles and the other ministers of the
primitive Church is also clearly implied in the 'Eucharistical'
prayers which precede the words *Receive the Holy Ghost.*
Thus the intention of our Fathers was to keep and continue
these offices which come down from the earliest times, and
'reverently to use and esteem them,' in the sense, of course, in
which they were received from the Apostles and had been up
to that time in use. This is a point on which the Pope is
unduly silent.

XVIII. But all this and other things of the same kind are
called by Pope Leo 'names without the reality instituted by
Christ.' But, on the contrary, our Fathers' fundamental principle was to refer everything to the authority of the Lord,
revealed in the Holy Scriptures. It was for this that they
rescinded ceremonies composed and added by men, even
including that best known one, common to the modern
Latin and Eastern churches, though unknown to the ancient
Roman church,[30] of holding a copy of the Gospels over the

---

30. See *Apostol. Const.* viii. 4 and *Statutes of the Ancient Church*, can. 2, which
appear to be of Gallican origin from the province of Arles, although they are sometimes published with the false title of the IVth Council of Carthage. That this rite was
foreign to the Church of Rome is clearly testified by the writer of a book *On the divine
offices* which is included in the works of our Alcuin and is perhaps of the XIth
century. '(The rite) is not found in either authority whether old or new, nor in the

head of one about to be ordained Bishop during the utterance of the blessing and the laying on of hands.

Thus then our Fathers employed one matter in imprinting the character, viz., the laying on of hands, one matter in the commission to minister publicly and exercise powers over the flock entrusted to each, viz., the delivery of the Bible or Gospels. This last they probably borrowed from the office of inaugurating a new Bishop and similar rites; thus in the Pontifical the Gospels are still delivered to the Bishop after the ring is given. Other ceremonies of somewhat later date and imported into the ancient Roman Ordinal from sources for the most part foreign and especially Gallican, such as the delivery of the instruments and ornaments, the blessing and unction of hands and head, with the accompanying prayers, they cut out as they had a full right to do. The porrection of the instruments came, as is well known, from the formularies of minor orders and was unknown to any Pontifical before the XIth century, which appears to be the earliest date of its mention in writing. When it was reformed, the new formula 'Receive the power of offering sacrifice to God and of cele-brating mass (or, as in the Roman Pontifical, masses) on behalf of both the quick and dead' was likewise dropped. The prayer for the blessing of the hands could be said or omitted at the discretion of the Bishop even before the XVIth century. The anointing is a Gallican and British cus-tom, not Roman at all. Not only is it absent from the 'Leonine' and 'Gelasian' Sacramentaries, but also from Mabillon's VIIIth and IXth Ordines and those of S. Amand, which apparently represent the custom of the VIIIth and IXth centuries.

Furthermore we find Pope Nicholas I. writing in the IXth century (874) to Rudolf of Bourges that in the Roman Church the hands neither of Priests nor Deacons are anointed

---

Roman tradition' (ch. xxxvii., Migne's *P. L.* vol. 101, p. 1237; and so Amalarius, *on the offices of the Church*, ii. 14, *P. L.* 105, p. 1092). On its use in the consecration of a Pope, see Mabillon, *Ord.* ix. 5.

with chrism.[31] The first writer who mentions anything of the kind is Gildas the Briton.[32] The same may be said of the anointing of the head, which clearly came, in company with much else, from an imitation of the consecration of Aaron, and makes its first appearance in the IXth and Xth centuries outside Rome,[33] as may be gathered from Amalarius (*On the Offices of the Church*, bk. ii. 14) and our own Pontificals.

There remains to be mentioned the Gallican Benediction *Deus sanctificationum omnium auctor*, which was added superfluously to the Roman Benediction (cap. XII.), and was rejected like the rest by our Fathers. This prayer, which is manifestly corrupted by interpolation as it stands in the Roman Pontifical, seemed to favour the doctrine of transubstantiation, rejected by us, and is in itself scarcely intelligible, so that it was singularly inappropriate to a liturgy to be said in the vulgar tongue for the edification of our own people. And yet this very prayer, whatever it may imply, teaches nothing about the power to offer sacrifice.

XIX. What wonder then if our Fathers, wishing to return to the simplicity of the Gospel, eliminated these prayers from a liturgy which was to be read publicly in a modern language? And herein they followed a course which was certainly opposed to that pursued by the Romans. For the Romans, starting from an almost Gospel simplicity, have relieved the austerity of their rites with Gallican embellishments, and have gradually, as time went on, added ceremonies borrowed from the Old Testament in order to emphasize the distinction

---

31. Migne, *P. L.* vol. 119, p. 884, where the letter is numbered 66. Cf. also Martenne *On the ancient rites of the Church*, bk. 1, c. viii. art. ix. §§9 and 14. This reply of Nicolas, beginning 'Praeterea sciscitaris,' is inserted in Gratian's *Decree, dist.* xxiii. c. 12.

32. *Letter*, § 106, p. 111 (Stevenson's edition, 1838). He mentions 'the blessing by which the hands of Priests or Ministers are dedicated' (initiantur). The anointing of the hands of Presbyters and Deacons is ordered in Anglican Sacramentaries of the Xth and XIth centuries.

33. Cp. Council of Trent, *Sess.* xxiii. *On the Sacrament of Order, can.* v, which, though it apparently admits that unction is not requisite in Ordination, anathematizes those who shall say that this and other ceremonies of Order are 'contemptible and harmful.'

between people and Priests more and more. That these ceremonies are 'contemptible and harmful,' or that they are useless at their proper place and time, we do by no means
assert—we declare only that they are not necessary. Thus in
the XVIth century when our Fathers drew up a liturgy at once
for the use of the people and the clergy they went back almost
to the Roman starting-point. For both sides alike, their holy
Fathers, and ours, whom they call innovators, followed the
same most sure leaders, the Lord and His Apostles. Now
however, the example of the modern Church of Rome,
which is entirely taken up with the offering of sacrifice, is
held up to us as the only model for our imitation. And this
is done so eagerly by the Pope that he does not hestitate to
write that 'whatever sets forth the dignity and offices[34] of the
priesthood' has been 'deliberately removed' from the prayers
of our Ordinal.

But we confidently assert that our Ordinal, particularly in
this last point, is superior to the Roman Pontifical in various
ways, inasmuch as it expresses more clearly and faithfully
those things which by Christ's institution belong to the nature
of the priesthood (§ 33) and the effect of the Catholic rites
used in the Universal Church. And this, in our opinion,
can be shown by a comparison of the Pontifical with the
Ordinal.

The Roman formulary begins with a presentation made by
the Archdeacon and a double address from the Bishop, first
to the clergy and people, and then to the candidates for
ordination—for there is no public examination in the ordination of a presbyter. Then follows the laying-on of the Bishop's
hands, and then those of the assistant presbyters, performed
without any words; in regard to which obscure rite we have
quoted the opinion of Cardinal de Lugo (chap. XV.). Then
the three ancient prayers are said, the two short collects, and
the longer Benediction (chap. XII.) which is now said by the
Bishop 'with his hands extended in front of his breast.' This
prayer, which is the 'Consecration' in ancient books, is con-

---

34. The English Version has 'office'.

sidered by weighty authorities,[35] since the time of Morinus, to be the true 'form' of Roman ordination, and doubtless was in old days joined with laying on of hands. Now however, 'extention of hands' is substituted for laying on of hands, as is the case in Confirmation (chap. X.), while even that gesture is not considered necessary. At any rate, if the old Roman ordinations are valid, directly this prayer has been said the ordination of presbyters is complete in that church even at the present day. For any 'form' which has once sufficed for any Sacrament of the Church, and is retained still unaltered and complete, must be supposed to be retained with the same intent as before; nor can it be asserted without a sort of sacrilege that it has lost its virtue, because other things have been silently added after it. In any case the intention of the more recent part of the Roman formulary cannot have been to empty the more ancient part of its proper force; but its object may not improperly be supposed to have been as follows, first that the priests already ordained should be prepared by various rites and ceremonies for the offering of the sacrifice, secondly that they should receive the power to offer it in explicit terms, thirdly that they should begin to exercise the right of the priesthood in the celebration of the Mass, lastly that they should be publicly invested with another priestly power, that of remitting sins. Which opinion is confirmed by the language of the old Pontificals, as for example in the Sarum Pontifical we read 'Bless and sanctify these hands *of thy priests.*' All therefore that follows after that ancient 'form,' just like our words added in 1662, is simply not necessary. For those powers above specified can be conveyed either implicitly and by usage, as was the method in ancient times, or at once and explicitly; but the method of conveyance has no relation to the efficacy of ordination.

Our Fathers then, having partly perceived these points, and seeing that the scholastic doctrine concerning the transubstantiation of the bread and wine and the more recent

---

35. See Martenne, *Anc. Rites of the Church*, book i. ch. viii. art. 9, § 18, tom. 2, p. 320, Rouen, 1700, and Gasparri, *Canonical Treatise on Ordination*, § 1059, Paris, 1893.

doctrine of the repetition (as was believed) of the sacrifice of the cross in the Mass, were connected by popular feeling with certain of the ceremonies and prayers that followed, asked themselves in what way the whole rite of ordination might not only be brought to greater solidity and purity, but might become more perfect and more noble. And inasmuch as at that time there was nothing known for certain as to the antiquity of the first prayers, but the opinions of learned men assigned all efficacy to the 'imperative' forms, they turned their attention to the latter rather than to the former.

With this object therefore in view they first aimed at simplicity, and concentrated the parts of the whole rite as it were on one prominent point, so that no one could doubt at what moment the grace and power of the priesthood was given. For such is the force of simplicity that it lifts men's minds towards divine things more than a long series of ceremonies united by however good a meaning. Therefore having placed in the forefront the prayers which declared both the office of the priesthood and its succession from the ministry of the Apostles, they joined the laying on of hands with our Lord's own words. And in this matter they intentionally[36] followed the example of the Apostolic Church, which first 'fell to prayer' and then laid on hands and sent forth its ministers, not that of the Roman Church, which uses laying on of hands before the prayers. Secondly when they considered in their own minds the various offices of the priesthood they saw that the Pontifical in common use was defective in two particulars. For whereas the following offices were recounted in the Bishop's address:—'It is the duty of a priest to offer, to bless, to preside, to preach and to baptize' and the like, and mention was made in the old 'form' for the presbyterate 'of the account which they are to give of the stewardship entrusted to them,' nevertheless in the other forms nothing was said except about offering sacrifice and remitting sins, and the forms conveying these powers were separated

---

36. See the Archbishop's address to the people in the consecration of a Bishop, and Acts xiii. 3: cp. vi. 6 and xiv. 22.

some distance from one another. Again too they saw that the duties of the pastoral office had but little place in the Pontifical, although the Gospel speaks out fully upon them. For this reason then they especially set before our Priests the pastoral office, which is particularly that of Messenger, Watchman and Steward of the Lord, in that noble address which the Bishop has to deliver, and in the very serious examination which follows: in words which must be read and weighed and compared with the holy Scriptures, or it is impossible really to know the worth of our Ordinal. On the other hand, as regards the sacraments, in their revision of the 'imperative' forms, they gave the first place to our Lord's own words, not merely out of reverence, but because those words were then commonly believed to be the necessary 'form.' Then they entrusted to our Priests all 'the mysteries of the sacraments anciently instituted' (to use the words of our old Sacramentary, see chap. XII.4), and did not exalt one aspect of one of them and neglect the others. Lastly they placed in juxtaposition the form which imprints the character and the form which confers jurisdiction.

And in these and similar matters, which it would take long to recount, they followed without doubt the example of our Lord and His Apostles. For the Lord is not only recorded to have said 'Do this in remembrance of me,' and 'Go therefore and teach all nations baptizing them'—in order to teach the due ministry of the Sacraments, but many things and those most worthy of attention about the pastoral office, both His own, as the good Shepherd, and that of His disciples, who instructed by His example ought to lay down their lives for the brethren. (Cp. S. John x. 11–18, and I Ep. iii. 16). Many things too did He deliver in the Gospel about the preaching of the Word, the stewardship entrusted to His chosen servants, the mission of His Apostles and His disciples in His stead, the conversion of sinners and remission of offences in the Church, mutual service to one another, and much else of the same kind. This then was the manner in which it pleased the divine Wisdom especially to instruct His messengers, watchmen, and stewards, in order that they might bear witness to the world after His departure and duly prepare a holy people until He should come again. And as the Lord had done, so did the Apostles. S. Peter is a witness to this, when as a Fellow-elder he exhorts the elders, that is the Presbyters and Bishops, to 'feed the flock of God which is among you,' and promises them that 'when the chief Shepherd shall appear, ye shall receive a crown of glory that fadeth not away' (1 Pet. v. 1–4). S. Paul is a witness, when he admonishes the Presbyters and Bishops of Ephesus with his own lips (Acts xx. 18–35), and instructs them in an Epistle of extraordinary spiritual power (Eph. iv. 11–13). A witness too is Pope S. Gregory, to whom the whole English race now scattered over the face of the earth owes so much, who in his book 'On the pastoral care' has much to say on these matters and on the personal life of pastors, but is almost or entirely silent on the offering of sacrifice. His book too was held in such high honour that it was delivered to Bishops in the XIth century, together with the book of the canons, at the time of their ordination, when they were further exhorted to frame their lives according to its teaching.[37]

S. Peter also himself, who commends the pastoral office so urgently to the Presbyters, exhorts the whole people, in the earlier part of the same Epistle, about offering, as a holy priesthood, spiritual sacrifices to God. This shews that the former office is more peculiar to Presbyters, seeing that it represents the attitude of God towards men (Ps. xxiii. [xxii.], Isaiah xl. 10, 11, Jerem. xxiii. 1–4, Ezek. xxxiv. 11–31), while the latter is shared in some measure with the people. For the Priest, to whom the dispensing of the Sacraments and especially the consecration of the Eucharist is entrusted, must always do the service of the altar with the people standing by and sharing it with him.[38] Thus the prophecy of Malachi

---

37. This is proved by Hincmar in the preface to his *Book of the LV. Chapters*; Migne, *P. L.* vol. 126, p. 292.

38. This is evident from the Greek Liturgies and the Roman Missal, where nearly everything is said in the plural number. Cp. *e. g.* the *Order of the Mass*: 'Pray, brethren, that my sacrifice and yours may be made acceptable in the sight of God the Father Almighty;' and in the *Canon*, 'Remember, Lord, Thy servants and

(i. 11) is fulfilled, and the name of God is great among the Gentiles through the pure offering of the Church.

We therefore, taking our stand on Holy Scripture, make reply that in the ordering of Priests we do duly lay down and set forth the stewardship and ministry of the word and Sacraments, the power of remitting and retaining sins, and other functions of the pastoral office, and that in these we do sum up and rehearse all other functions. Indeed the Pope himself is a witness to this, who especially derives the honour of the Pontifical tiara from Christ's triple commendation of His flock to the penitent S. Peter. Why then does he suppose that, which he holds so honourable in his own case, to contribute nothing to the dignity and offices of the priesthood in the case of Anglican Priests?

XX. Finally, we would have our revered brother in Christ beware lest in expressing this judgment he do injustice not only to us but to other Christians also, and among them to his own predecessors, who surely enjoyed in an equal measure with himself the gift of the Holy Spirit.

For he seems to condemn the Orientals, in company with ourselves, on account of defective intention, who in the 'Orthodox Confession' issued about 1640 name only two functions of a sacramental priesthood, that is to say that of absolving sins and of preaching; who in the 'Longer Russian Catechism' (Moscow, 1839) teach nothing about the sacrifice of the Body and Blood of Christ, and mention among the offices which pertain to Order only those of ministering the Sacraments and feeding the flock. Further it thus speaks of

---

handmaids N. and N. and all here present . . . (for whom we offer unto Thee, or) who offer unto Thee, this sacrifice of praise,' and later: 'This oblation of us Thy servants, and also of all Thy family,' etc. On this point see e. g. S. Peter Damian in his book, The Lord be with you, in ch. viii. on the words 'for whom we offer unto Thee.' 'It is clearly shewn that this sacrifice of praise, although it seems to be specially offered by a single Priest, is really offered by all the faithful, women as well as men; for those things which he touches with his hands in offering them to God, are committed to God by the deep inward devotion of the whole multitude'; and on 'This oblation.' 'From these words it is more clear than daylight that the sacrifice which is laid upon the sacred altars by the Priest, is generally offered by the whole family of God.'

the three Orders: 'The Deacon serves at the sacraments; the Priest hallows the Sacraments, in dependence on the Bishop; the Bishop not only hallows the Sacraments himself, but has the power also to impart to others by the laying on of his hands the gift and grace to hallow them.' The Eastern Church is assuredly at one with us in teaching that the ministry of more than one mystery describes the character of the priesthood better than the offering of a single sacrifice.

This indeed appears in the form used in the Greek Church to-day in the prayer beginning *O God who art great in power*:—'Fill this man, whom Thou hast chosen to attain the rank of Presbyter, with the gift of Thy holy Spirit, that he may be worthy blamelessly to assist at Thy Sanctuary, to preach the Gospel of Thy Kingdom, to minister the Word of Thy Truth, to offer Thee spiritual gifts and sacrifices, to renew Thy people by the laver of regeneration,' etc. (Habert, *Greek Pontifical*, p. 314, ed. 1643).

But let the Romans consider now not once or twice what judgment they will pronounce upon their own Fathers, whose ordinations we have described above. For if the Pope shall by a new decree declare our Fathers of two hundred and fifty years ago wrongly ordained, there is nothing to hinder the inevitable sentence that by the same law all who have been similarly ordained have received no orders. And if our Fathers, who used in 1550 and 1552 forms which as he says are null, were altogether unable to reform them in 1662, his own Fathers come under the self-same law. And if Hippolytus and Victor and Leo and Gelasius and Gregory have some of them said too little in their rites about the priesthood and the high priesthood, and nothing about the power of offering the sacrifice of the Body and Blood of Christ, the Church of Rome herself has an invalid priesthood, and the reformers of the Sacramentaries, no matter what their names, could do nothing to remedy her rites. 'For as the Hierarchy (to use the Pope's words) had become extinct on account of the nullity of the form, there remained no power of ordaining.' And if the Ordinal 'was wholly insufficient to confer Orders, it was impossible that in the course of time it could become sufficient, since no change has taken place.[39] In vain those who from the (VIth and XIth centuries) have attempted to hold some kind of sacrifice or of priesthood (and power of remitting and retaining sins), have made some additions to the Ordinal.' Thus in overthrowing our orders, he overthrows all his own, and pronounces sentence on his own Church. Eugenius IVth indeed brought his Church into great peril of nullity when he taught a new matter and a new form of Order and left the real without a word. For no one knows how many ordinations may have been made, according to his teaching, without any laying on of hands or appropriate form. Pope Leo demands a form unknown to previous Bishops of Rome, and an intention which is defective in the catechisms of the Oriental Church.

To conclude, since all this has been laid before us in the name of peace and unity, we wish it to be known to all men that we are at least equally zealous in our devotion to peace and unity in the Church. We acknowledge that the things which our brother Pope Leo XIIIth has written from time to time in other letters are sometimes very true and always written with a good will. For the difference and debate between us and him arises from a diverse interpretation of the self-same Gospel, which we all believe and honour as the only true one. We also gladly declare that there is much in his own person that is worthy of love and reverence. But that error, which is inveterate in the Roman communion, of substituting the visible head for the invisible Christ, will rob his good words of any fruit of peace. Join with us then, we entreat you, most reverend brethren, in weighing patiently what Christ intended when He established the ministry of His Gospel. When this has been done, more will follow as God wills in His own good time.

---

39. (The English of this and the following sentence seems hardly to represent the Latin. 'Quum tale ipsum permanserit' might rather be translated 'since it (*i. e.* the Ordinal) remained such as it was.' The following sentence might be rendered:– 'And they laboured in vain who from the time of Charles Ist onwards attempted to introduce (admittere) something of sacrifice and priesthood by making some additions to the Ordinal.')

God grant that, even from this controversy, may grow fuller knowledge of the truth, greater patience, and a broader desire for peace, in the Church of Christ the Saviour of the world!

F. CANTUAR:
WILLELM: EBOR:

Dated on Friday the 19th day of
February A.D. 1897

A ROMAN DIARY

T. A. Lacey

[The personal diary of T. A. Lacey (1853–1931) is not an official document in any sense. It is included in this collection as an Anglican voice reporting on events as they were perceived at the time. Lacey was a distinguished Anglican priest and scholar who eventually became a Canon of Worcester. He was devoted to the cause of unity between the Church of England and the Church of Rome. With E. Denny he wrote *De Hierarchia Anglicana* in 1895, producing a Supplement when in Rome the following year. The main work was produced in direct support of the 'Campaigne Anglo-Romaine'. Lord Halifax was instrumental in arranging for Lacey to go to Rome, with a friend and fellow scholar Fr F. W. Puller SSJE, to be unofficially available to the theological commission. Lacey kept a day to day diary which he eventually published.[1]

The diary itself runs to 54 printed pages. Much Roman colour and conversation are described. Necessarily this edited version loses almost all of this personal flavour by reproducing only the strictly relevant theological material. In the original there are references to Gladstone's interest in the question – Halifax keeping Gladstone closely informed; liturgical customs are described in some detail as well as Roman personalities. Even in this edited version however we can feel something of the electric atmosphere generated by the enquiry. Lacey's later footnotes occasionally repent of partisanship; in particular against Moyes. But the objectivity of

---

1. [*A Roman diary and other Documents relating to the papal inquiry into English Ordinations* MDCCCXCVI. Longmans Green and Co., London, 1910.]

the unofficial Anglican observers is impressive, as when they pass on what appears to be evidence against their case in the matter of the Marian re-ordination of Anglican priests ordained with the Edwardine Ordinal by Bishops Bonner, and King of Oxford (entries of May 3 and 4).

Much of the work of Lacey was concerned with the then disputed question of whether Archbishop Parker's principal consecrator Bishop Barlow had been consecrated with the Sarum Pontifical, and thus indisputably ordained bishop in Roman eyes. This is no longer generally questioned. Investigations initiated by Lacey from Rome and conducted by W. H. Frere established a confusion between Barlow's consecration as Bishop of St David's and his subsequent royal nomination and election to the See of St Asaph (for which, of course, he was not consecrated again). The sudden completion of the work of the theological commission meant that perhaps more significant work on the theological and liturgical aspects of the question with the assistance of the Anglican scholars was attenuated.]

Ap. 9. Arrived Rome 6.15. Portal met us at station, and took us to our rooms at 36 Via del Tritone.... After déjeuner we drove – still with Portal – to St Peter's; thence to the Farnese Palace to see Duchesne.... Afterwards to see Gasparri.... He is full of Ferrar's case. The enemy are maintaining that Ferrar was consecrated according to the Ordinal, in order to adduce him as an instance of a bishop consecrated by the Ordinal, who might nevertheless have conferred *minor* orders – an instance such as is needed for their interpretation of the Breve *Regimini* of Paul IV.

The Commission consists of Cardinal Mazzella, president, Dom Gasquet, Moyes, and a certain Father David representing one side; Duchesne, Gasparri, and de Augustinis on the other side, specially appointed by the pope, and last an unknown Spaniard.[2] Father Scannell also has been summoned.

---

2. He was sufficiently well known as a theologian, the Capuchin Fr. Jose Calasanzio de Llevaneras, afterwards Cardinal.

Ap. 10. Mgr. Gasparri came to see us in the morning, with two questions: (1) about Ferrar's consecration, and (2) about certain Legatine acts of Pole's supposed to involve the invalidity of the Edwardine Orders.

Ap. 11. Called on Gasparri at 8.30 to take him a copy of the register of Ferrar's consecration, and some notes. The session of the Commission at 10 a.m. . . .

Afternoon: Sir Walter Phillimore[3] called on us. Then came Duchesne, bringing two Jesuit fathers, Lapôtre and another, who is a Bollandist. Finally came Portal, who carried off us and Phillimore to the Villa Medici and the Pincio. Duchesne reported that our information had been very useful at the morning session, and had fully established the fact that Ferrar was consecrated according to the Pontifical.

Ap. 12. Low Sunday. Duchesne and Gasparri came by appointment and we did three hours' hard work investigating the cases alleged by Moyes as showing that Pole rejected the Edwardine Orders. Duchesne is satisfied that Pole made no distinction between the men ordained by the two rites, but Gasparri is of contrary opinion.

Ap. 13. I spent the morning at the Biblioteca Nazionale consulting Wilkins' Concilia: found that Pole in the second Legatine Constitution referred to the *Decretum ad Armenos*, without, however quoting it in full. . . . Father Puller went to the Vatican Library and . . . verified, in Gairdner, the letter of 12 June 1536, in which, according to Estcourt's copy, Barlow was called '*elect* of St Davye's'; but in Gairdner's he is called 'Bishop, then elect of St Asaph, now of St David's'.[4]

Afterwards a long discussion with Portal. . . . The secretary to the commission, son of the Spanish Ambassador and of an English mother, is very fierce against us. Mgr Merry del Val

---

3. [W. G. F. Phillimore, was a distinguished ecclesiastical and secular lawyer, eventually to become Lord Chief Justice of Appeal in 1913.]

4. See below, April 17th, and Letters of April 14th, May 18th and 24th.

his name.[5] Calling on Gasparri we were introduced to the Catacomb of St Priscilla.

Ap. 14. Afternoon to Catacomb of St Priscilla; Duchesne, Portal, Canon Bright [*church historian and hymn writer, Regius Professor of Ecclesiastical History and Canon of Christ Church, Oxford*], Scannell, Father Puller, and I. All came to tea with us afterwards.

Duchesne reports that out of forty cases alleged by Moyes, in which Pole or those acting under his authority had refused to recognise the Edwardine Orders, he has demolished thirty-eight *and a half*. This has much impressed de Augustinis.

Ap. 15. Gasparri has seen Cardinal Rampolla, spoken about us, and obtained permission to show us anything and consult us. Apparently some one had been objecting.

Ap. 17. Telegram from Father Waggett saying that the copy of the letter of 12 June 1536, in the Harleian collection, which Gairdner refers to, agrees with Estcourt's copy in speaking of Barlow as *elect* of St David's.

Ap. 18. Sir Walter Phillimore saw Cardinal Rampolla; half an hour's conversation, which he then came and reported to us. The Cardinal was rather shy of speaking on the question of Orders, but called attention to the impartiality of the Commission. Phillimore spoke of the growing desire for union – of the English Church Union – of the Bishop of Lincoln and his good works and saintliness – of the Lincoln trial and the Bishop's refusal to plead before the Privy Council. Also of political matters.

Ap. 19. Sunday. Discussed with Scannell the difference between a decision allowing Anglican priests to minister in the Roman Church, and one admitting the validity of our Sacraments, but not allowing ministrations on the ground of *praxis*. The latter would not in any way prove a barrier to re-union. Adversely it would affect *converts* only, with

---

5. Now Cardinal Secretary of State.

whom we have no concern. Scannell frankly says he does not believe in the validity, but he is working for *no decision at all*.

Afternoon, Portal came, and I discussed this same point with him. He pointed out that a decision *confirming* the *status quo* would be mischievous, but if no decision at all is given no harm is done, though the *status quo* is maintained in practice.

At three o'clock Duchesne, with his friend M. Fabre, an historian of merit, Gasparri, Sir W. Phillimore, and Scannell arrived. A long discussion on Barlow.

Ap. 21. In the morning Mgr Gasparri came with questions about Barlow.

Ap. 22. I found that some of my information given to Gasparri was inexact, and drew up a memorandum showing that the king's mandate for confirmation and consecration of a simple bishop went to the Archbishop alone. Who must then proceed according to *jus commune*, which moreover had just been confirmed by statute (Act of Submission of Clergy). Therefore Cranmer, having received the Mandate for Skyp and again for Bulkely, had to see that he was consecrated by three true bishops according to *jus commune*. Neglect of this would bring him and all concerned under pains of *praemunire*.

Gasparri came in the morning, bringing notes of some things put forward by Moyes at the previous sitting of the Commission. Moyes alleged fourteen possible *documents* in Barlow's case, nine dealing with appointment, and five with consecration. All the former, he said, were extant; all the latter wanting.... Referring to Moyes' own articles in *The Tablet*, we find that these are the documents relating to St Asaph.... I drafted a memorandum showing that in point of fact the *only* documents extant are 1^0 those entered in Cranmer's Register,[6] and 2^0 the Concessio temporalium.

Observed and showed Gasparri that in the Sarum Pontifical the Consecrator does not impose hands at the

---

6. Inaccurate. See below, April 28th, and further developments.

Oratio ad instar praefationis, but afterwards at the prayer *Pater Sancte, omnipotens Deus.*

Afternoon, we and Portal went to see Duchesne at the Farnese palace. He had been arguing that the Bulls both of Julius III and of Paul IV were favourable to us. Moyes retorted that they must be read together and were then unfavourable. 'Then,' said Duchesne, 'put them together and there is one Pope for you, take them apart and there are two Popes for me.'

He entrusted to us the memoirs of Moyes and Co.[7] and of De Augustinis, and his own.

Abstract of De Augustinis, written in Italian

1. In the year 1684 no papal decision against Anglican Orders had been given, and in 1685 a case submitted to the Holy Office was 'Dilata.'
2. Gordon's case was purely personal, and the decision was not grounded on his Supplica.
3. The Bull and brief of Paul IV do not refer to the Anglican rite.
4. Paul IV did not condemn Cranmer for changing the essential form of Orders. He had offended only *sentiendo et docendo* against the Sacrament of Order.
5. Men ordained according to the Anglican rite were received by Pole *in suis ordinibus*.
6. The Nag's Head Fable is rubbish and Parker's Register is genuine.
7. Hodgekyn validly consecrated Parker.
8. Barlow was unquestionably a true Bishop.

The Rite

9. Traditio Instrumentorum is no essential part of Ordination, but only a declaratory ceremony.
10. Council of Mainz in 1549. 'In collatione Ordinum, quae cum impositione manuum veluti visibili signo traditur,

---

7. I regret this rudeness of style, here and elsewhere.

doceant rite ordinatis gratiam divinitus conferri, qua ad ecclesiastica munera rite et utiliter exercenda apti et idonei efficiantur.'

11. Council of Trent, 1562, demonstrates the sacramental nature of Order by a reference to St Paul's words, 'Admoneo te ut resuscites gratiam Dei quae est in te per impositionem manuum mearum.'

12. The form in the Anglican rite must not be considered to be the *Accipe Spritum Sanctum* alone, 'But with these words is conjoined the Prayer which precedes them, and of which they are in a sense the conclusion. The sacramental form of Ordination consists properly of Prayer, according to the teaching of Scripture and of tradition.'

13. He analyses the rite for the consecration of a Bishop and determines that the *Signum* is *massimamente determinato*. The elect is presented *to be consecrated* Bishop, and then prayer is made that the heavenly grace may descend on him so that *as Bishop* in the Church, and according to God's institution, he may serve faithfully to the glory of God's name and the good of the same Church.

14. The concluding words about the *spirit of soberness*, etc., cannot be taken to destroy this determination.

15. If, juxta communem sententiam, the words *Accipe Spiritum Sanctum* alone are sufficient to make a Bishop, much more are they sufficient when determined as in the English rite.

16. He briefly analyses the rite for the ordination of Priests, and shows that it contains the necessary *sign*, namely, imposition of hands with a corresponding form, and this is determined by the concluding words, 'Whosoever sins, etc.,' by the preceding prayer, and by the general drift of the rite.

Objections

17. 'The rite was drawn up and introduced by heretics, with an heretical intention, therefore it cannot be valid.' Answer: If it contains a sufficient matter and form the

intention of the compilers is of no account; for the Arians baptized validly though they used the formula with heretical intention, and St Thomas (3, 64, 9) says that faith is not necessary to the minister of a Sacrament.

18. 'The Anglicans have corrupted the sacramental rite of the Church; therefore they confer no true sacrament.' (Summa Th. 3, 60, 7, ad 3.) Answer: They have altered only accidentals, not essentials. By *verba sacramentalia* St Thomas means the *form* of the Sacrament.

Intention of the Minister

19. It is *not* required that the minister should intend to produce the *effect* or *end* of the Sacrament. Thus a man who does not believe that a Sacrament confers grace or imprints character may nevertheless validly minister the Sacrament. Quotes Sum. Theol. 3, 64, 9, ad 1, and 10, ad 3; also Bellarmine against Tilman and Kemnitz showing that the Council of Trent required not that a man should intend 'quod ecclesia intendit, sed quod ecclesia facit.'

20. He takes the case of a Bishop saying, 'I do not intend to ordain you to be sacrificing priests,' and shows that this declaration does not destroy the intention to do what the Church does. 'He who simply wishes and intends to ordain a priest, in spite of such a declaration, does in fact ordain him as he is according to the divine power conferred on him – that is to say, with the power of offering the holy Sacrifice.' This he defends by the decree of the Holy Office about Baptism conferred with a similar declaration, 18 December 1872.

21. What *is* necessary? 'To constitute ecclesiastical ministers by a sacred rite, and to do what has been done from the beginning of the Christian Society.'

22. The expression of this intention is found in the Preface to the Ordinal, and is illustrated by various extracts from the rites.

23. 'We conclude: The English Ordinations, on which the
    Holy See has not yet given a doctrinal judgement, are
    valid by reason of their being effected by a competent
    Minister, with a valid rite, with the intention of doing
    what the Church does.'

In an appendix he argues that Julius III ordered Pole to
receive those ordained by the Edwardine Ordinal 'non servata
forma Ecclesiae *consueta.*'

Duchesne tells how he used with great effect in the commission an argument which I supplied a few days ago. Pole, on
the receipt of the Brief *Regimini*, must have verified the consecration of all bishops promoted during the Schism, to make
sure they had been consecrated *in forma ecclesiae*, in order
that the ordinations they had performed might stand good. In
doing this he must have either verified Barlow's consecration,
or found that he was not consecrated; and in the latter case it
would certainly have been heard of. Moyes replied that there
was no proof that Pole did so. 'Then,' said Duchesne, 'he was
a very unfaithful representative of the Pope.'

I told Duchesne of Mr Lunn's suggestion about the
Answers of 1540. He was much struck by it, and at once
noticed that the word *consecrare* is especially used in the
Pontificals in connection with the anointing. 'Consecrentur
istae manus,' etc.

Ap. 24. Mgr Gasparri came to us with questions. Still
Barlow. He wished to establish definitely the fact that the
bishops sit in the House of Lords according to the order of
consecration.

Today Gasparri saw the Pope, spoke to him of the help we
were rendering and our attitude generally. The Pope spoke of
us as being *at the door*, 'et je vais l'ouvrir à deux battants.[8]
The question is, What does that really mean?

After dinner I went to the Farnese to restore Duchesne his

---

8. Italian was presumably spoken, but the conversation was reported to us in
French.

copies of the Memoirs, and had a long talk with him about the possibilities of the Commission. It seems that the actual decision of the Holy Office in Gordon's case was based not on his own Supplica at all, but on the report of Genetti, or even on a direct examination of the rite. They took the *forma essentialis* to be exclusively the *Accipe Spiritum Sanctum*, and declared this insufficient, on the express ground of its not being a prayer. For this reason Duchesne thinks it is impossible in the Commission to argue in favour of the validity on the ground of this form. Only the prayer which precedes can be treated as the form. In the presbyteral ordination he is himself satisfied that this contains a prayer for the ordinand, but it is slight and obscure: that for the episcopate is beyond challenge. We spoke of the practical difficulty of an affirmative decision as affecting the internal practice of the Roman Church. Duchesne also pointed out the difficulty of deciding dogmatically on the matter and form when the Council of Trent had declined to do so. I suggested that this had been done to all intents and purposes by acknowledging the validity of the Greek rite. He thought a *practical* decision might be come to, saving the actual praxis by requiring conditional reordination,[9] but expressly leaving open the theological question. I pressed the danger of any decision, short of an absolute affirmative, which could even be represented to English people as final, and as settling the terms of a future reconciliation. We cannot ever press for reunion if our people are made to think that it would involve even conditional reordination. The utmost that could be made tolerable to our people would be an arrangement by which Anglican priests, wishing to exercise their office within the Roman Church, should have to undergo some sort of *sanatio*.

Ap. 25. A letter from Mr Gladstone sent on from Lord Halifax. Writing wonderfully firm. M. Portal has seen Cardinal Rampolla again today, speaking about Mr Gladstone among other things.

---

9. 'I cannot understand,' he said, 'why you should object to this. It is no more than your own St Chad endured, for the sake of peace.'

Ap. 26. Mgr Gasparri came, reporting that Moyes declared the Congé and Assent for Barlow at St David's were in the Records. Telegraphed to E. G. W.[10] to search.

In the sitting of the Commission on Saturday N. challenged A.'s statement about the Barlow documents. B. intervened, declaring that he had seen the documents. 'You say so?' said N., 'Yes.' 'I believe you,' said N. with a little emphasis.[11]

Ap. 28. Telegram from Wood explaining the mystery about the Barlow documents. The *Patent Rolls* contain nothing about Barlow's promotion to St David's. The reference given by Moyes is for St Asaph. But the *Privy Seals* records contain Congé and Assent for St David's.[12]

Ap. 30. In the morning Gasparri came. We could not get anything out of him about the effect of the telegram at the meeting of the commission yesterday.

The question now was about rite. Was it true, as recently stated in *The Tablet* by A. G. Clark, that the prayer, 'Almighty God, giver of all good things, etc.,' in the rite for the consecration of Bishops, was sometimes said by another than the Consecrator? I pointed out that the corresponding prayers in the rites for diaconal and presbyteral ordination since 1662 have been said as the Collect of the Mass, and so of course are said by the ordaining Bishop. Formerly they were said after the Litany, as is still the case in the consecration of a Bishop. In all cases the rubric directs the Bishop or the Consecrator to say the Litany with this prayer. But is this rubric adhered to in practice?

Our impression was that in the actual practice, though the Litany is commonly said by a priest, yet the special suffrage and the prayer in question are always said by the ordaining or consecrating Bishop.

10. [i.e. the Revd E. G. Wood, a Cambridge historian of Canon Law.]

11. This petulance was quite unjustified, as the sequel shows. The documents were found, as noted below, and there was no cause for any reticence about them. I should like to expunge the story, as well as the names, but it would not be fair to suppress evidence of our own suspicious temper.

12. The significance of this last was not yet understood. See below, May 6th and 12th, and the letter of April 29th to W.H.F.

It was agreed that we should write to the Archbishop of York, now at Florence, to ask for information as to the existing practice.

Gasparri contends that these prayers are unquestionably sufficient as *forms*, that there is sufficient moral union between them and the imposition of hands, on the ground of the unity of the whole rite as maintained by De Lugo and many others, and that, therefore, if it is certain that they are always said by the proper Minister, there can be no question as to the validity of the rite.

Father Puller wrote to the Archbishop.

M. Portal came with an important letter from Lord Halifax about Mr Gladstone. Mr Gladstone is quite willing under certain conditions, e.g. if asked to do so, to write a letter either to the Pope or to anyone else, for publication at an opportune moment. A draft of a letter to the Pope, on which Lord Halifax and Mr Gladstone were agreed,[13] was enclosed. We talked this over. M. Portal thought he must see cardinal Rampolla and sound him. But he would put it that Mr Gladstone would certainly do *something*: the only question was *what*?

He waited on the cardinal after Ave Maria, and returned to us about half-past nine to report. The cardinal was keenly interested. It would not do for Mr Gladstone to write to the Holy Father a letter intended for publication, but it would have a good effect if he would write such a letter to someone else; Lord Halifax, for example. To the Abbé's idea of Mr Gladstone's coming to Rome he would not commit himself: he must think it over.

May 1. Father Puller found at the Casanatense the Acts of the Council of Mainz in 1549, in which the matter and form of Order are treated exactly as in the English Ordinal: for a priest the matter being imposition of hands, and the form 'Accipe Spiritum Sanctum, quorem remiseris, etc.' Moreover,

---

13. This, my interpretation at the time, was incorrect. (marginal note of June 12th, 1896.)

this is spoken of as occurring at the *beginning* (principio) of the rite.

This is interesting either as (1) having suggested the arrangement in the Ordinal of 1550, or as (2) evidence of contemporaneous opinion.

In the evening we all went to Duchesne's. He, too, thinks this Council of Mainz important.

He described the procedure in Commission. The Cardinal President puts questions. Gasparri, being a prelate, speaks first – and generally says all there is to be said. Then come the seculars, then the Jesuit, the Benedictine, and the Franciscans. N.'s mode of arguing, he says, is exactly like that of the Donatists in the great conference at Carthage, which Duchesne – alone probably – has read right through: the same wearisome insistence on trivial points, the same determination never to acknowledge a mistake.

May 3. Father Puller received a letter from Frere[14] giving account of certain *reordinations* by Bonner, and King of Oxford, in Mary's reign, before the arrival of the Legate. There is no indication in the registers that these are reordinations, but the conclusion is arrived at by noting that the same names appear in the registers as ordained between 1550 and 1553. On the other hand, there are men ordained during these years who retain benefices without any mention of reordination. Frere is inclined to draw the inference that in some cases reordination was resorted to on the ground of private scruples, but that there was no settled policy.

We determined to place this evidence at once in the hands of Duchesne. M. Portal came with a letter from Lord Halifax, saying that the Bishop of Stepney was sending an account of these matters to *The Times*. We went to Duchesne's; found

---

14. In reply to one written by him on April 27th about a report which had reached him from Mr. Birkbeck. He wrote: 'If you have discovered facts which prove that Bonner did repudiate Edwardine Orders, we should feel bound to communicate such facts to our friends on the Commission. They have acted so very loyally towards us, that, besides the general obligation of perfect openness in such matters, we are specially bound to be open with them.'

him not at home; then on to St Peter's, where was a baptism. Back to Duchesne's, whom we now found at home, very tired and pining for some mountain or sea air. He took our information very seriously.

May 4. We called on Mgr. Gasparri, and gave him a short paper which I have drawn up respecting Frere's information. (i) We have merely identity of *names* in the registers, nothing to show clearly identity of persons. (ii) Some ordained by the Edwardine rite are shown to have retained their benefices, no mention of reordination; therefore either there were no reordinations, or else different cases were differently treated. (iii) All was done before the coming of the Legate, and by individual Bishops – especially Bonner. But Bonner rehabilitated Scory: therefore he either reordained none, or treated different cases differently.

May 6. After breakfast M. Portal came with important information. The Commission will probably finish its work tomorrow, meeting again only once next week to draw up the *procès-verbal*. They hardly touch at all on the question of intention, merely stating a few general truths. Apparently things have been hurried. All graver considerations are to be reserved for another Commission of Cardinals, either of the Holy Office, or that of the Reunion of the Churches, or a special one appointed *ad hoc*. Nothing is yet known. Mgr. Gasparri is inclined to raise the question of Baptism, some one having described a careless case of *sprinkling* to him as if typical. He will probably have no opportunity of doing this, and will immediately return to Paris. Duchesne, he added, wished to see us.

We went on to the Farnese. Duchesne had much to say. We must on no account leave Rome when the Commission is finished. The report will be submitted in about a fortnight to the Cardinals. Until we know what Cardinals, nothing can be done. He described various Cardinals. Rampolla, 'très saint homme,' bent on doing all he can to further the pope's policy, but likely to be influenced theologically by

Mazzella. About Mazzella his mouth is shut. He has learnt what he knows in the Commission, and so can say nothing.

They are nearly all of the old school. They will ask what is the *intention of the English Ordinal*? What was the meaning of its compilers? Either heretical opinions or the change of the rite alone would not present much difficulty, but the combination is awkward. We must be on the spot to meet it. After all, a majority of the Cardinals will not decide. It will be not *maior pars*, but *senior pars*. Of that the Pope will judge himself.

After dinner a great surprise. A telegram from E. G. Wood, saying that he has found the *mandate to consecrate Barlow*. We all went straight off to Duchesne with the telegram for him to produce at the Commission to-morrow. The question is, Where has it been found? If in the Privy Seals, did Moyes know of it, and is that the reason why he was so unwilling to give the reference to the Privy Seals for the Congé and Assent?[15]

May 7. By the next post came a letter from Frere stating that the Literae certificatoriae about Consecrations are preserved in the Privy Seals and Signed Bills, and calendared in the Domestic State Papers; but they are very imperfect. E.g. Repps' consecration is thus recorded, but the letter about Sampson is wanting. Sent this on to Gasparri at the Vatican while the Commission was actually sitting.

The Commission has held its last meeting. At present we have to wait and see to what Cardinals the matter will be referred.

Frere writes that he has a conviction, growing stronger as he works out the evidence, 'that in the first blush of Marian revulsion they were inclined to dispute the orders of the English Ordinal,' but he is coming to suspect more and more, and hopes to prove, 'that this doubt was a steadily diminishing quantity: possibly even that the influence of

---

15. I am sorry to put on record this imputation of bad faith, for which there was not the smallest foundation, but as a matter of fact some of us did talk so, and I must not falsify the record.

Pole or even Rome was exerted against it, and that the reordinations which prevailed in the early months were afterwards discouraged.'

May 8. Duchesne saw Cardinal Rampolla, who expressed a
wish that we should stay in Rome for the present, and hold
ourselves in readiness to give information to the commission
of Cardinals which is now appointed.

Letter from the Archbishop of York, who is at Florence,
giving assurance that the prayer after the Litany in the
Consecration of Bishops is, by the unvarying use of both
provinces, said by the Archbishop himself.

May 12. Letter from Wood enclosing documents. The
Mandate to Consecrate is what is usually known as the
Royal Assent: but a full explanation of the whole process of
issuing Letters Patent shows that this is the original Sign
Manual which set the whole thing in motion, and that the
king gave this order only, which was afterwards expanded in
the routine of the office to the usual form.

May 14. Ascension Day. Father Puller and I called in the
morning on Cardinal Mazzella at the German college, giving
him the Archbishop of York's letter, and a passage from
Pilkington received this morning from Mr Ross-Lewin to
the effect that the Edwardine priests were reconciled in
Mary's time by unction only. He was stiff and grumpy, but
speaking English seemed to express himself with great difficulty. He could not think why so much fuss was made about
Orders. The *Pope* was the great question.

May 23. In the afternoon Scannell called, a priest of the
English College accompanying him. He explained that he
had been keeping out of our way because of the fashion he
was spied upon. He spoke as if he were certain there would be
a negative decision of the question. It was impossible, said
Portal. 'C'est l'impossible qui arrive,' said Scannell. Still he
was very friendly and pleasant, and appears to be much dis-
gusted with *The Tablet*.

May 24. Whitsunday. Afternoon. Portal came full of news. Letter from Lord Halifax enclosing a copy of one he has written to Cardinal Rampolla requesting a memoir by Mr Gladstone, which we are to translate into French and give to the Cardinal.

May 28. Breakfast with M. Duchesne. Duchesne let out that the Description of the Rites by Pole was *not* before the Commission.

May 29. Evening. I called on the Cardinal Vicar. I spoke pretty fully of the state of things in England; he asked particularly if it were certain that *we* can get behind the prejudices of the people and bring them on gradually to Catholic truth. He did not actually make the comparison, but obviously meant to ask if we can do it more effectually than the Romanists. I illustrated the progress made by showing that it is easy now to speak in public about reunion and about the Holy See in a way which would have been impossible twenty years ago. Portal describes the Cardinal Vicar as very intelligent, very pious, but thoroughly suspicious of the reunion movement. He could not keep me long, as he had several people to see, and the Ordinations tomorrow; but he asked me to call on him again before leaving Rome.

June 1. Called on Cardinal Serafino Vannutelli. He was keenly interested in Mr. Gladstone's letter. I asked him directly whether he was seised of our question. He said, not yet, but he expected to be so shortly: meanwhile he thought it was in the hands of some consultors. I went on to Cardinal Vincenzo Vannutelli. He had read the pamphlets and found them clear. I would rather have had a request for explanation than the compliment. I spoke about Mr Gladstone's letter. It was pretty obvious from his manner that he had seen it, but he too asked for information about it. He thought we ought not to leave Rome yet. I tried to find out why, but without success. I asked him if he could tell me what is the actual state of affairs. He told me that so far as he knew Cardinal Mazella had presented his report to the Holy Father, who since then

had spoken not a word about it to any one; but he thought –
emphasizing this as a mere personal impression – that the
Pope might perhaps take occasion from Mr Gladstone's letter
to put something out of his own motion.
Afterwards I went to the Cardinal Vicar, who saw M.
Portal before me. As soon as I got into the room he burst
out about some new discovery to the effect that St Pius V had
withdrawn, or wished to withdraw, the Bull *Regnans in excel-
sis*, but it had passed too soon into promulgation.

June 5. Afternoon, called on Cardinal Steinhüber. Found
him extremely pleasant, but in no way encouraging.

June 6. Father Puller called on Cardinal Serafino Vannutelli,
who told him that a commission of Cardinals was forthwith
to take up the question of the Ordinations. He would receive
the dossier on Monday, and the first meeting would be on
Wednesday or Thursday. Father Puller asked him directly
whether it was a special Commission or the Holy Office. He
replied, 'I am on this Commission: I am also in the Holy
Office.' Father Puller concluded from his manner that it
was *not* the Holy Office.

June 7. Heard Pope's Mass in the private chapel of the apart-
ment at 8 o'clock. Portal called on Cardinal Serafino
Vannutelli, who told him that the instruction to the
Commission was to study the documents for a month. He
said among other things that we had made a good impression;
we have made it evident that the question is a serious one.
They are much struck by the absence of timidity or supplica-
tion in our manner. I suppose there is no 'drop-down-dead-
ativeness'.

June 8. Afterwards to the Vatican to see Cardinal Rampolla
by appointment at one o'clock. Congregations were just
breaking up. Cardinals Serafino Vannutelli, Segna, and
Steinhüber met us in the antechamber and greeted us warmly.
Father Puller and I went in first to the Cardinal. He was
curiously nervous in manner, but most encouraging. He
sent a message for Mr Gladstone direct from the Holy

Father, that he was much touched by the expressions used in the memoir. He said with great emphasis, 'Le Saint Père s'est occupé beaucoup lui-même de votre question, et vous pourrez vous assurer qui'il la traitera avec la plus parfaite impartialité. Il ne cherche que la vérité, mais le plus possible de la charité.' He repeated this several times, and added, 'Voilà en deux mots notre politique.'

Father Puller then left for Milan.

We afterwards drove round the Villa Borghese, and after dining left Rome at 10.20 for Pisa and Genoa.

June 10. Arrived at Paris soon after seven and drove to the Lazarists.

June 11. Got the *Monde* for to-morrow, containing a very remarkable communication from the Roman correspondent. He speaks of our hearing the Pope's Mass last Sunday, with comments which could hardly have been inspired by any one but Cardinal Rampolla. He adds that the Pope will shortly have ready an utterance on the Anglican question, which will *not* be a reply to Mr Gladstone, as it was begun before Mr Gladstone's letter appeared.

June 12. Arrived Holborn Viaduct 6 a.m. Went up to Highgate. Afterwards called on Lord Halifax, and stayed to dine with him.

LETTER OF LORD HALIFAX TO F. PORTAL

21 September 1896

[Portal had written to Halifax
on the publication of *Apostolicae Curae*]

Your letter fills my eyes with tears; but it does me inexpressible good. Assuredly it was love of souls that moved us: we did not think of anything else. May something be done to put an end to the divisions among those who love our Lord Jesus Christ – those divisions that keep so many souls far away from Him – so that those who love each other, communicating at the same altars, may love each other more; in short, so that the essential unity of the Church of Jesus Christ may be recognized by everyone. To bring that about we must come together in a spirit of love and of charity, in a spirit also of penitence for all the faults committed on both sides; with a view to dispelling misunderstandings; to distinguishing what is of faith and what is merely a matter of opinion; to dispelling prejudice and, quite simply, to seeking the will of God, as He made it known to His Holy Apostles, and as it has been understood by the Church from the earliest times; and finally to establishing ourselves upon the grounds of Christian faith and practice required by the Encyclical (*Satis Cognitum*).

That, my friend, is all that we wanted. I suppose the others wanted it also. But in order to arrive at this much love is necessary, much charity, much patience, great self-denial, the wisdom that discriminates. Above all is needed that love-inspired spirit which, above all difficulties and in spite of all appearances, sees the essential truth as it actually is in itself, and neglects every personal consideration, trusting others as oneself, in order to make that truth prevail. ... We tried to do something which, I believe, God inspired. We have failed, for the moment; but if God wills it, His desire will be accomplished, and if He allows us to be shattered, it may well be because He means to do it Himself. This is no dream. The thing is as certain as ever.

There are some bitter things which are worth all the joys of earth, and I prefer, many thousand times, to suffer with you in such a cause, than to triumph with the whole world. Your letter is more precious to me than I can possibly say. Troubles shared are already half assuaged; only I know that if we suffer, you are suffering still more, and it is this thought that hurts me most.

SOURCES AND FURTHER READING

SOURCES

The documents which comprise this collection, in some cases in translation, come from the following sources:

F. Portal's letter from AHP [= *Archivum Historiae Pontificae*] 19 (1981), pp. 339–341;

P. Gasparri's *votum* was published as *De la valeur des ordinations anglicanes*, Paris 1895;

L. Duchesne's *votum* from *Gregorianum* 62 (1981), pp. 709–746;

E. De Augustinis' *votum* from *Archivum Historicum Societatis Iesu* 30 (1981), pp. 55–74;

The Westminster theologians's Exposition was printed privately, London 1896;

T. B. Scannell's letter from *The Tablet*, 24 August 1895, p. 305;

R. Pierotti's summary and *votum* from AHP 20 (1982), pp. 355–388;

Apostolicae Curae is given in the translation published from time to time by the Catholic Truth Society;

Saepius Officio was published in 1897 and was reissued by SPCK in 1943 and in subsequent impressions;

T. A. Lacey's diary was published as *A Roman Diary and other Documents relating to the Papal Inquiry into English Ordinations 1896*, London 1910;

Lord Halifax's letter is quoted from H. Hemmer and A. T. Macmillan, *Fernand Portal (1855–1926), Apostle of Unity*, London 1961.

FURTHER READING

F. Clark, *Anglican Orders and Defect of Intention*, London 1956.

F. Clark, *Eucharistic Sacrifice and the Reformation*, 2nd edn, Oxford 1967.

G. Dix, *The Question of Anglican Orders*, 2nd edn, London 1956.

E. Echlin, *The Story of Anglican Ministry*, Slough 1974.

R. W. Franklin (ed), *Anglican Orders: Essays on the Centenary of apostolicae Curae 1896–1996*, London 1996 (previously published in *Anglican Theological Review* 78/1 (1996)).

Lord Halifax (C. L. Wood), *Leo XIII and Anglican Orders*, London 1912.

J. J. Hughes, *Absolutely Null and Utterly Void*, London 1968.

J. J. Hughes, *Stewards of the Lord: A Reappraisal of Anglican Orders*, London 1970.

G. H. Tavard, *A Review of Anglican Orders: The Problem and the Solution*, Collegeville 1990.

J. Willebrands, Cardinal, Letter to the Co-Chairmen of ARCIC II, and their reply in *Anglican Orders – a New Context*, ed. E. J. Yarnold, CTS London, 1986.

INDEX

343

Baptism. G 10, G 34–35, G 39–40, G 45, G 47, G 72, A 27, A 32, W 12, W 17, W 27, W 52, P 54, SO 10, L *Ap22*, L *Ma6*
   repetition of. D 42, A 24, A 30
Barbaro, D., Coadjutor of Aquileia. D 56
Barlow, William, Bishop of St David's. I 14, I 25, I 26, G 7, G 21–25, G 30, G 49, G 51, G 80, D 2, D 4, D 7–15, D 16, D 48, A 11, A 12, A 14, A 28, W 43, W 45–46, W 49, P 37, L 2, L *Ap13*, L *Ap17*, L *Ap19–24*, L *Ap26–28*, L *Ma6*
   nephew of. G 22.
Bellarmine, Robert, St. A 29n, A 30, L *Ap22*
Belson, Lord. P 29
Benedict XIII, Pope. G 62n
Benedict XIV, Pope. G 41–42, G 67n, SO 3, SO 4
Benson, Edward, Archbishop of Canterbury. I 1–2, I 5, I 31, FP 3, SO 1
Bickersteth, E. H., Bishop of Exeter. W 20
Billuart, C.-R., o.p. G 57n, G 76n
Birkbeck, Mr. L *Ma3n*
Bishop, Edmund. I 2
Bishops, priesthood of. SO 13
Bobbio. D 19
Boleyn, Anne. P 20
Boniface, St. G 31, P 48
Bonner, Edmund, Bishop of London. W 36, P 17, P 36, L 1, L *Ma3–4*
Book of Common Prayer. D 3, D 17, W 31–32, W 34, W 41, W 48, SO 13
Bossuet, Bishop J. -B., G 19
Boudinhon. G 59, G 69n
Bourne, Gilbert, Bishop of Bath and Wells. P 17
Brady, Maziere. W 5
'Branch' theory. W 9, W 21, W 62, P 59
Bright, Canon W. D 17, L *Ap14*
Brown, George, Bishop of Stepney. W 23, P 18
Bucer, Martin. W 11, W 28–29, W 33, W 60
Bulkel(e)y, Arthur, Bishop of Bangor. G 22, L *Ap22*
Bullinger, J. H. W 11, W 29
Bunsen, Christian von. W 54

Cajetan. G 72n
Calvinist, unnamed French. I 11, I 28, W 3, P 22, AC 17–18
Calvinists, Calvinism. G 35, G 41, A 30, W 29, W 34
Camm, Dom Bede. G 24n, G 26
Cappaddocia. D 42
Carne, Sir Edward. P 10
Casanata, Cardinal. I 11, P 22–29, P 32, P 35, P 53
Casoni, Mgr. P 29
Castoria, Bishop of. W 4
Catherinus. W 35
Cecil, Lord D 9

Grindal(1), Edmund, Archbishop of Canterbury.   A 9, SO 13

Hadrian I, Pope.   SO 12n
Hadrian II, Pope.   D 44
Hales, A.   W 29
Halifax, Lord.   I 1–2, I 5, FP 2–6, L 1–2, L *Ap25*, L *Ap30*, L *Ma24*, L *Jul2*
Hands, imposition of.   I 31, G 7–8, G 21n, G 52, G 55–57, G 61–2,
    G 64–73, D 16, D 18, D 21–25, D 35, D 54, A 11, A 12, A 13, A 16,
    A 17, A 18, A 19, A 20, A 21, A 22, W 53, W 55–57, W 59, P 40, P 44,
    P 45, AC 24, SO 3, SO 6, SO 8–10, SO 12, SO 15, SO 18–20, L *Ap22*
Harding, Thomas.   P 24
Hardouin, Jean, S. J.   G 62n
Harley, John, Bishop of Hereford.   G 4
Henry VIII, King.   I 7–8, G 2, G 22, G 24, D 3, D 4, D 9–15, D 53, A 14,
    W 23, W 26–28, W 45, P 4, P 14, P 17, P 20, P 51, AC 9
High Church.   P 59
Hilsey, John, Bishop of Rochester.   W 27
Hippolytus, St.   W 54, P 40, SO 20
Hodgkin(s) (Hodgekyn), John, Bishop of Bedford.   G 7, G 21n, D 4, A 11,
    A 12, A 13, W 43, W 49, P 37, L *Ap22*
Holbeach, Henry, Bishop of Lincoln.   A 14, W 27, P 51
Holland, Vicar Apostolic of.   P 23, P 25
Holy Office (Supreme Council).   I 5, I 9, I 11, I 12, I 31, G 19, G 34, G 40,
    G 45, G 69n, A 2, A 3, W 3–7, P 3, P 18, P 20–23, P 30–32, P 34, P 35,
    P 45, p 57, P 58, P 61, P 62, AC 5, SO 7–8, L *Ap22–24*, L *Ma6*
    judgment in Case of Calvinist deferred.   P 27–28
    Commission of Cardinals.   I 4–5, I 11–12, L *Ma6–8*, L *Ju6–8*
Holy Spirit, invocation of.   G 59
'Holy Spirit, receive the': recent origin of formula.   G 57, W 16, W 56–57
Holywood, John.   A 9, D 6n, P 24
Homilies, Books of.   W 17, W 35, W 48
Hooper, John, Bishop of Gloucester and Worcester.   W 29, P 51
Hopton, John, Bishop of Norwich.   I 8, G 15, P 8–9, P 12, AC 10,
    AC 12–13
Horne, Robert, Bishop of Winchester.   A 9
Howell, M. I. D. (Editor of *The Times*).   G 26
Hughes, J. J.   I 5n

Innocent III, Pope.   G 41, SO 3
Innocent IV, Pope (S. Fieschi).   G 61
Innocent XI, Pope.   W 3, P 29
Institution by Christ.   I 23, G 59, G 62, G 65, G 69, A 15, A 24, A 25,
    A 30, W 51, W 62, P 40, P 49, AC 3, AC 29, SO 19–20, L *Ap22*
    generic/immediate determination by Christ.   G 54–55, W 52, W 65
Instruments, handing over of.   I 1, I 28, I 31, G 4, G 52, G 55–57, G 62n,
    G 64, G 67–68, G 80, D 16, D 18, D 54, D 56, A 16, A 17, W 16, W 55,
    W 56, W 60, W 63, P 26, P 32, AC 21, SO 4, SO 6–7, SO 18, L *Ap22*

a late rite. G 56–57, G 62n, D 16, D 18, A 16, SO 18
handing over of Gospels. SO 15, SO 18
rite changed in 1552. G 4, SO 6
Intention. I 1, I 8, I 25–27, I 31–32, G 15, G 17, G 25–51, G 80, D 2,
    D 36–40, A 1, A 11, A 23, A 27–35, W 4, W 7, W 59, W 64, P 9, P 12,
    P 14, P 16, p 19, P 29, P 35, P 37, P 46–47, P 53, P 56, P 57, P 62, AC 12,
    AC 20, AC 33, SO 5, SO 8, SO 12, L *Ma6*
  of doing what the Church does. I 25, G 26, G 28, G 31–43, D 39–40,
    A 26–36, W 62–63, S, P 48, AC 33, SO 6, L *Ap22*
  externally manifested. AC 33, SO 8–9, SO 14, SO 19
  invalidated by deliberate change of form. G 49, P 48–50, P 53,
    L *Ap22*, L *Ma6*
  not invalidated by accidental change. P 48
  not invalidated by error. I 25, G 34–36, G 39–48, A 26, A 29, A 31–2,
    D 39–40
  not required in minister. W 12
  positive exclusion of effect. I 25, I 26, I 27, G 42–50, W 62, W 66,
    AC 33, D 40
Invalid, distinguished from illicit. P 19
Invalidity, opportuneness of declaration of. P 58–61

Jacobites. D 37, P 26, P 40
James I, King. P 20
James II, King. P 28
Jesuits. FP 4, D 48
Jewel(l), John, Bishop of Salisbury. P 24
John IX, Pope. D 44
John X, Pope. D 45
John Paul II, Pope. I 32n
Julius III, Pope. I 7–10, I 34, G 5, G 14–15, D 50–51, A 38, P 5–10, P 12,
    P 14, P 16, P 19, P 21, P 32, P 36, P 57, P 62, AC 7, AC 9–10, AC 15,
    SO 6, L *Ap22*
  distinction between Bull and Brief. I 9, P 6
Justification by faith. W 12, W 29

Kemnitius (Kemnitz). A 30, L *Ap22*
King, Edward, Bishop of Lincoln. L *Ap18*
King, Robert, Bishop of Oxford. A 7, W 46n, L 1, L *Ma3*

Lacey, T. A. I 1, I 3–4, I 14, I 31, G 7, G 38
Lapôter, Fr, s.j. L *Ap11*
Latimer, Hugh, Bishop of Worcester. W 27
Laud, Archbishop William. W 19, P 20
Leo I, Pope. SO 20
Leo IX, Pope. I 1, I 5, D 46

Sins, power of remitting. W 12, W 17–18, W 20, W 22, W 61, SO 12, SO 19–20
Siricius, Pope. A 24
Skip (Skyp), John, Bishop of Hereford. G 22, L *Ap22*
Smith, S., s.j. G 18
Somerset, Duke of. W 28, P 4
Soto, D., o.p. G 72n, D 54
Stapleton, T. P 24
Steinhüber, Cardinal. L *Ju5*, L *Ju8*
Stephen I, Pope. D 42
Stephen II, Pope. D 44
Stephen VI, Pope. D 45
Straton, Norman, bishop of Sodor. W 20
Strype, J. P 50
Syrian Church. D 37, D 42, P 26

Tavard, G. H. I 31n
Taylor, John, Bishop of Lincoln. W 37
Temple, Frederick, Archbishop of Canterbury. I 5, I 31–32
Tertullian. D 34
Thirlby, Thomas, Bishop of Westminster etc. A 7, W 32, W 39, P 16, AC 11
Throckmorton, Nicholas, Bishop of Ely. D 57
Timothy, St. P 46
Treason to celebrate Mass. W 18
Trent, Council of. I 25n, I 32, G 26, G 34n, G 39, G 54, D 16, A 17, A 30, P 21, W 51, W 52, W 53, W 60, W 65, AC 8, SO 3, SO 8, SO 11, SO 13–14, L *Ap22–24*

Urban VIII, Pope. G 53n

Validity, no longer an open question. W 1, P 1, P 16, P 57, AC 22
    doubtful. P 1–3, P 56, P 57, P 59
Vannutelli, Cardinal Serafino. L *Ju1*, L *Ju6–8*
Vannutelli, Cardinal Vincenzo. L *Ju1*
Vatican I, Council. P 61
Vatican II, Council. I 34
Vaughan, Cardinal Herbert. I 1–3, I 32, G 26, G 38, G 44, G 46, G 48, G 81, P 15, L 1
Veni Creator. P 44
Vernacular prayers, replace Latin. D 53
Vicar, Cardinal. L *Ma29*, L *Ju1*
Victor, Pope. SO 20
Von Hügel, Baron F. I 3

Waggett, Fr. L *Ap17*

Also published by
The Canterbury Press Norwich

'A BROTHER KNOCKING AT THE DOOR'

by Dr Bernard Barlow, OSM

Foreword by Bishop Geoffrey Rowell

Traces the history of the Malines
Conversations, 1921–1925

'painstaking and scholarly ...
All concerned with the unity of
Anglicans and Roman Catholics ...
can be encouraged by this detailed
and moving account of a pioneering
ecumenical encounter.'

ISBN 1-85311-135-X